D0522689

My Journal: Remembering and Growing

A Biblical context to life's journey.

Edition 1

Dan L Bragg, Ed-D

WESTBOW PRESS®
A DIVISION OF THOMAS NELSON & ZONDERVAN

Copyright © 2016 Dan L Bragg, Ed-D.

All rights reserved. No part of this book may be used or reproduced by any means, graphic, electronic, or mechanical, including photocopying, recording, taping or by any information storage retrieval system without the written permission of the author except in the case of brief quotations embodied in critical articles and reviews.

THE HOLY BIBLE, NEW INTERNATIONAL VERSION®, NIV® Copyright © 1973, 1978, 1984, 2011 by Biblica, Inc.® Used by permission. All rights reserved worldwide.

Visit the author's website: www.bleabundantlife.com

Author Photo: Cynthia Reilly

WestBow Press books may be ordered through booksellers or by contacting:

WestBow Press
A Division of Thomas Nelson & Zondervan
1663 Liberty Drive
Bloomington, IN 47403
www.westbowpress.com
1 (866) 928-1240

Because of the dynamic nature of the Internet, any web addresses or links contained in this book may have changed since publication and may no longer be valid. The views expressed in this work are solely those of the author and do not necessarily reflect the views of the publisher, and the publisher hereby disclaims any responsibility for them.

Any people depicted in stock imagery provided by Thinkstock are models, and such images are being used for illustrative purposes only. Certain stock imagery © Thinkstock.

ISBN: 978-1-5127-6734-6 (sc)
ISBN: 978-1-5127-6735-3 (hc)
ISBN: 978-1-5127-6736-0 (e)

Library of Congress Control Number: 2016920506

Print information available on the last page.

WestBow Press rev. date: 12/14/2016

Thank you to my wife Annette, the boys and my whole Family! You have given me love, laughter, context for ambition, focus and purpose! I like who we are, and I am excited what we can become through God's grace and His principles!

I pray the generations coming proclaim us faithful!

I love the journey God has for me as I get to do it with you all!

The Abundant Life for sure!!

Dan

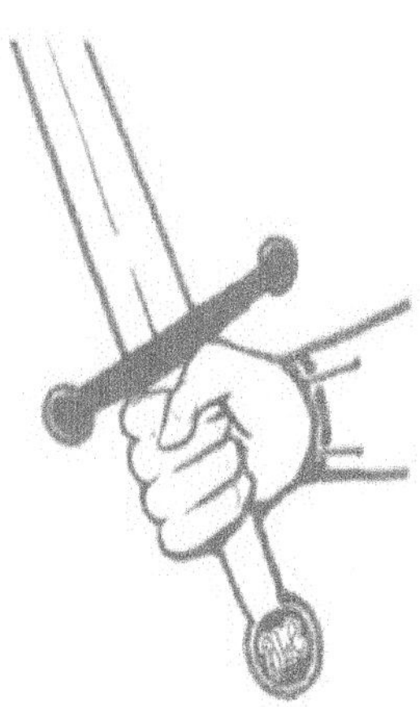

Welcome!

Life is a great journey and I believe this journal will help you think it through as you grow and discover what God has for you.

This is your life and this journal is your book, how could it not be exciting? Make it your own. You are the center of every page!

I believe as you walk with God, read, reread, and know His Word, pray and commune with Him, while going through whatever He has for you, good things (though not always easy) will come your way and the perspective and wisdom you will gain...**priceless!**

The key to all of this is that you must be in God's Word. I hope you will follow the Bible reading plan laid out in the following pages. It takes you through the whole Bible in one year. But if it is too much, just choose the Old Testament, or the New Testament, or half of it, or some system that makes sense to keep you grounded in God's Word. The Bible is the original "self-help" best seller! I believe following this plan and using this journal can have a real impact on your life!

Journaling requires active participation. You are the evaluator, thinker, self-coach in the driver's seat of this program. Take the opportunity to listen to people, write down the questions you have, take sermon notes, list important events, record advice you receive, and follow some of my ideas here. Work out the system that is best for you.

Each day I have included my thoughts, but this is really the least important part! I would like to be a whisper in your ear, a little bit like a coach who is cheering you on or telling you to consider some big issues. But I know that my ideas and thoughts will not always connect. That is okay! Blow me off and move on! The system is too good to let me get in the way!

Happy journaling, thinking, and remembering! Go and Grow!

In His Grip,

Dan

Why Journal?

I was in 10th grade. My English teacher, Mr. Sawyers, gave us an assignment to write entries in a journal and turn it in at the end of the quarter for a grade.

I found it freeing. It was more than just another assignment! I could write things I was not allowed to say. I could think better. I was hooked.

Thirty-five years later I am still writing in my journal. It is a part of my Bible study, my brain-storming, and my thought process. It helps me to let off some steam and remember important stuff.

There are lots of journaling methods out there. I have used everything from a blank notepad to some of the best published journals available in the book store. It is my hope and my goal to put the best possible system and structure in place to help you journal effectively. I believe this system can help you to remember, facilitate personal growth, push you to think Biblically, and keep you accountable as you journey through life.

The Bible tells us hundreds of time to "remember." We humans have a knack for remembering what we should forget, and forgetting what we should remember!

I want to remember the right things. I want to throw my life, the hopes, joys, dreams, and even the difficulties and struggles up against the truth of God's Word! I want to examine my life and character in such a way that I can improve and become the person God has designed me to be! I have heard it said: "You will never become what you are not now becoming."

I want to become the best me possible! And I believe you should too!

I also want to remember and contemplate the process. Plato once said that the unexamined life was not worth living. So let's examine life! Let's remember the good stuff. Let's categorize and index how things have transpired and gain understanding and perspective.

I hope this journal and the ideas behind it become a life long passion of yours that enrich you and those around you greatly!

Perspective Check

Deuteronomy 6:4-9 (NIV) lays out God's curriculum for his people. "Love the Lord your God with all your heart, with all your soul, and with all your strength." In Mark 12:30 Jesus helps us understand this even more by adding the word 'mind'.

In order to implement this curriculum, we need a successful strategy. For the family and the Body of Christ, we need to have an intentional plan with our kids. The directions in Scripture go on to imply we have to have a 24/7 approach to our parenting, to our teaching, and to a mentoring process that gets to the core of our young people.

What are we learning in school? What if we had teachers and staff at school ready and willing to partner with families and the Church to implement this Biblical strategy?

Read the following passages:

Deuteronomy 6:4-9	Mark 12:30
Colossians 2:2-4	Judges 2:9-12

How can we fight deception today? How can we increase knowledge and experience complete understanding without the truth of God, His Word, and His principles?

Consider what the outcomes of deviation from God's curriculum, even slightly, could look like down the road.

What are those "slight" deviations? What can you do about it? What is your obligation? Is this downward slope inevitable? How is the Church solving the problem?

Is God's curriculum being ignored? It reminds me of the beautiful orchestra music that was being played on the Titanic while it sank. Let's not get so caught up in our own things that we miss the important stuff!

Moses told the children of Israel in Deuteronomy exactly what God expected of them. By the time you get to Judges 2:10, the Israelites are worshipping Baal, they don't remember Moses or his miracles. Why weren't they doing what seemed so obviously right? Moses was the leader of leaders. Wouldn't you think a message from him would stick? What was the disconnect?

A missionary to Spain came by my Church. He said that only .07% of people in Spain claim to be Christian. Yikes! This is very similar to our Judges 2 passage when you consider Spanish history. Did you know that the Spanish people were very religious back in the day? Spanish kings were expected to be devout to the powerful Catholic Church. Church and State were aligned. Crusades were launched from Spain. What happened?

How is America like Spain? How is America like the Judges 2 passage?

If a family moves away from Jesus only slightly now, what might that look like 10 years from now, 50 years from now, or generations from now?

In both of the examples we find it very difficult to find strong remnants. Give it enough time and no one "survives."

What is the key to stopping this tragedy?

How can we be different?

What are you personally going to do about it?

Thinking About Learning

As I think about education in America, I believe there are many problems.

What is the cultural temperature of today's youth? What about our own kids? You may see positive things forming around you that are in sharp contrast to the negative reports you will hear about children and families in our country and our communities.

One plan for correction, training, hope, cultural making is Christian Education. Did you know only about 2% of the population is educated in a Christian school? So how are we ensuring our kids are getting the most important information they need to live a godly life? You will likely see my Christian Education background and bias come out through my brief thoughts and written encouragement as you go through this book.

But what is the plan, how will we turn our generation back to the ways of the Lord? What do you think will work?

How will the next generation learn the things of the Lord? How will the current culture lead them astray? How do you and I stay focused on God and His Word so that we are not swept away?

Read II Corinthians 13:5

I am praying that you will not go with the flow without a reflection process to think about the future of the Church, the family, and even the Christian faith.

II Chronicles 7:14 tells us that the prayer of a righteous person is worth so much! Lets pray hard!

The Idea Behind the Blank Index Pages

There are several pages available for you to index and categorize life happenings.

Maybe it has to do with your New Year's resolution, your budget, your weight loss plan, or your exercise plan. Maybe its your kid's statistics and progress in a sport, the books you read, or the movies you watch. It could be a prayer list, or the key God moments or days that you don't want to forget. Maybe it's a system to remind you which are the most important pages to go back to and read in your journal. You might just want to remember and list your achievement at work or at school. Whatever it is, figure out the system that works best for you!

Categorizing your life and some key impact moments will help a lot as you seek to remember and grow. One day you may find you can go back to these index pages and quickly see the significant things that happened in the particular year.

In the end, the Bible reading, the character development, your use of God's gifts, along with your words, thoughts, reactions, pictures, and artifacts will help you to understand the year and grow! It is my prayer that this journal will help you become exactly what God wants you to be for Him!

Index Options/Suggestions

1. New Year's Resolutions
2. Goals, Objectives, Plans for the year.
3. Budget
4. Weight loss progress
5. Exercise plan
6. Kids statistics, sports, hobbies, grades.
7. Movies you watch, or favorites with synopsis
8. Books you have read—synopsis/summaries
9. Prayer lists
10. Key journal days, the page number, God moves
11. Important days that God revealed something to you, taught you.
12. Progress at work, goals achieved, promotions, bonuses.
13. Sermon notes.
14. Big Questions you want a mentor or respected leader to answer.
15. Amazing current events, happenings of our day, culture shifts.
16. Friend list. Salvation targets.
17. Gifts given. Pay it forward acts.
18. Actual night dreams.
19. Great ideas, inventions, thoughts you refuse to forget.
20. New games to play. Conversation starter ideas.
21. Favorite sports teams/progress.
22. List of the artifacts/pictures you have stored in the pockets.
23. Websites, blogs you want to keep going back to.

Index

Index

Index

Index

Index

The Educational Quandary

Public education in America has been under scrutiny over the last few decades. In 1983 President Ronald Reagan's National Commission on Excellence in Education published a report called "A Nation at Risk" declaring that at the current rate of our educational failures the country would collapse.

Several attempts have been made to fix the American education system. New systems and methods are constantly being implemented and developed. The resources and attention devoted to education reform today are massive and ever-increasing.

It has always been an American belief that education can solve the problems of our society. But what is the value of education that has been cut loose from the absolute standards of the Bible?

Read II Peter 1:1-21

Peter tells us here that God has given us everything we need for a good and abundant life. He makes it clear that the learning we go through must include a spiritual component. The mind is only a part of our necessary growth. The heart must also be considered. Not just a nice prayer before an activity or a weekly moment of silence but an intentional progression of learning that combines our mind with our heart.

If we could pull together this combination of God's standards, and His way of learning we are given a promise that any educational establishment can never give... Guaranteed Success!

Verse 8 in II Peter 1 says our kids will be productive and effective. Reminds me of the Jabez prayer in I Chronicles 4:10.

I want to see the Body of Christ, you, the Church, reap the benefits of verses 10 and 11, "you will never stumble, and you will receive a rich welcome into the eternal kingdom..."

How can the Body of Christ encourage Biblical education? How might these ideas integrate into a school or a church? Can this reformation take place in your life or within your church?

Week 1—Example page/Getting started (52 weeks in a year)

Date: <u>Write in today's date</u>

Getting Started—The title for the day

Bible Reading: Genesis 1 - 8

Focus Word: Initiative - A word to consider

I get excited about new beginnings.

But keeping that initial motivation can be hard. As you begin this journal commit in prayer to a process of Bible reading and reflection.

Make your life an act of worship as you grow and learn from the Lord. Be quick to see and notice what God is doing in the circumstances of your life. Write down what you see and experience. I have a feeling you are going to be amazed at the Father's love for you and the great plans He has in store!

I am also sure you will have many tough days. Hang in there! Journal on those days as well. This is a journey worth taking!

1. This is the scripture reading for the day. They always have implications to the thoughts at the left. The pace of reading is around 10 pages for the OT, and two or 3 pages for the NT and the Psalms and Proverbs. Approximately 30 minutes for Bible reading and reflection and writing.

2. There are 5 devotional thoughts per week paired with a Bible reading. If you were to miss a day or two you can catch up. The key is your reflection of the Bible passage.

3. The sections with the gripped sword has lines and blank spaces for you to write your thoughts. Use this journal space to reflect on what God is teaching you. You will continue to decide, and evolve, about how much you write, what you write about, and who you share it with. This is your documentation for the year!

4. There are twenty "teaching sections" through the journal book that might help you process your journey. Blank pages could be used for sermon notes, Indexing, and more space for your writing! This arrow is pointing to page 19 as one of the example lessons.

Week 1

Date: ________________

Getting Started

Bible Reading: Genesis 1 - 8

Focus Word: Initiative

I get excited about new beginnings.

But keeping that initial motivation can be hard. As you begin this journal commit in prayer to a process of Bible reading and reflection.

Make your life an act of worship as you grow and learn from the Lord. Be quick to see and notice what God is doing in the circumstances of your life. Write down what you see and experience. I have a feeling you are going to be amazed at the Father's love for you and the great plans He has in store!

I am also sure you will have many tough days. Hang in there! Journal on those days as well. This is a journey worth taking!

Thanks for getting started, but thanks too for hanging in long term. I am telling you...you will be blessed!

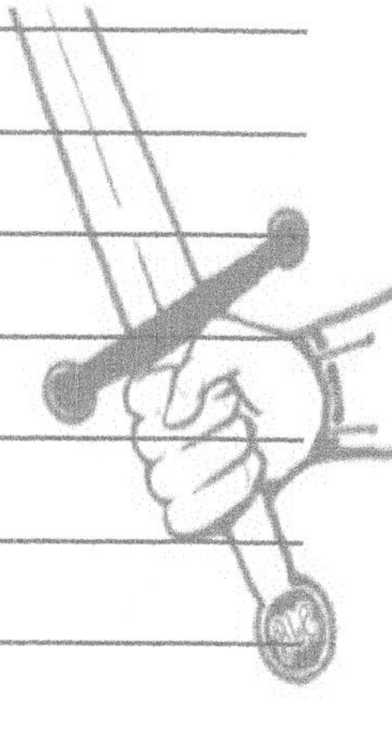

Date: ________________

The Body of Christ and Leadership

Bible Reading: Genesis 9 - 17

Focus Word: Alertness

Is it possible for the body of Christ to actually work together and create something great and amazing? I know it is possible and I have seen it, but I have to tell you, I see us failing more than not!

What gets in our way?

One issue is that we often struggle to follow our leaders. Rather than stand by a good leader we are quick to put down, criticize and find fault. No one is ever good enough to be offered our full loyalty and support.

On the other hand, the leaders can be the issue as well. Some leaders think they own the world and their pride creates problems.

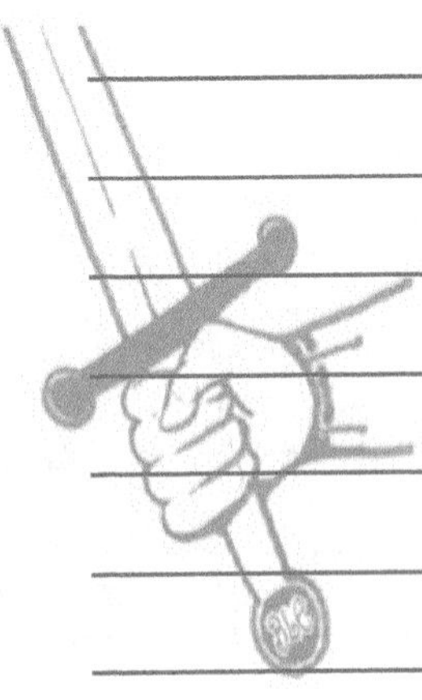

How can you apply the Bible's many examples of leadership? When do the following words make sense? Subdue, manage, direct, inspire, create, accomplish, improve, discover, learn and grow.

What does this look like in me?

Date: ________________

How Does Influence Work?

Bible Reading: Psalms 1 - 7

Focus Word: Joyfulness

Did you know that you become like those you hang around? You begin to think like those you pay attention to.

Who or what has a big influence on you?

Who are you influencing? Sometimes I think I am having an influence on others, and maybe I see a particular person as a project, but the truth is that I am the one being changed and influenced! If I am not careful then those people I hang out with, the shows I watch, and that Web site I frequent all have an influence on me rather than vice versa.

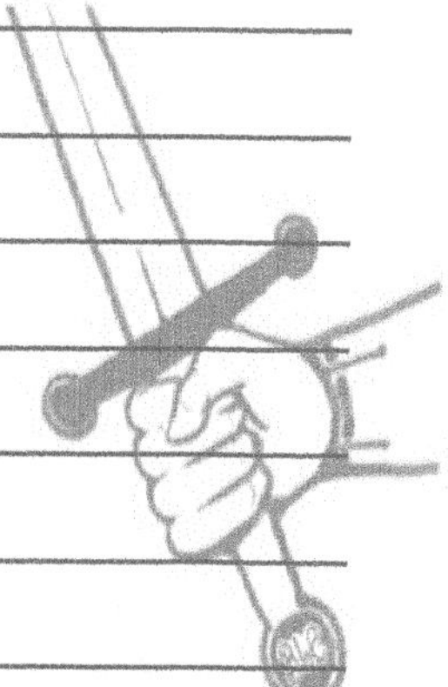

Stay grounded in the Bible in order to avoid being blown in the changing winds of popular culture or the latest fad. Make a positive difference today and tomorrow!

What is your influence on those around you? Are you positive or negative? What is the tone of your conversations?

Date: ____________________

Deal with it!

Bible Reading: Matthew 1 - 3

Focus Word: Attentiveness

Introspection is good. It is important to me and key to why I believe in journaling. I love to talk about growth and becoming better.

As sinful people we are quick to notice the flaws in others but fail to consider our own weaknesses. Do I allow my introspection to point me to my problems, my weakness, and my sin? How often do I confess and seek forgiveness?

I never want to forget that Jesus came to fix the sin in me!

Though I don't yet comprehend exactly what heaven will be like, I am excited to be in the presence of Jesus. Even now Jesus can fix my seemingly endless capacity to mess things up and spoil relationships. How cool is it to think that my walk with Jesus can cure my propensity for sin and positively effect every relationship I value!

How is your sin wrecking things in your life and what are you doing about it?

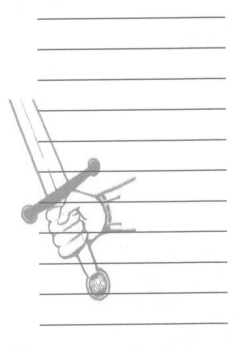

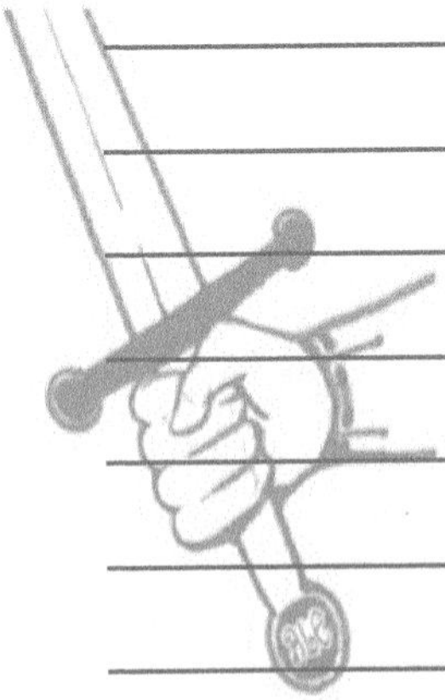

Date: ____________________

Blessed

Bible Reading: Matthew 4 - 5

Focus Word: Kindness

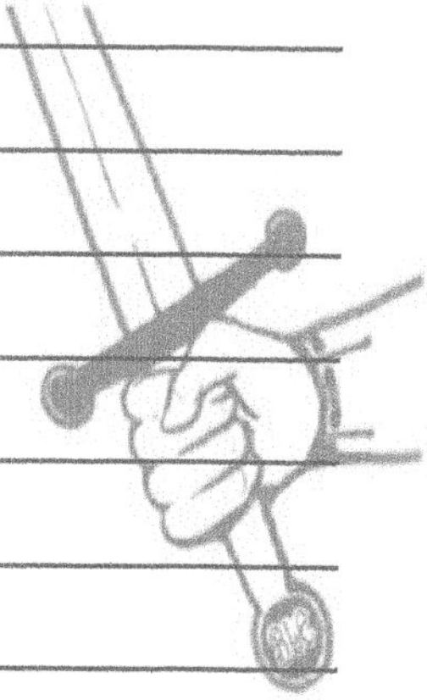

Prayer of Saint Francis of Assisi:

"Lord, make me an instrument of thy peace! That where there is hatred, I may bring love. That where there is wrong, I may bring the spirit of forgiveness. That where there is discord, I may bring harmony. That where there is error, I may bring truth. That where there is doubt, I may bring faith. That where there is despair, I may bring hope. That where there are shadows, I may bring light. That where there is sadness, I may bring joy, Lord, grant that I may seek rather to comfort, than to be comforted. To understand, than to be understood. To love, than to be loved. For it is by self-forgetting that one finds. It is by forgiving that one is forgiven. It is by dying that one awakens to eternal life."

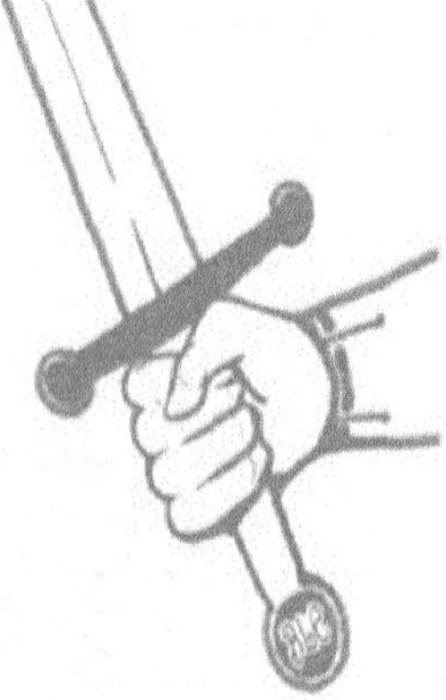

What is your view of Creation?

Does the teaching and understanding of creation change anything in a practical way?

Read the following passages:
Psalms 19:1-4
Romans 1:18-20
Job 38 through 42

Does the study of science help us to look closer at God and cause us to appreciate the amazing things He has created, or does it make us feel we need God less? Perspective and worldview are critical as we consider this.

Darwin's theory of evolution leaves a lot of questions unanswered. The 2nd Law of Thermodynamics says that all things move from structure to chaos, from high power to low power: entropy. This law tells us that things dissipate or lose energy. How can this be reconciled with the randomness of evolution?

This amazing world we live in did not just show up.

William Paley used the metaphor of a watchmaker. When you see the wonder and detail of a watch, you do not assume it just happened thanks to time and chance, but you understand there was a watchmaker behind the little machine.

Are the ideas of evolution really the intellectual high ground?

Biochemistry professor Michael Behe, the originator of the term irreducible complexity, defines an irreducibly complex system as one "composed of several well-matched, interacting parts that contribute to the basic function, wherein the removal of any one of the parts causes the system to effectively cease functioning".

Does the creation story help give you direction and purpose to life? How important is this?

Week 2

Date: ________________

When Is Laughing Good for the Soul?

Bible Reading: Genesis 18 - 24

Focus Word: Cheerfulness

Life can be tough, difficult, and serious! But sometimes we just need to laugh.

On the other hand, when is it the wrong time to laugh? Our culture laughs a lot, and sometimes at the wrong things. There is a lot of cynicism, -or humor at others' expense, -and everything is pretty much a joke. How can we get the balance right?

Isn't it interesting that when God tells Sarah she will experience childbirth in old age, she thinks He is joking and she laughs! Probably not the right time to laugh at God's promise. She even tried to cover it up with a lie!

Turn a couple pages and find Lot telling his sons-in-law that God will destroy Sodom; they thought Lot was joking -and then they perished!

When are the times we need to laugh more, and when does our culture laugh too much?

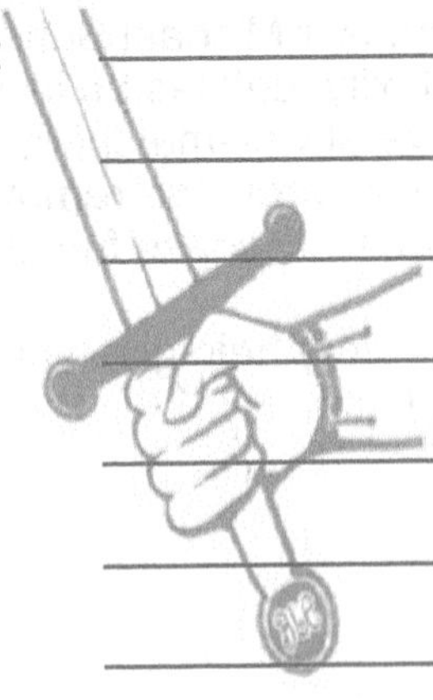

Date: ________________

Bad examples

Bible Reading: Genesis 25 - 30

Focus Word: Living a Holy Life

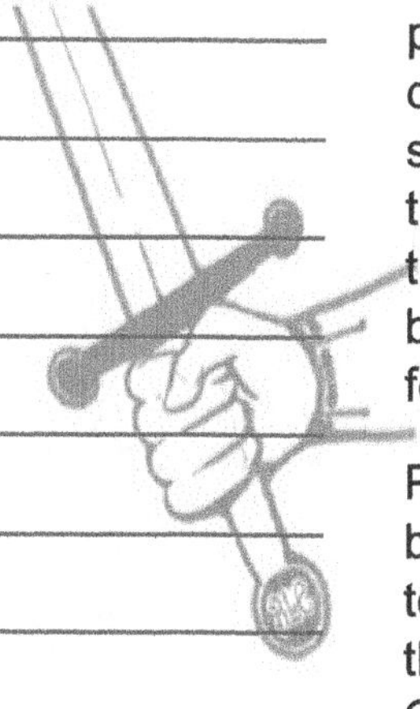

Have you ever heard he expression, "do as I say and not as I do"?

Sometimes it is shocking how many bad examples show up in the Bible. In Genesis 28-30, we find Jacob deceiving his father for a blessing and then we witness the hostile rivalry of sisters Leah and Rachel. Again and again we are reminded that we are all, including our biblical heroes, fallen and sinful.

But let's not use our sinful nature as an excuse! The Bible is also filled with good examples of people who did the right thing in difficult circumstances. We should not be so quick to proclaim that "no one is perfect" as though this gives us an excuse to just get by or that it provides a free pass for our own sinfulness.

Plan to do better, work hard to do better, and be what God wants you to be. Not only is this the right thing to do, but when we do things God's way, everyone benefits.

Date: ________________

God's Best: You!

Bible Reading: Psalms 8 - 14

Focus Word: Confidence

I get excited when science helps us get a glimpse of just how big, great, and amazing this world is!

The same kind of thinking can then dive into the small things, like electronic waves, the intricacies of molecules, and other powerful parts of our world that are hidden to the unaided eye.

We have so much to praise the Lord for every day! This world He created is incredible!

Catch this! As amazing as God's world is and as impressive as all these natural systems are, there is nothing more amazing or more cherished than *you*!!!

Today's passage contains the imagery of God creating the world with His finger tips, -no big deal. But when He creates people, now that is where He rolls up His sleeves and gets to work!

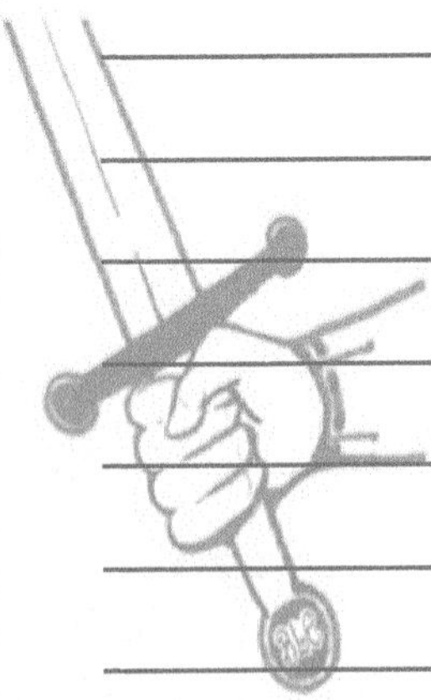

Date: ____________________

The Life of Faith

Bible Reading: Matthew 6 - 8

Focus Word: Discernment

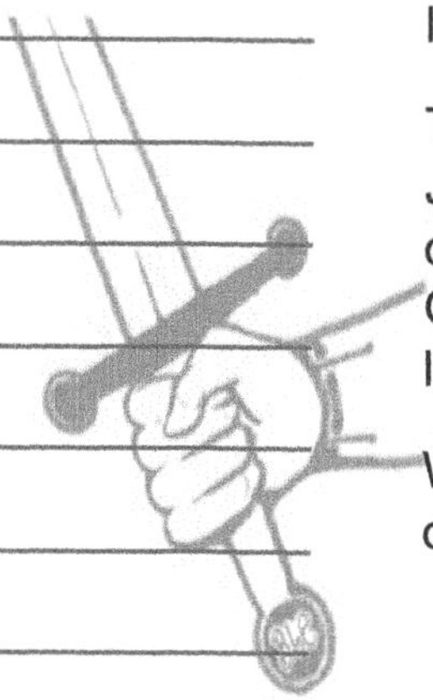

Christianity is based on faith. But Christianity is not alone in this, -every philosophy, worldview, or system of thought is based on faith.

Interesting that Jesus is amazed at the faith of the Centurion. Why do you think He was so impressed?

What does the walk of faith look like? Have you seen it in others? What behaviors, attitudes, and practices are typical of such people?

What needs to change for you so that you demonstrate to others a life of faith?

The quandary of the book of James comes to mind. What is our response to the free gift of God's grace and salvation in our life?

What are the practices (and fruit) of faithful people?

Date: ________________

Shake Off the Dust

Bible Reading: Matthew 9 - 10

Focus Word: Perseverance

Jim Elliot, a missionary to the Auca Indians, made this statement: "He is no fool who gives away what he cannot keep to have what he cannot lose."

This comes very close to what Jesus said in Matthew 10:39 about how losing your life for His sake is the only way to really find life at all!

I like to think I have control over my life and that my decisions will result in a great life. I usually have it figured out that my actions should merit joyous, wonderful results or effects that benefit me and make me happy and prosperous.

Newsflash: It doesn't always work that way!

Quit being surprised when things do not go your way. Life can be tough and we never have as much control over our circumstances as we think we do. But take heart; God has so much to teach us when life is difficult.

Week 3

Date: ________________

Wrestling with God

Bible Reading: Genesis 31 - 37

Focus Word: Courage

"What goes around comes around."

Many people seem to love this phrase, but what does it mean?

It is often refers to those who create or sow their own problems will eventually reap the results of those problems.

That is certainly true of Jacob.

Am I self-aware enough or, humble enough, to realize when I am reaping some of my own problems? It is easy to rationalize and blame everyone else and never own up to my part.

I love the imagery of wrestling with God like Jacob did in Genesis 32. Not that we can ever win, but that we can struggle to find God's truth. In the struggle we can be serious, blunt, honest and even wrong, so long as it finally opens us to what we need to do and how we need to own up to our situation!

And yes, all this can be very good for us, even if we end up limping!

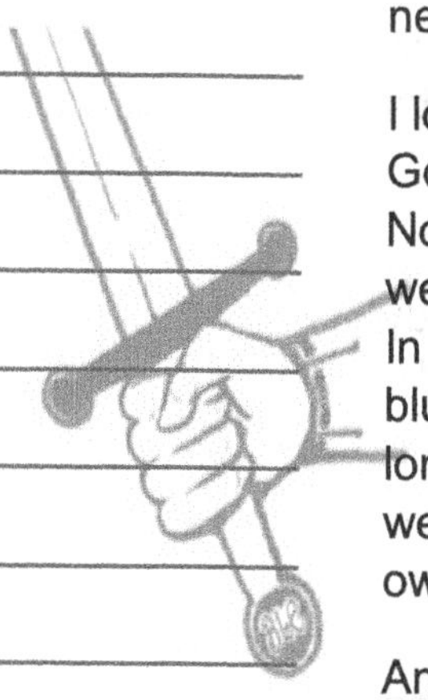

Date: ________________

So, Lead!

Bible Reading: Genesis 38 - 43

Focus Word: Persistent

Leadership is tough. God's call to leadership can be seen from the very beginning in His expectation that humanity exercises "dominion" and "subdues" the earth.

Romans 12:8 gives no indication that this will be easy —"lead diligently."

Look at Joseph as a leader. He was dependable, he was creative, and he was a problem solver. He had a lot of success, but he was also misunderstood. Remember the story of Potiphar's wife In Genesis 39. One moment Potiphar trusted Joseph with everything he owned, and the next moment Joseph was in prison after being wrongly accused by Potiphar's wife!

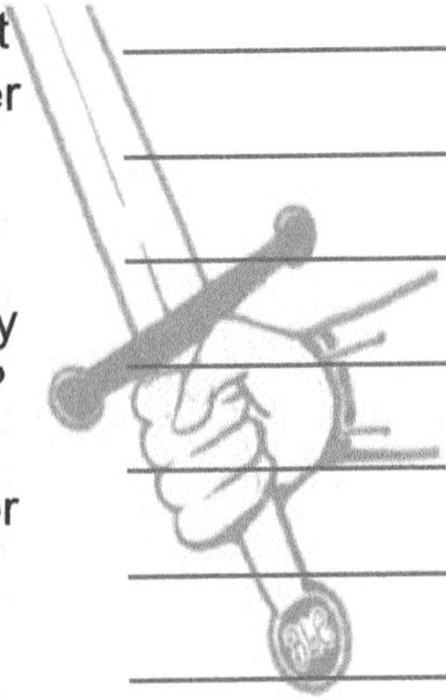

Leadership is a risk. Are you ready to put yourself out there and lead? Do not be surprised if you are rejected, at least by some group or someone!

God is in the business of using people. Are you open to Him using you?

Date: ________________

God is Good

Bible Reading: Psalm 15 - 18

Focus Word: Gratefulness

"God is good. God is great. Now we thank Him for our food, amen."

You may have been taught this simple prayer when you were first learning to talk.

Sometimes I need to allow the Psalms to remind me that in my complicated world God is still good, His word is still flawless, and that He in fact equips me with strength I need. He trains me and He enables me. God makes my way perfect.

I must remember to take refuge in this rock solid deliverer, the creator God who loves me more than I can imagine!

How is God showing himself to you today?

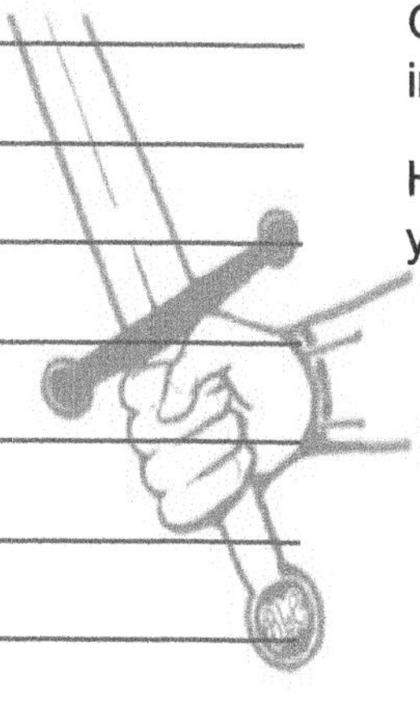

Date: ________________

Forceful Advance

Bible Reading: Matthew 11 - 12

Focus Word: Boldness

John the Baptist was the man! From his wild clothes to his all natural diet, he was tough! Probably a little weird, but no one can question his commitment.

I am prone to give up too quickly. I think the American culture in general is very willing to let things slide and it often fails to take a stand on important issues! No conviction and nothing worth fighting for!

As Christians we have to be willing to take a stand when the time comes. Heaven forbid that we stand up for nothing!

"Forceful advancing" of he kingdom of heaven sounds like a difficult path, but it may be exactly what is needed to accomplish great things!

Don't give up. Be part of God's kingdom advancement!

Where do you need to add resolve to your life? What do you need to see through to the end?

Date: ____________________

I Am Not Worrying, Just Concerned!

Bible Reading Matthew 13 - 14

Focus Word: Responsiveness

When does worry become a sin? Isn't it funny how so many people want to rename it and claim that they are just showing concern!

And yet I understand that people who are trying to flourish and succeed in this world will find many hurdles. There are all sorts of problems, dilemmas, and setbacks that make us anxious, stressed, and WORRIED!

I was told that 90% of what we worry about will never come to pass. But then again I have also heard that 90% of all statistics are made up!

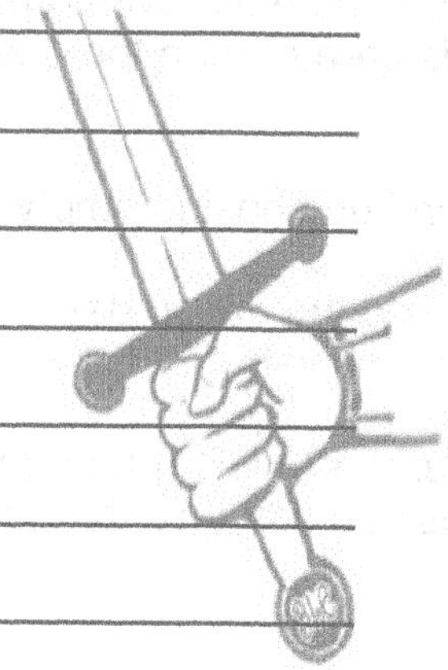

I think my problem is what I worry about. When it is all about me and my comfort and my happiness, then my worry is definitely headed toward the thorns as in the parable of the sower.

How do you overcome worry?

The value of Learning

Statistics make a strong case for the value an education has on one's career. The more degrees, the more money you make. Is a job the only thing, or the main thing, we expect from our education?

Read Matthew 11:12
Read I Peter 1:13 through 2:3

Not only do we want our children and those in the Body of Christ to be materially successful but we need them to be wise and discerning.

The next generation will have some very difficult issues to negotiate and they need to be ready.

Anything we do, anything we believe, starts with our mind. Are we prepared? To move the kingdom forward, the next generation will have to be people of conviction, people who have enough fortitude to push back. Matthew gives the impression that when you are up against a force, you have to be like John the Baptist and push back!

Peter says in the reading listed above that ignorance is the way for evil to take root and that the Body of Christ must prepare ourselves for action which requires self-control.

"You, dear children, are from God and have overcome them, because the one who is in you is greater than the one who is in the world." I John 4:4 (NIV)

How do we get distracted and end up chasing empty things in life?

How can our children taste and see the day to day implications of "growing up" in our salvation?

What might the future look like and how will you be prepared? What are you learning that helps you advance the gospel?

Week 4

Date: ________________

God's Ways/Man's Ways

Bible Reading: Genesis 44 - 50

Focus Word: **Acceptance**

I think Joseph was amazing!

He had so many setbacks and yet kept persevering through life making the most of every situation.

The epitome of this ability is when he comes to terms with the fact that his brothers have done him wrong and yet God has used their evil, their bad intention, their misguided decisions and conclusions for a purpose much bigger than anyone could have initially thought possible! He forgives.

This sort of forgiveness can be hard to understand! In fact, I do not think I like it! Good story for Joseph, but what about when it happens to you and me? Would I be able to forgive my family after being sold into a life of slavery?

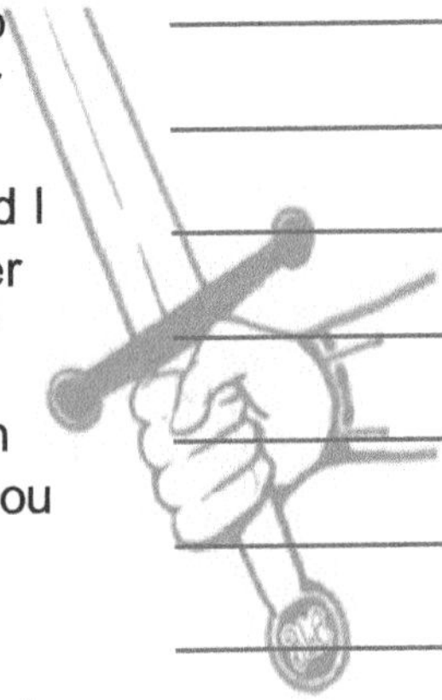

Have you ever been "stabbed in the back"? Even worse, have you been hurt by a family, friend, or Christian?

Where does God fit in this? Am I willing to forgive?

Date: ________________

Lead like Moses

Bible Reading: Exodus 1 - 8

Focus Word: Leadership

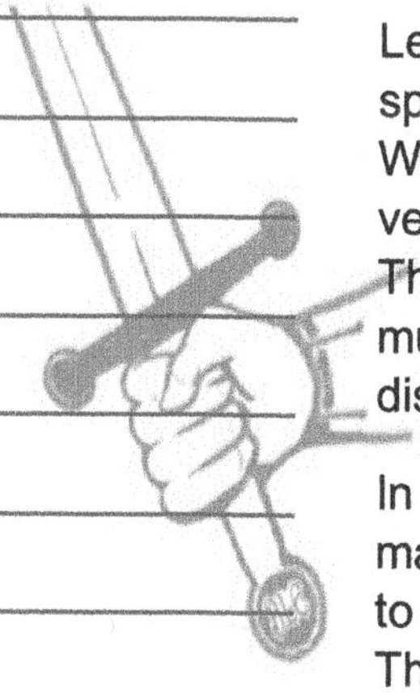

Moses rocks! Maybe that is why Hollywood has long been fascinated by this Biblical figure. Check out a few of these movies to get various views on his life.

He had a crazy, interesting life, but what stands out most is his incredible leadership ability! After his years of hiding and wandering he developed into an amazing leader!

Romans 12:8 tells us that leadership is sometimes no more than just hard work and perseverance. Leadership skills can take time to ripen.

Leaders are people in the spotlight. People are watching. While this can be fun it can also be very difficult, tough, and lonely. Those who want and hope for much, can also be greatly disappointed!

In light of the fact that there are many things we forget, work hard to remember the right things. Think about leadership lessons that Moses' life can teach us.

Date: ____________________

Thinking Like God

Bible Reading: Psalms 19 - 23

Focus Word: Wisdom

I would like to think that as I get closer to the Lord, I will think like Him and be passionate and excited about the things He wants me to be passionate and excited about.

My own sinfulness and selfishness can reek havoc on my thinking! Thinking like God seems distant and impossible when my every thought is turned towards myself. I get this messed up more than I would like to admit.

But somewhere there is a desire to do God's will and to fulfill His purpose in me in such a way that I am a blessing to others. And maybe, just maybe, you and I can experience success in doing the desires of our hearts in a way that glorifies God. This is a type of success that is bigger and better than money, promotions or fame.

Be careful! Check your intentions! This purpose driven mindset takes wisdom!

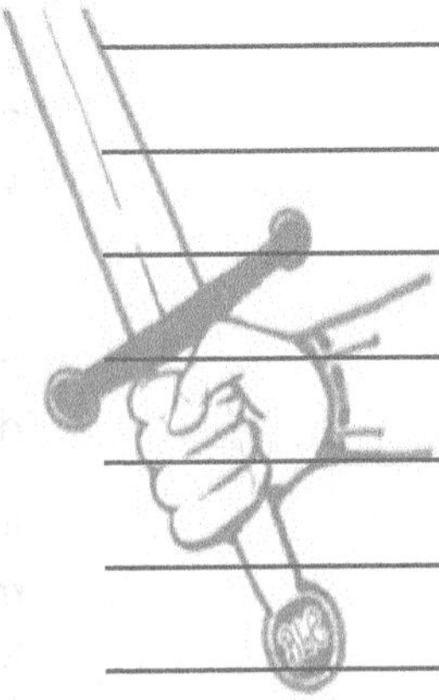

Date: ________________

Learning From Others

Bible Reading: Matthew 15 - 17

Focus Word: Mentoring

Just like Paul mentored Timothy you and I also need good mentors. And yes, you need to be a mentor for others as well.

The call to mentorship is clear, but establishing a quality relationship is very difficult. Just because someone is older doesn't qualify them to be a mentor.

So how does one go about seeking mentorship? Maybe it is best to use several people? Or possibly even books and other remote sources will work.

I hope that your reflection here on God's Word and observation of people in your life will have a positive mentor effect on you. I believe that journaling can be key to your personal growth. As we pay attention to things God directs us to, write it down, categorize it, think about it, and maybe even share it with others, we learn and grow. As strange as it sounds, we often mentor ourselves.

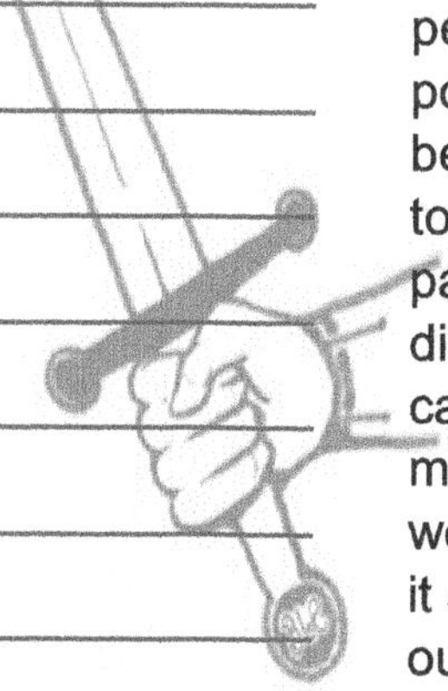

Date: ________________

Dealing With Conflict

Bible Reading: Matthew 18 - 20

Focus Word: Courageous

Have you ever seen church discipline work?

To many the idea doesn't even sound right today. Our culture is not open to being told what to do or what is wrong.

So how do we handle conflict and confrontation in the church and in Christian organizations?

In my world we turned Matthew 18 into a verb! It meant the process of confrontation and how that works. It is very difficult to do in a Christ-like way. But in light of Galatians 6:1 it is possible to have great results if the motivation is love and restoration.

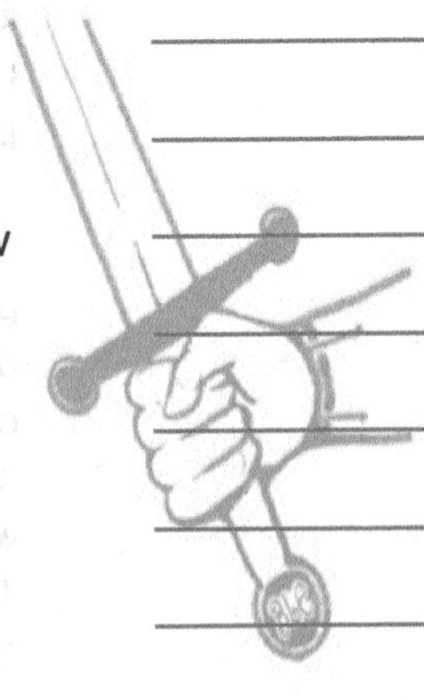

Church discipline and conflict are really two different things. But how you handle conflict, while keeping the problems in tight circles, will help you solve people issues successfully!

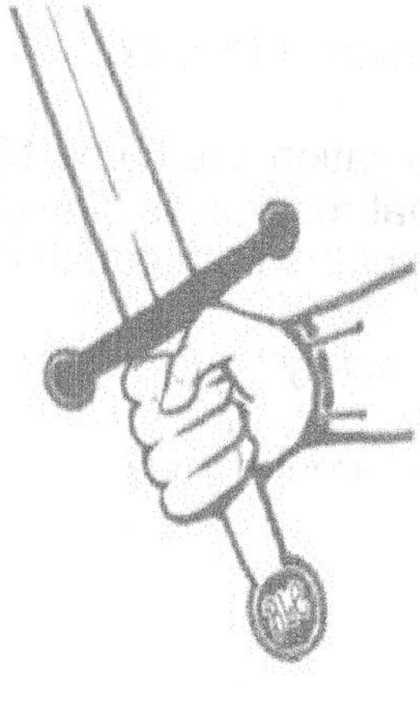

Proclaiming the Truth!

You can start a great discussion by asking people why they think Jesus came to earth.

You might get several different answers.
He came to save us.
He came to heal us.
He came to set us free.

Read John 18:27-37

Jesus came to do many things. But isn't it interesting that when He is pushed to declare his purpose, He tells Pilate he came to testify to the Truth.

Truth is interesting. Most of us like for people to speak the truth and even expect it. The problem is that truth is not as clear as one might think, it is often a perspective issue. We often believe that "Truth" can be discovered through scientific reasoning. Although this is an important way to find some truth, science has obvious limitations when you consider ideas such as morality, ethics, metaphysics, epistemology and then consider these concepts in light of postmodernism.

Where do you find truth?

Who is teaching the next generation truth?

Read Romans 12:1-2
What is required to have the mind of Christ?

How does a public school population overcome 16,000 hours of secular teaching in K-12, that regardless of negative or positive intent, keeps God out of the truth equation?

How important is truth to our society?

How important is truth to those around you?

Week 5

Date: ________________

A Good Team

Bible Reading: Exodus 9 - 15

Focus Word: Mindfulness

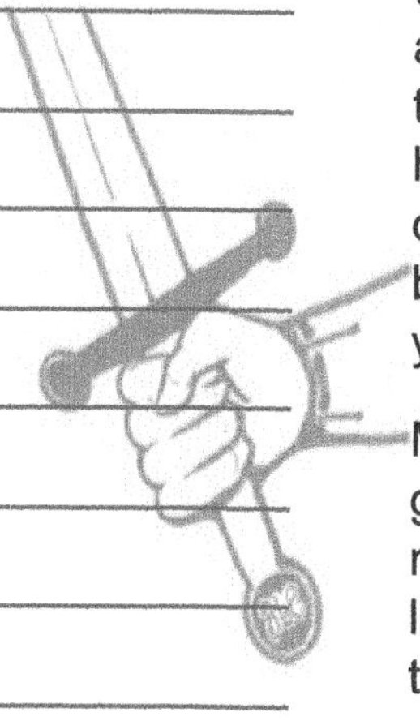

Some people are just fun to be around. Just think about some of the friends or family who give energy to your life.

Unfortunately there are also people out there who seem to make life harder. Can you think of people in your life who steal energy from others?

Be careful how you sort it out. Sometimes we need several perspectives and viewpoints as we walk through our journey.

I do not like that Pharaoh's heart was hardened! I have to work through how that fits my theology and doctrine, but I also noticed that those around Pharaoh had hard hearts as well. There is no opportunity for checks and balances when your friends have your same weaknesses!

My take away here is I need a good group around me pointing me to the abundant life I want to live. I also want to think about how to be a helpful friend to others!

Date: ________________

Good Planning

Bible Reading: Exodus 16 - 23

Focus Word: Orderliness

Moses was such an example of a life of faith and dependence on God that his family began to take notice. His father-in-law, Jethro, after years of observing Moses, accepted God as the one and only true God.

Go Moses! May we all be a testimony of praise that points people to Jesus!

Consider Exodus 18:17-27. Jethro also had much to teach Moses. He analyzed the dispute resolution methods Moses was using. He noted that there is a better system and use of people that could make life more productive and sustainable if Moses would just think it through and delegate.

What awesome lessons of leadership! Here is a great example of the power of teaching, training, and what discipleship can do for the body of Christ!

Don't skip good planning and thinking!

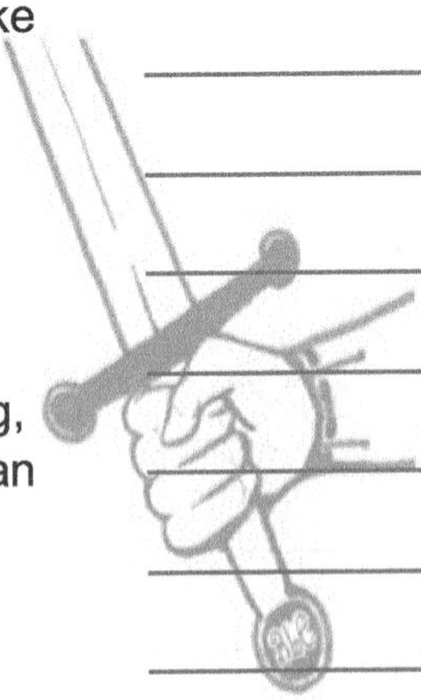

Date: ________________

Good Thoughts

Bible Reading: Psalms 24 - 29

Focus Word: Confidence

It is easy to get discouraged and find yourself full of negative, even self-destructive, thoughts.

Oh the power of positive thinking (google Norman Vincent Peale)!

But don't take it too far! I think we should be careful of the mind over matter, hocus-pocus, meditation, and self-talk quick fixes that our culture so often proclaims.

This is another of the many good reasons we need to be in God's Word! The power of the Holy Spirit combines with the words we read to guide and direct the kind of thinking we need to practice.

The Psalms is an awesome place to build hope and confidence in what God is doing and can do through your life.

The Lord is my light and my salvation-whom shall I fear? That is real confidence!

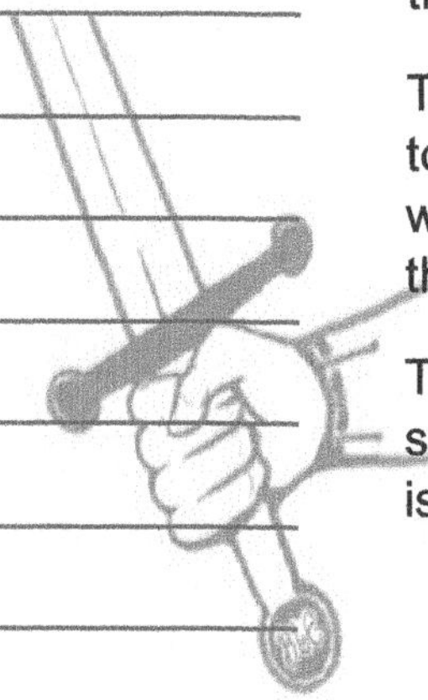

Date: ________________

The Greatest Commandment

Bible Reading: Matthew 21 - 22

Focus Word: Love

Love should drive our actions as we pursue the good life with Christ!

One of my favorite scripture lessons comes from Deuteronomy 6:4-9 where Moses explains the most important thing people can do is to love the Lord with all your heart, soul, and strength. Too bad we mess this up more than not!

In today's passage you will find that Jesus reasserts and reaffirms Moses' words to love God with your heart, soul and mind and then follows it up with a command to love your neighbor as yourself.

Life can be so complicated! Sometimes it helps to focus and gain perspective by taking your complicated life and realize how simple God's plan is. Love God and love others.

Love is motivating, powerful, and so very useful. Allow love to order your day today!

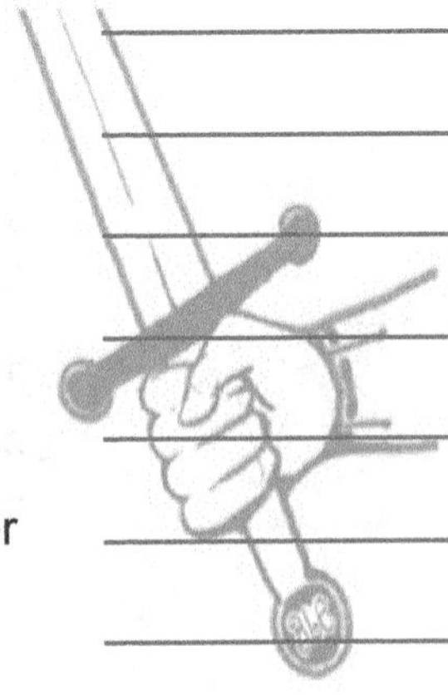

Date: ________________

Who Do I Listen To?

Bible Reading: Matthew 23 -24

Focus Word: Authority

In America we love the idea of a self-made man. You know, the guy that doesn't have everything handed to him on a silver spoon but he makes his life amazing anyhow!

These are the kind of people who solve all their own problems and follow the American dream while doing whatever they want. You know, listening to no one!

Who is on the throne of your life? Who (maybe it is you) calls the shots? Who do you like to listen to (are you old enough to remember EF Hutton commercials?)?

If you have a "Red Letter" edition Bible you will see that today's passage is all red. It is the words of Jesus.

Listen to Jesus, He won't lead you astray.

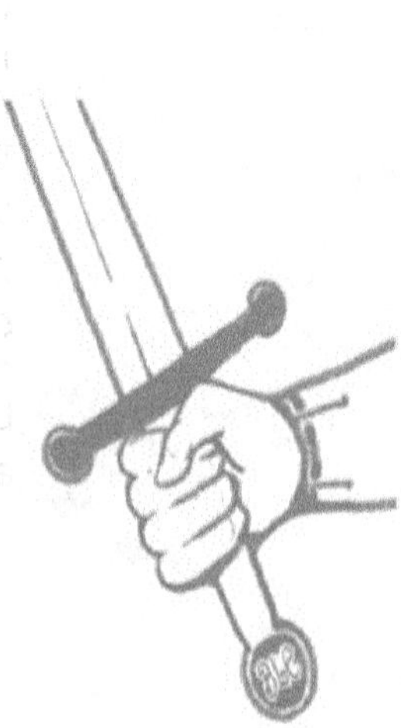

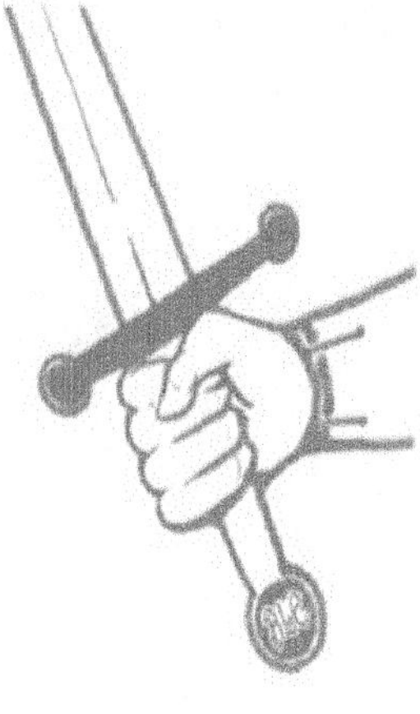

Week 6

Date: ________________

Skill Development

Bible Reading: Exodus 24 - 31

Focus Word: Competent

So what are you good at doing?

What are you doing to develop your skills? How much effort are you putting into being a better person?

Have you ever heard of Bezalel or Oholiab? A couple of guys who might be easy to miss!

It turns out these guys were good at several types of craftsmanship. They were artist who used their God-given abilities to glorify the Lord in ways I do not always put in the "ministry" category. Yet, the Lord told Moses in Exodus 31 that he had filled these two men with the Spirit of God to get an important job done!

Truth is, we need to do whatever we do in such a way that honors the Lord! See Colossians 3:23!

Commit to developing your skills. You never know where the Lord will take you and put you to work!

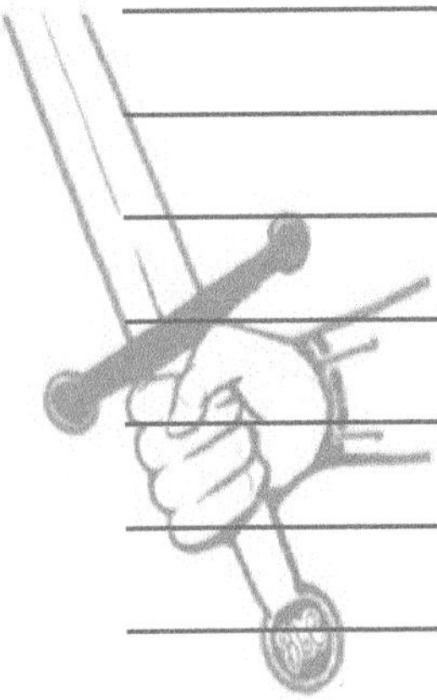

Date: ________________

Rationalize

Bible Reading: Exodus 32 - 40

Focus Word: Integrity

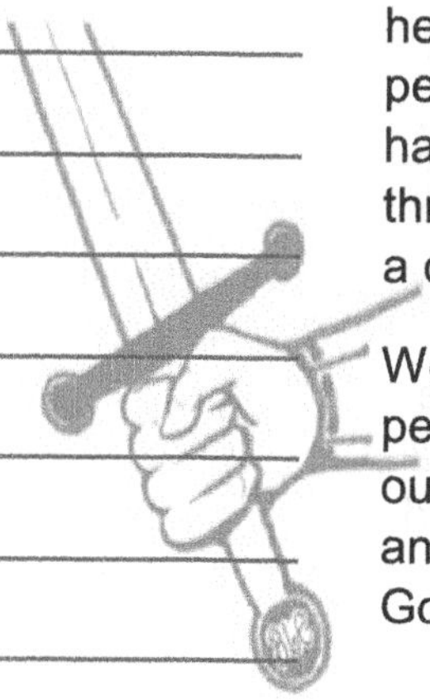

I have a gift of making everything seem right in my own eyes! And no this "gift" is not a fruit of the spirit!

I blame sin nature and the fall of man! But the truth is, it is not a good trait and I need to stop rationalizing my actions.

In Exodus 32 Moses leaves Aaron in charge while he speaks with God on the mountain. When he comes back the people are going crazy and they are worshipping a golden calf that Aaron made.

When Moses asks Aaron about it he blame shifts to the "bad people" and some crazy thing that happened to jewelry when he threw it in the fire (bam—out pops a calf).

We need to fight for truth and be people of integrity. Rationalizing our sin away only hurts ourselves and others and falls far short of God's standard.

Date: ________________

Use Me Lord

Bible Reading: Psalms 30 - 33

Focus Word: Worship

One of my favorite verses is II Chronicles 16:9.

"For the eyes of the Lord range throughout the earth to strengthen those whose hearts are fully committed to him." (NIV)

You get a sense here that the Lord is looking for good people to carry out His will. He wants to use me and you. In fact, He not only wants to put you on the team, He wants you to play and He wants you to score! Pretty important stuff.

Psalms 33:18 says that same kind of thing. The Lord is looking for the kind of people He can bless and use.

It is a great honor to be part of important work.

Praise the Lord today for what He is doing in your life and how He is using you to accomplish great and mighty things. Your joy might even result in dancing!

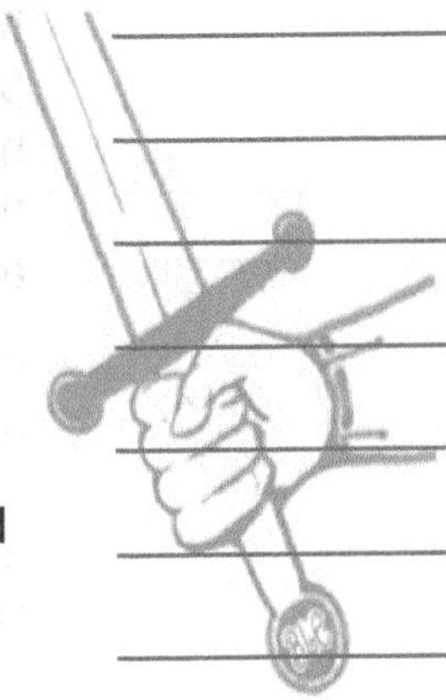

Date: ________________

Kingdom Math

Bible Reading: Matthew 25 - 26

Focus Word: Stewardship

Math is the elementary school subject that you just can't argue with as 2 plus 2 always equals 4.

But consider this, everyone of us has gifts and talents. These gifts and talents are part of God's plan for each of us. From the beginning He tells us we are fearfully and wonderfully made.

So, what is kingdom math? If you have one talent and you use it and develop it well He will give you two. If you have five talents that you dedicate for His work and His glory he will give you ten!

The down side is that if you do not use and steward the gifts and talents He has given you he will take them away.

So the math looks like this:

Use 2 get 4; develop 5 reap 10!
Or: 2 + effort = 4; 5 + effort = 10.

Do things God's way and let Him multiply your effectiveness!

Date: ________________

The Great Commission

Bible Reading: Matthew 27 - 28

Focus Word: Simplicity

Christianity hinges on the truth that Jesus lived a sinless life and chose to die on a cross for each of us out of His great love. Three days later He rose from the grave.

He is alive! He wants to live in you. He wants you to have a relationship with Him.

It is so crazy, so fantastic—so amazing—and so unbelievable!

But really, what else have you got to depend on? Does anything make more sense?

God the creator puts it all together for us. There is no way we can comprehend it all and explain everything. But if you give it your best shot, and learn from His Word and the wisdom of those around you, you will see the pieces fitting together.

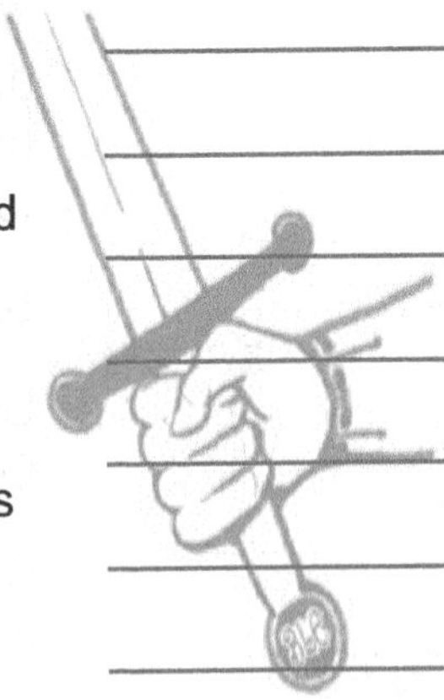

In the end He loves you and wants you to participate in building His kingdom.

Go for it!

Growing the Mind!

I have been an educator my whole career. I love it! I am in the growth business. What a joy to see kids, teens, and even parents grow and become better!

It takes motivation and hard work!

The Bible is filled with lessons and encouragement about growing and getting better. To be a virtuous person is of great value. To grow in character, in the fruits of the Spirit (Galatians 5:22-23), and train yourself in godliness is a wise and smart thing to do!

Considering all the hard work that goes into growing in our faith its no surprise that sin, foolishness and simple thinking can really mess people up! Immorality corrupts your ability to think straight. I will say it another way, sin has a way of making you stupid!

But the good news of Romans 12:1-2 is that you don't have to be stupid, you can be transformed. This transformation and all that is included actually makes you wiser, smarter, more helpful, and a better problem solver!

There is a link between IQ, EQ (emotional intelligence), and other measures of intelligence (tactile, creativity, etc.) and biblical disciplines and growth. Commitment to grow in your faith actually makes you smarter!

So you want to be smarter? You want to be successful? Start with humility and realize that you have weaknesses (and yes, strengths too), and that you are a vulnerable, fragile human depending on miracles and God's grace to function well!

Now start learning. Come up with a process. Discover new things, be teachable, curious, and persistent. Apply your knowledge with courage, and systematic thinking, as you read God's Word. Think introspectively. Think critically with honesty and integrity.

Maybe the statement in Daniel 1:20 can be you? "Ten times better!"

Week 7

Date: ____________

Dealing with Sin

Bible Reading: Leviticus 1 - 9

Focus Word: Reverence

Keep your head up as you jump into the Old Testament book of Leviticus! It is difficult reading.

Maybe now is a good time to talk about sin. Sin is bad. It not only hurts others, but it is self-destructive.

Sometimes our sin is the evil stuff we do on purpose. These are sins of commission. Sometimes it is the good stuff we refuse to do. These are sins of omission.

Sometimes the sin we commit are out of ignorance and we just do not know any better.

Either way we need to be serious about our sin and about confession. When sin is taken care of, we can get on with fulfilling the mission God has for each of us!

There is no sense acting like we are perfect! Ask others to evaluate your life and help you thrive. What a blessing when people are honest in evaluations and willing to grow!

Date: ________________

Parenting

Bible Reading: Leviticus 10 - 17

Focus Word: Obedience

Good parenting is so, so important and yet so, so hard to do!

Are you a good parent? Were you parented well?

Most people have a story here.

It can be hard to find good parenting advise. Sometimes it can be even harder to give parenting advice! There are so many opinions out there. Pride or maybe embarrassment often get in the way when we consider our own parenting and some people simply do not want your parenting advice.

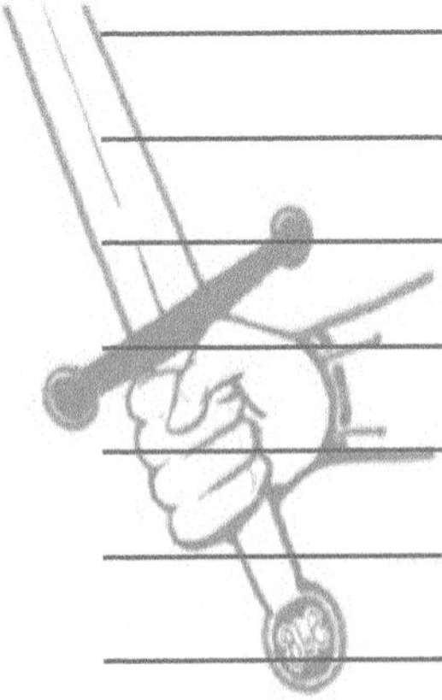

The Old Testament is filled with bad parents. Aaron, the brother of Moses, was a disaster of a parent. When his sons were immoral and irreverent priests, he said nothing. He just let them get away with it! The consequences were so final - death! (Leviticus 10)

So what does good parenting look like today?

Date: ________________

Wanting Stuff

Bible Reading: Psalms 34 - 37

Focus Word: Maturity

I want so many things. By popular definitions they are usually good things, but some of my desires are not so honorable.

It is tough to think like Jesus in such a materialistic culture, especially when we have so many resources. Poor people in America are still in the wealthiest 10% of world population.

We are blessed. Use the Psalms to praise Him! Be thankful but consider what obligations we have for our blessings. To whom much is given much is required, right?

So my wrestling match is when the desires of my heart are not met, do I consider why this might be and consider that I may be falling short in some capacity?

Truth is, I already have far more than I deserve and I need to be more thankful. A heart for the Lord wants the things the Lord wants!

Date: ________________

Prayer Challenge

Bible Reading: Mark 1 - 2

Focus Word: Assurance

Prayer is talking to God. Praying to Jesus, in Jesus name, Holy Spirit quickening, or praying in the Spirit are all part of the combinations.

At times it is helpful to have a guide to your prayer. I like the ACTS acronym which stands for Adoration, Confession, Thankfulness, Supplication (or specific requests).

Pray before meals. Pray for each other. Pray for healing and pray without ceasing.

The perfect God/man Jesus needed to pray. He often went to a quiet place where He could be alone and commune with His Father. In these verses in Mark, He prayed early in the morning.

We need to be people of prayer. Prayer is a key part of the relationship with our Savior. We also need to allow God to speak back to us through His Word and Spirit.

Supernatural God = Mystical applications. Be ready and open.

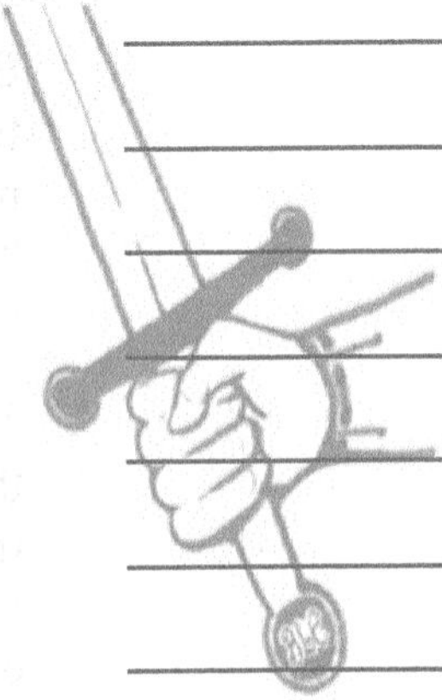

Date: ________________

Parables

Bible Reading: Mark 3 - 5

Focus Word: Belief and Faith

Good creative writing or speaking contains many techniques and innovations to get the audience involved. One of my favorites is a deep, "make the point stronger" metaphor!

Jesus often uses parables. Parables are a way to hide deep meaning in a story that the folks of that day, that culture, could understand.

Thing is, if people did not have help from the Holy Spirit they sometimes missed the point entirely.

I love the perspective I gain by thinking about the parable of the sower. The four paths are 1) rocky soil, 2) thorny soil, 3) hard path, 4) good soil.

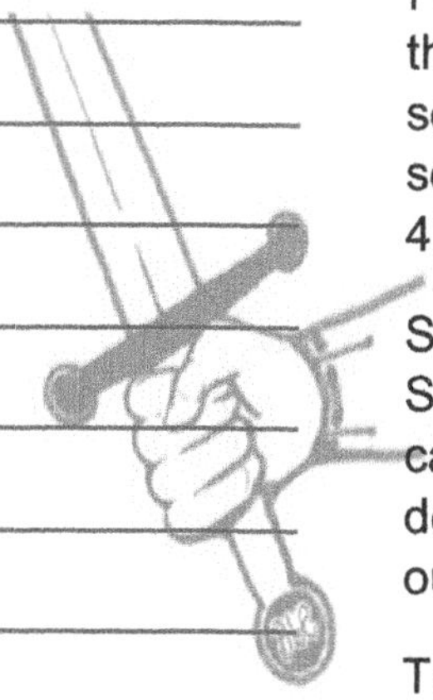

So, easy conclusion, go be Good Soil! But it's not always easy. We can be tripped up by deceit, wrong desires, and sin. We find ourselves in less than good soil.

Think it through and pray for God to use you as a product of good soil!

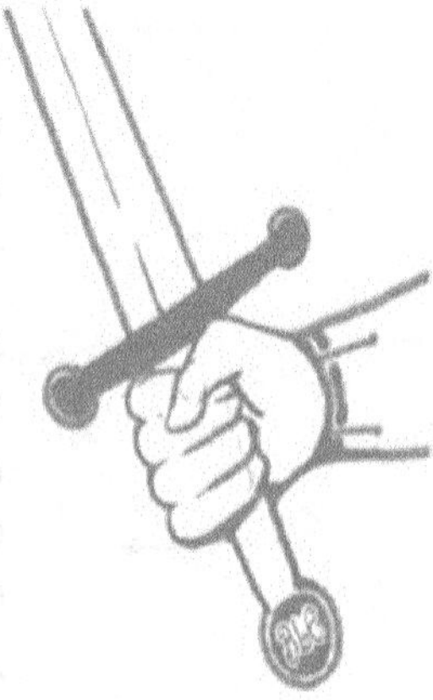

Week 8

Date: ________________

Systems for Success

Bible Reading: Leviticus 18 - 25

Focus Word: Orderliness

I love grace! I need grace! Jesus Christ is a giver of grace.

It is easy for me to want to focus on grace and overlook the value and the need for rules and rule following.

With that in mind and the readings in Leviticus to sort out I want to proclaim, there is value in structure! There is value in habits and making decisions to do certain things in certain ways to keep you on the straight and narrow. I am often my own worst enemy because I do not stick with the systems that work.

So consider your habits, the things you do that are helpful and the things you do that always lead to problems.

Are you under conviction? Are you being challenged? Give yourself some rules to follow!

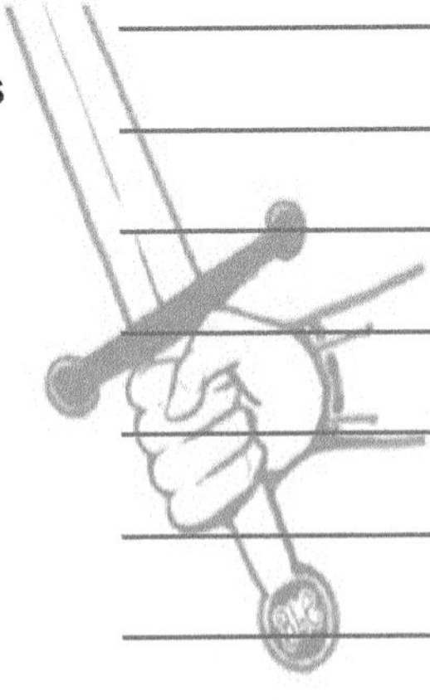

Date: ________________

Reasons Behind the Plan

Bible Reading: Leviticus 26 - Numbers 4

Focus Word: Reliability

One of the greatest gifts you can give to your boss, or those you work for, is to be reliable!

Are you the one that others can count on?

Following the leader can be tough. Especially when you are wondering if their instructions, their expectations, or their rules have any benefit whatsoever!

Don't be afraid to look into the issue, but also be willing to consider that you do not know everything. Perhaps doing as you are told is the most Godly and wonderful thing you could do at that moment.

Living out the instructions of the Lord will give you rewards and blessings. But that doesn't mean it always makes sense. Ask the Lord to guide you!

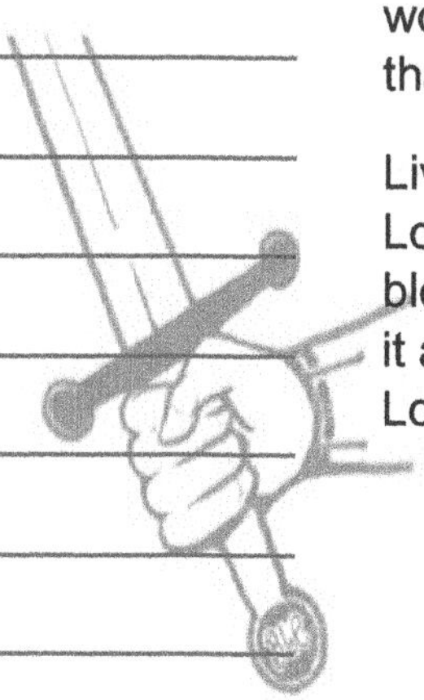

Date: ________________

The Habit of Confession

Bible Reading: Psalms 38 - 41

Focus Word: Forbearance

Honesty with yourself is tough. Be ruthless. I know I am so quick to give myself a break. My rationalizations always seem to make so much sense!

It takes a type of courage to be honest with yourself and with God. I hate to do it, but sometimes the best thing I can do is just write the sin and failures out right on the page. Seeing your sins spelled out before you hurts. It looks terrible!

We need to look at our sin, the way we hurt God and others, and be grieved by it!

Then we have to work at the turn around. Not just a satisfaction with status quo, but really be different!

David was so good at confessing his sins in the Psalms. I pray God uses these readings to help you get closer to Him and turn from sin.

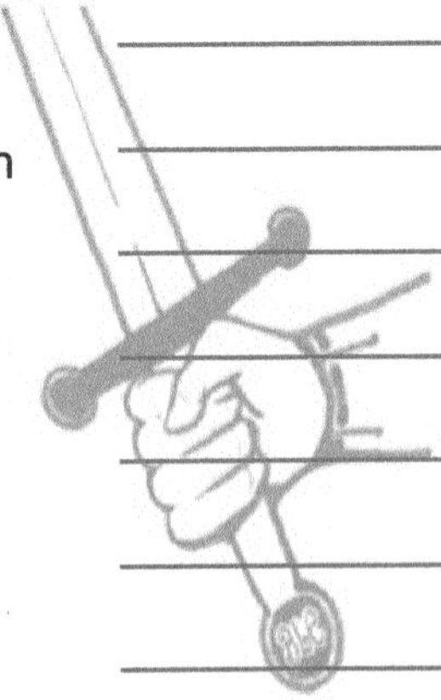

Date: ____________________

Miracles

Bible Reading: Mark 6 - 7

Focus Word: Faith

Salvation is an act of faith. Trusting Jesus to do what he says he will do takes faith.

It also takes faith to believe that Jesus wants to use you. As you give him what you have he will multiply it and use it in powerful ways.

Watch for Miracles. Jesus is still in the miracle business today. Make sure you are paying attention.

Consider the miracles He is doing in you and for you.

I, like you, do have faith, but it is a valuable prayer to ask the Lord to increase your faith! Make it fresh and make it real.

Some of the best miracles are the ones the Lord uses to develop you and me. Be ready!

Date: ________________

Great People Serve

Bible Reading: Mark 8 - 9

Focus Word: Tenderheartedness

Isn't it crazy that the savior of the world came to us as a baby? He grew up in normal skin, with parents, friends, struggles, and even experienced some of the physical limits of the human body.

But He did this to serve others, to serve you and I. He did it to be the perfect man and die in our place as the perfect sacrifice.

Okay, so this is a Sunday school lesson you have heard 100 times. But as we get ahold of this, we can realize better it is our job to serve others like Jesus did.

I am in the teaching business and I can tell you it is an awesome thing to serve kids as they grow into adults. To be a part of a child/student's life is to serve with purpose. To mentor and disciple a growing person who is still forming and developing is powerful!

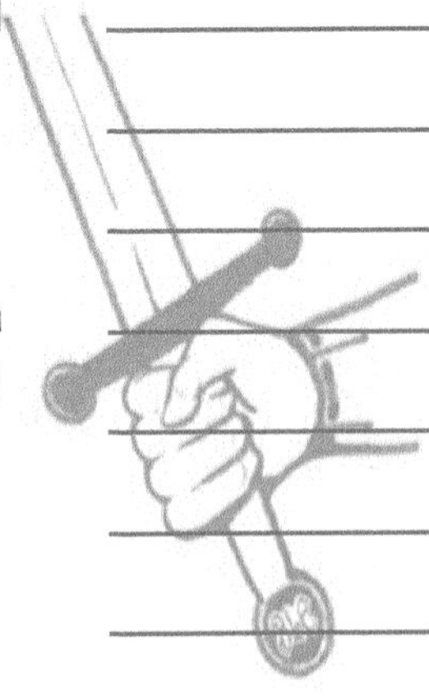

Do not sit on the sideline! Touch the future—teach (including Sunday school, AWANA, youth group, etc.)!

More Thinking About Thinking

Have you heard the brain teaser that goes something like this: Do not think about a big pink elephant.

How did you do?

We have an amazing brain. The science and biology behind it are incredible. But what about the mind, the spirit, the heart? The mind goes far deeper than a mechanical process of taking in information.

Read the following:

II Timothy 2:23-26	II Corinthians 10:2-5
Philippians 4:8	Colossians 2:2-4

Have you ever been deceived? Have you ever been tricked? Have you gone through a time when you thought you understood a situation only to find out the rest of the story? We all are prone to make mistakes. We are all fallible.

Satan's biggest strategy is to take captive our minds. The prodigal son was considering eating pig feed, when he finally came to his senses. It was at that point he turned from his selfish life and headed home to his father (Luke 15:17).

What are the conditions that help us to come to our senses?

How important is it to realize that our thoughts are not God's thoughts and His ways are not our ways?

Read Isaiah 55:8 and I Corinthians 1:18

Where will the natural flow of thinking take you?

Where will it take your children?

What powerful forces are controlling how we think today?

Can we afford to just go with the flow and hope it all works out!?

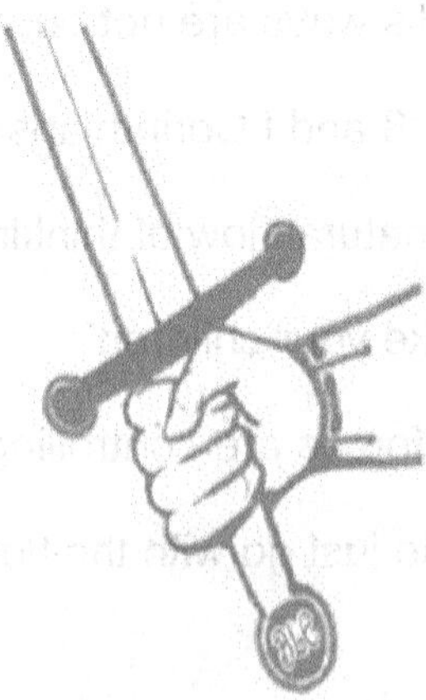

Week 9

Date: ________________

Speak the Truth

Bible Reading: Numbers 5 - 10

Focus Word: Purity

Integrity means that we speak the truth. We care enough to be truthful. We want to live for the right things in the right way. We want all the parts of our life to match up.

By the way—kids are great at spotting when our life and talk do not match up!

Interesting story here in Numbers about the Test of Adultery. The priest mixes up a goo of some sort, spreads it on your leg and says, "now, tell me the truth about…" And if you lie some disease or plague is coming your way.

I would think everyone would just fess up!!

Truth is, sometimes I too fail to confess! Only Jesus can make you pure through his saving grace!

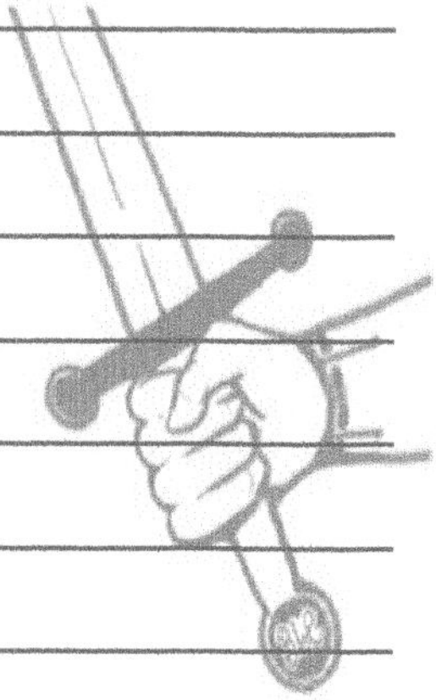

Date: ________________

More Complaining

Bible Reading: Numbers 11 - 18

Focus Word: Cheerfulness

How much time do you spend whining and complaining about your issues? Maybe you just whine and complain about other people?

A negative disposition is tiresome.

Moses is surrounded by complainers and their endless stream of complaints. His siblings, the leaders he puts in place, and the people he is trying to lead are all upset at one time or another. They are quick to belly-ache about the food, the heat, what is fair, and what isn't. They seem to think that God is just too hard on them.

Maybe this crew from the Old Testament sounds like some people in your life! If you are called to leadership then follow Romans 12:8 and lead diligently!

But for most of us, have some courage, a little optimism, and give your leaders and the people around you a break by being cheerful!

Date: ____________

Count Your Many Blessings

Bible Reading: Psalms 42 - 45

Focus Word: Hope

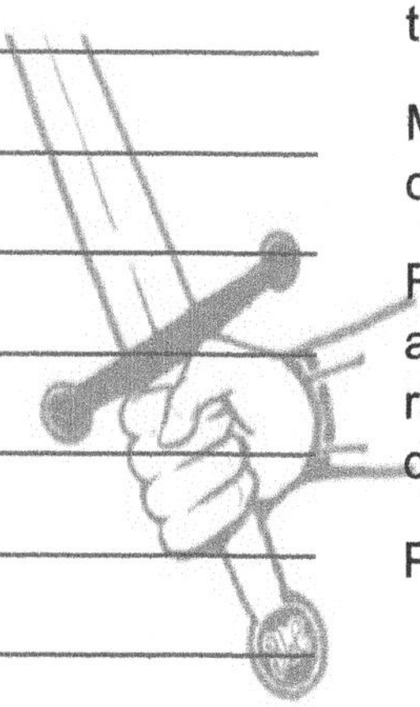

Hope is powerful!

May God give you hope today.

I pray you see a working out of Gods plans in your life that brings you enthusiasm and excitement about the future.

I believe there is a powerful boost of energy when we live in hope and joy! I may not have it every day, but I notice that my mind, spirit, and disposition can turn towards this strength if I am in His Word! I can find the joy of the Lord by my prayers, by my thankfulness, and by my attention to the things of God!

Maybe today is a great day to count and recount your blessings!

Remember that your hope and joy are not in your own hands, but rather come from what God is doing in and through you!

Praise the Lord!

Date: ____________

Leadership Challenge

Bible Reading: Mark 10 - 11

Focus Word: Gentleness

I love to feel like I am making things happen!

But sometimes I get so full of myself and my plans that I do not keep pace with God's will and His plans.

Are you aware of God's patience with you? He constantly provides each of us a second chance, and when we mess up He forgives us.

Notice that God is working on you! Sometimes it happens through His Word or through other people. He mentors you, looks out for you and gently nudges and pushes you where He wants you to go. He may be opening an opportunity or telling you to slow down.

Several times in the gospels we see the disciples or a large crowd of people were astonished by what Jesus did or said. He still does amazing stuff in this day and age!

Watch for, and pay attention to Jesus today and be wowed!

Date: ________________

Repeat the Important Stuff

Bible Reading: Mark 12 - 13

Focus Word: Consistency

The greatest commandment is to love the Lord your God with all your heart, with all your soul, with all your strength and with all your mind.

This was discussed a few different times in the Old Testament and it is repeated in the gospels.

Important stuff gets repeated.

Do you need to repeat any messages to your family, friends, or co-workers?

Interesting that as we get this greatest commandment right, it has impact on how we treat everyone else.

This is way better than just "pay it forward." Instead of doing good for others because they were kind to us or our circumstances are good at the moment, we do good to others because we love God!

If this was important enough for God to repeat it, we better make it a part of our lives!

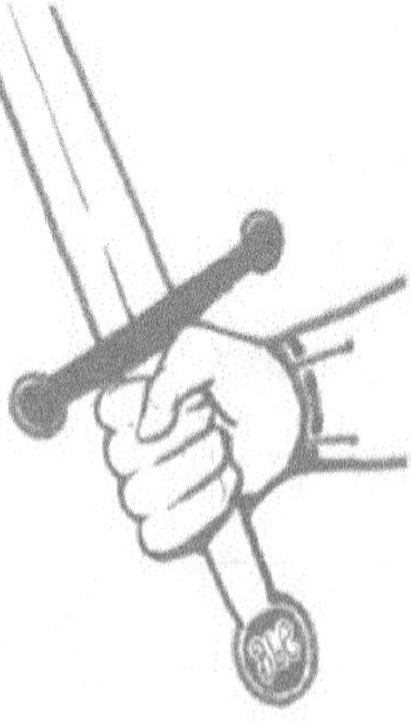

Week 10

Date: ____________

Faith and Belief When it is Confusing

Bible Reading: Numbers 19 - 24

Focus Word: Committed

Okay, let's just admit it, some of these stories in Numbers have me reeling! What is going on here!?

Here is a plague created by snakes as a consequence of bad behavior. Many have died and many more will die. The only hope is to look at a bronze snake. If you follow the prescription, do what is asked, in faith, you will be healed.

I had a mentor who used to tell me to pretend the Bible is true, do what it says and see what happens.

Lord help me to have the faith, the commitment, the belief, the follow through, to live out what you say. To actually do it.

To stop explaining away everything that does not go well for me or that I do not like!

I am committed to you!

Date: ________________

Our Words are Trustworthy

Bible Reading: Numbers 25 - 32

Focus Word: Reverence

So who in the world is Balaam and did that poor donkey ever recover?

The systems in place for holiness and purity are wild! Keep wrestling with the point of it all!

You will find this in other places, but notice the importance of a person's word, their vow, or pledge in chapter 30.

To say something and actually do it is a big deal. It is actually an area where you can stand apart as different from our current culture.

How can I use a vow to align my life with Christ? What vow or pledge do I need to make? Is this an area to challenge others in? Maybe it is something to do with abstinence? Maybe it's a pledge to leave behind drinking or drugs or pornography? Could a vow be helpful today? Or will it just make us feel more guilty and defeated?

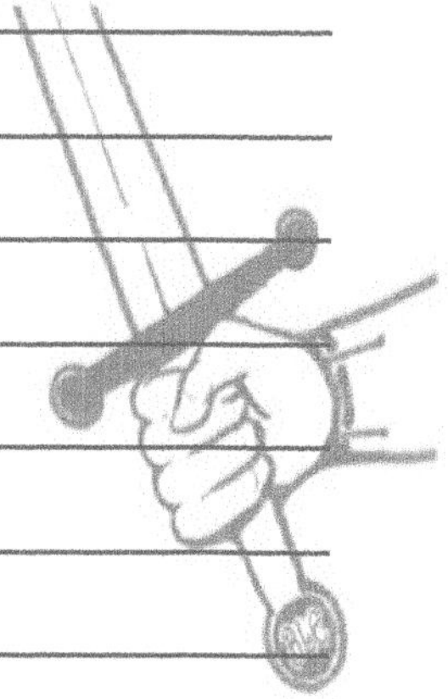

Date: ____________________

A Mighty Fortress

Bible Reading: Psalms 46 - 50

Focus Word: Confidence

Hundreds of years ago world-changer Martin Luther proclaimed his confidence in God. He challenged the Catholic church and the order of the day and was a key part of the protestant reformation. Maybe Luther was reading today's Psalms when he penned these two verses?

"A mighty fortress is our God,
a bulwark never failing;
our helper he amid the flood
of mortal ills prevailing.
For still our ancient foe
doth seek to work us woe;
his craft and power are great,
and armed with cruel hate,
on earth is not his equal."

"Did we in our own strength confide, our striving would be losing, were not the right man on our side, the man of God's own choosing. Dost ask who that may be? Christ Jesus, it is he; Lord Sabaoth, his name, from age to age the same, and he must win the battle."

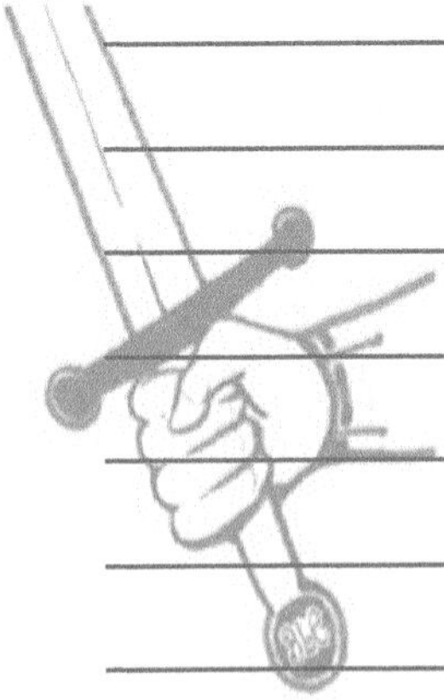

Date: ________________

Value of a Ritual

Bible Reading: Mark 14

Focus Word: Purpose

The idea of rituals seem to come and go. Some people like them and many do not. Some churches embrace them and others do not.

Do you have any purposeful rituals in your life?

Do you have ceremonies or celebrations that are fun, helpful and important? You might consider studying the Jewish feast system.

Of course we have to be careful of routines. They can be so common place we simply go through the motions. But they can also be valuable.

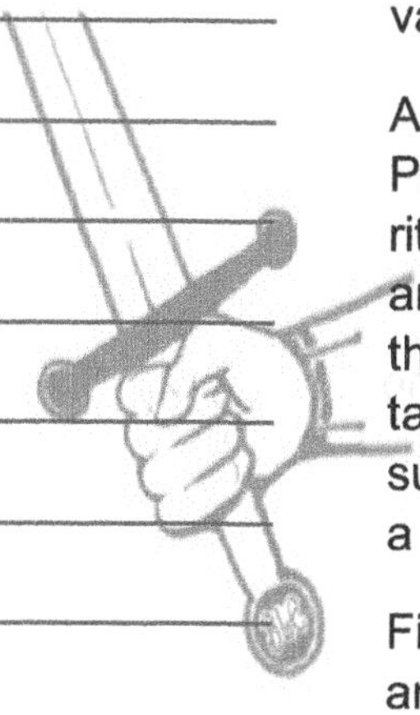

Analyze the Passover. The Passover is certainly an important ritual to many Jewish people today and throughout history. What are the important lessons being taught? And why is there a suggested need that we do this on a regular basis?

Figure out who the naked guy is and you get a bonus! Why is that here in Mark 14:52?

Date: ________________

You Just Never Know

Bible Reading: Mark 15 - 16

Focus Word: Sensitivity

Who was Joseph of Arimathea?

There is some idea that he was a respected member of a Jewish council. I am not so sure his fellow council members where thrilled about the way he cared for Jesus post crucifixion! But I bet they were watching and that his actions caused quite a stir!

You never know who is watching, paying attention, taking it all in!

On the one hand, be on your best behavior!

On the other hand be ready to share the rest of the story.

People around you may be going through things that finally humble them in such a way that they are ready to give up and listen.

So what is your answer to one who wonders why you seem to have such hope?

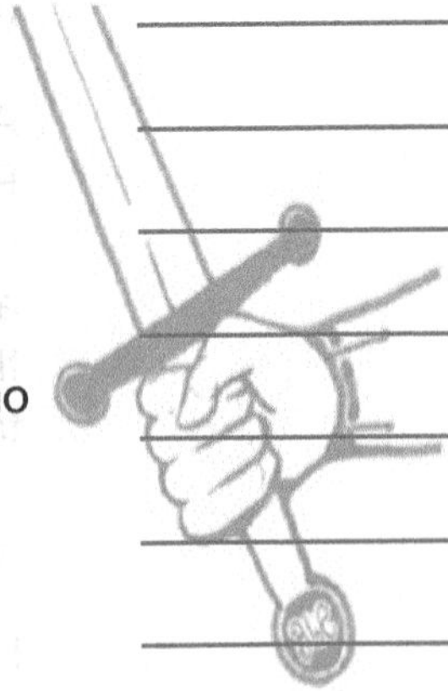

What in The World Is Up with My Kid!?!

On the one hand it is shocking, but on the other hand when I look at myself, it is very explainable. Our children, all children, have a propensity to misbehave, usurp authority, and do as they please instead of what we tell them to do.

Educators, parents and the Church must consider the best approach to honestly deal with the sinfulness of human nature. Sin is right at the center of our human condition. No one likes it, but it has to be dealt with righteously.

Read the following:

Galatians 5:16-17	Romans 7:15-25
Romans 6:12	Romans 8:5-14
Genesis 6:5	Hebrews 9:27
Colossians 3:5-10	Romans 3:23

The book of Judges tell us that God's people did that which was right in their own eyes (Judges 21:25).

There is a process that requires us to teach, discipline and correct our kids. Left unto themselves, bad decisions will take place. Sin nature can get each one of us into a lot of trouble.

The good news is found in II Corinthians 7:9-11 that tells us when we face our sin for what it is and repent, we can become over-comers and victorious over sin.

How can discipline, rules, policies, and structures be helpful to the process of dealing with sin?

How well is our American culture doing in the area of discipline today? How would you evaluate the American culture on what sort of behaviors are permitted and what requires punishment? What can we do to make it better?

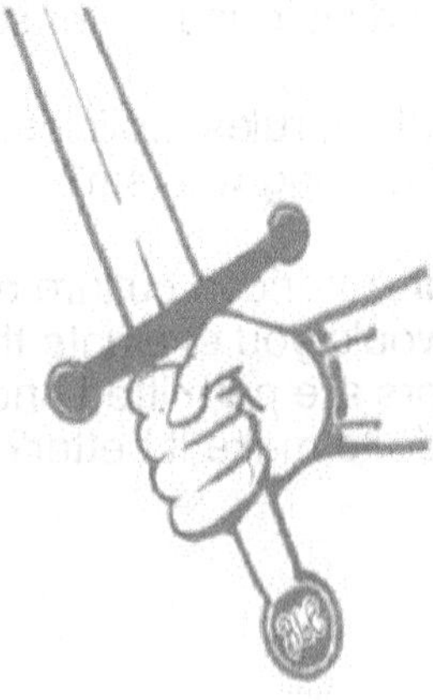

Week 11

Date: ________________

Leaders Make Decisions and Lead

Bible Reading: Numbers 33 - Deuteronomy 2

Focus Word: Humility

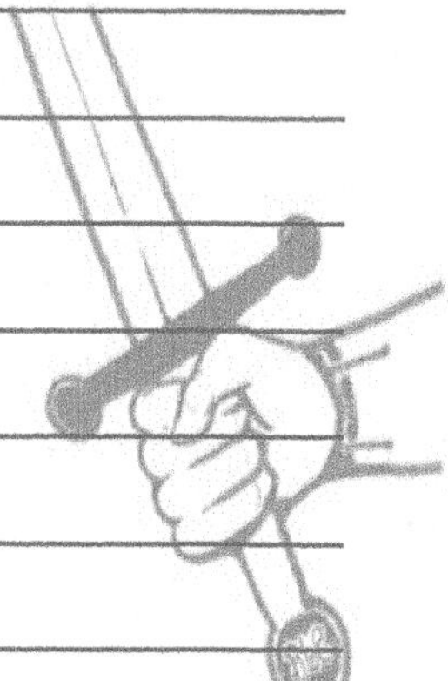

I love the HBO mini-series *Band of Brothers*.

There is one scene where a commanding officer is fearful in the moment of battle to make a decision. His unwillingness to decide creates a terrible situation for all his men. Failing to act can be just as bad as making the wrong decision!

Then a new commanding officer takes over and just starts pointing, deciding, moving and leading. The men are encouraged and good things start happening!

Being placed in a position of leadership can feel good! I like to be honored and respected. But sometimes it is just about seeing the needs and making things happen. Sometimes it's about having the courage to act!

It also takes humility.

Someone has to get the work done, so be willing to be His tool and let God use you!

Date: ________________

Get Organized!

Bible Reading: Deuteronomy 3 - 6

Focus Word: Diligence

Do you ever have one of those days where you are pumped to start working on your to-do list, but by the end of the day not only have you failed to mark off tasks on your list, but the list has grown?

I hate that! But sometimes I have days where I just throw stuff on the desk and work seems to pile up! As the stacks of paper rise I become more and more likely to forget an important issue or due date! Soon my effectiveness is lost due to my failure to keep organized!

Work hard! But work smart too. Get organized. Put systems in place. Get the help you need, share the load. Get rid of time wasters. Assess and re-assess your priorities.

I have never heard someone say that organization is a spiritual discipline, but it just may be! Don't let your clutter get in the way of effectively serving God!

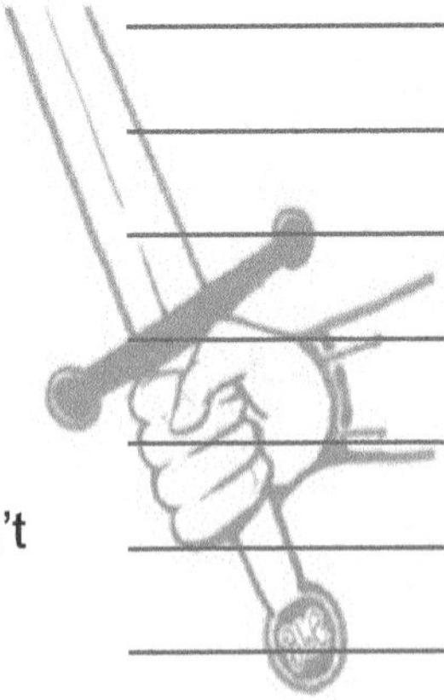

Date: ________________

You've Got to "Crave it!"

Bible Reading: Psalms 51—55

Focus Word: Service

God's Word is the key to the good life!

God's Word can provide a foundation for joy, success, and happiness in this life. And that is not all! Through the Bible God teaches us so much about ourselves and makes us better people.

God shows us where we fall short and how amazing He is so that we want to confess, make the bad stuff right, and move forward in a positive way to chase our dreams and honor the Lord.

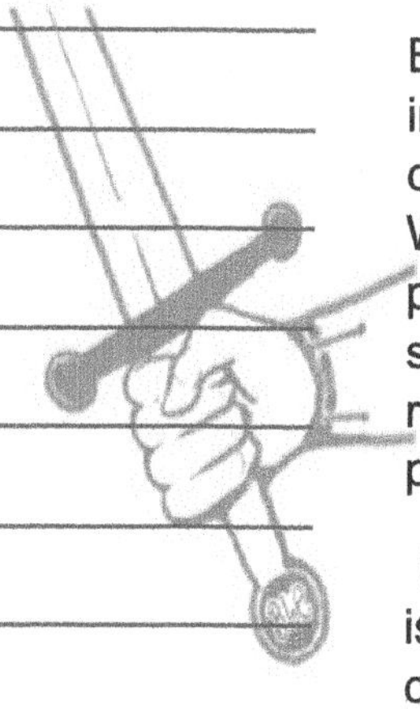

But it's up to you to stay immersed in scripture! I certainly cannot make you read God's Word or force the correct perspective in your head. I sometimes find the task of reading and working through the points a challenge as well.

Peter 2:2 has a word/phrase that is key to our growth and success; we need to "crave" spiritual growth! Lord help me to crave

Date: ________________

Working Within God's Plan

Bible Reading: Luke 1

Focus Word: Availability

Dig into these chapters in Luke and you will see the birth of Jesus is much more than a cheery Christmas story that warms your heart.

Notice the participation of normal people in the midst of the supernatural. The shepherds, a father, a mother, old people, Anna and Simeon, John and Elizabeth. Check out the growth of children, John the Baptist and Jesus ,who became stronger, wiser, and were prepared to do incredible things for God's glory.

Lord use me! Use me even when life looks chaotic and random. Help me to be a part of your plan, even when I cannot see the final destination or when my path looks insignificant or meaningless!

In this "mess" I want to look deeper and live greater than the circumstances seem to require.

Give me more insight!

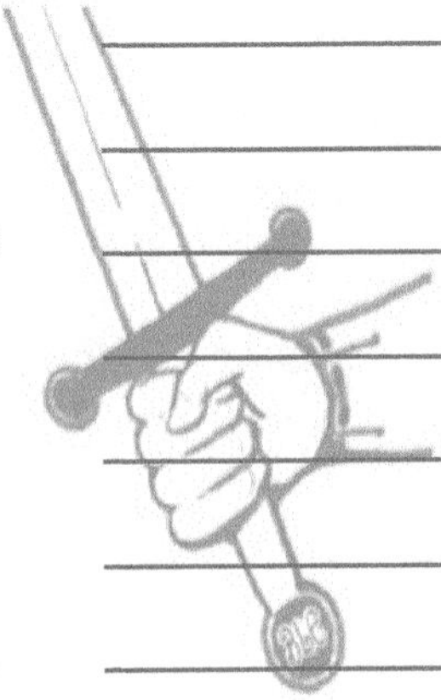

Date: ________________

Use Me!

Bible Reading: Luke 2 - 3

Focus Word: Loyalty

It is an amazing thought that the Lord would use a regular olé' person, guy, gal, like you or me. But He has been doing it that way for a long time!

I hope that while God is using me, teaching and training me, that somewhere along the line I am a blessing to others.

While life throws a lot of curve balls, cheap strikes, and even wild pitches that scare us to death, may I not only think about myself, my problems, but how I can love and serve others.

Luke 2:52 says that Jesus grew in favor with God and man. While you and I will never grow up to be the savior of the world I do believe each of us can grow in faith and grow in favor with God and man! What a great testimony to the power of the God of the universe who says nothing is impossible!

That includes using you or me!

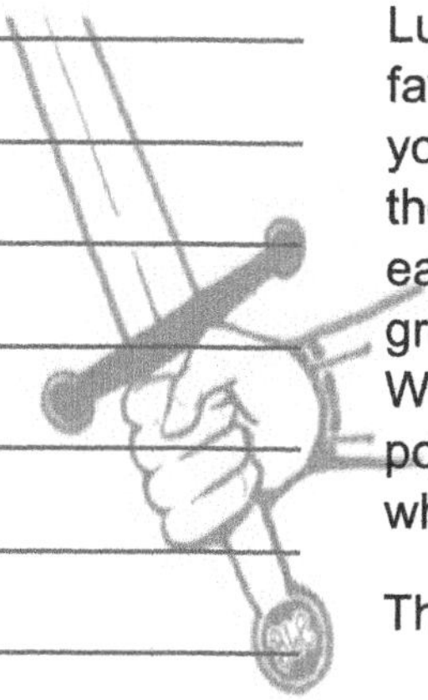

Eleven Weeks Down and Forty-one to Go!

If you are getting into this journal that is great! Victory. You hear different things about how long it takes to develop a habit. I have been running for almost forty years and most the time I dread it, especially when it is cold outside. Yet the habit is important to me and hopefully beneficial to my health!

So I do not know if you are hooked yet, but it seems to me you have been doing a great job! Keep it up!

Writing a useful journal is a dream I have had for a long time. It seems a little counter intuitive in this day and age that people would enjoy using pen and paper, an actual book, over a smart phone, tablet or some other electrical device. But even in this age of technology I still believe in the power of the written word!

It may be that I am "old school" but there is something special about the pen I use, the feel of it when I write. Sometimes my thoughts seem incomplete and unformed unless I write them down. Once written down I feel I have a legitimate thought ready for reflection and revision.

I love the feel of a book. Not only this journal, but any book I am reading. I can see the progress I am making as I move through the pages. There is some tactical magic that takes place when I turn the pages, or remember to take "my book" to church, or the seminar, or even with me for devotions, because I know it is "learning time."

I feel I am less distracted when I work with my book. The computer and the internet are quick to move me to other rabbit trails.

Someday I may figure out how to turn this journal into the perfect app, but I guarantee you it will not be for me! Give me... my book!

I hope you are enjoying this journal! It is your book—your story. With eleven weeks down, you may be hooked. Congrats! Stay strong. Keep learning and happy journaling!

Week 12

Date: ____________________

Remember What???

Bible Reading: Deuteronomy 7 - 11

Focus Word: Sensitivity

If you have a moment check out Dr. Caroline Leaf's brain research. Her work concentrates on unlocking the power of the human brain by training ourselves to think in a healthy manner. It is pretty cool, very interesting, and some of it may even be true!

Seriously, I like it, and her work on the brain makes sense, but some will say it is not scientific or properly peer reviewed.

I love research and I love to learn. Knowledge and the vast universe of what we can know is expanding at rates none of us can keep up with. It is hard enough to remember people's names, let alone all the other stuff we hope to recall! Remembering, storing information, learning, is a very big deal!

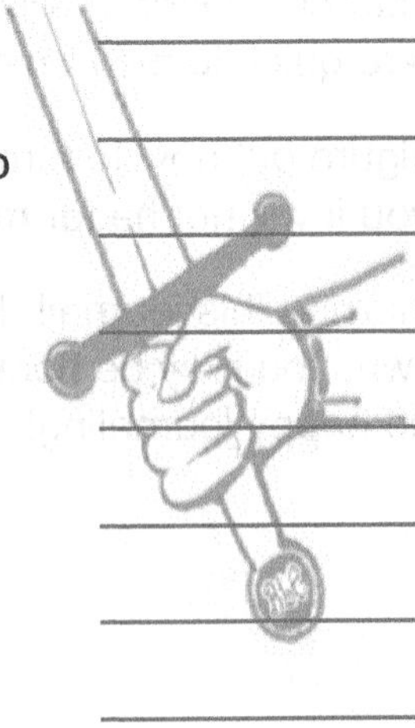

God often called the children of Israel to remember! We should remember what God has done for us in the past and what He has promised to do in the future!

Date: ________________

Increasing Your IQ

Bible Reading: Deuteronomy 12 - 20

Focus Word: Compassion

Thinking about learning capacity today.

I want to remember more!

I want to be smart!

I think you will find Biblical claims, especially in the proverbs, that say we can remember more, we can be smart, and we can be wise!

God can help us to expand our memory capacity!

So what gets our attention? What gets our focus and brain power?

Here is a warning: some of our learning choices, and the things we store in our memory, may actually sabotage our ability to remember.

I believe your work with this journal is a quest to know the right things and to remember the right things.

So consider this idea, that your work in God's Word, that your walk with the Lord, are factors that are making you smarter!!

Date: ____________________

Lost Sheep

Bible Reading: Psalms 56 - 60

Focus Word: Holiness

Simple, lowly sheep seem to be the stars again and again in several different Bible verses. Luke 15 provides us with the parable of the "Lost Sheep."

I bring it up here because in Psalms 56-60 we see the author calling on the Lord to save him from the clutches of lions and evildoers. Just like a sheep in need of a shepherd! We are continually confronted with our own weakness and our need for God!

I remember thinking it was a bad move for a shepherd to leave ninety-nine sheep to find the one missing straggler. I get a bit irritated that "Mr. Missing-Sheep" got away, messed up, and put the rest of us, the other ninety-nine, in trouble!

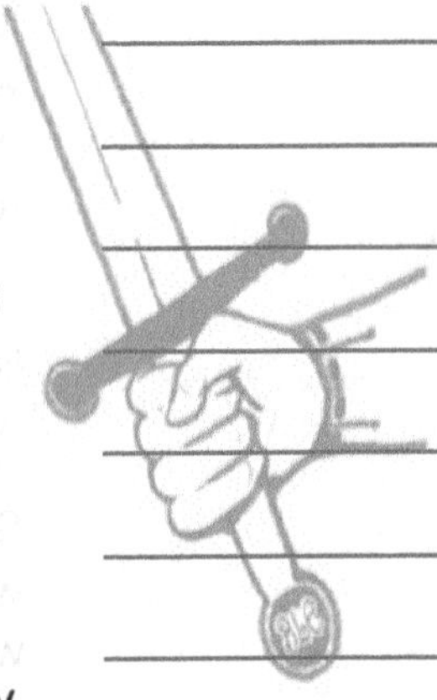

In the end I am so glad the Good Shepherd went after that missing sheep, because there are days when I am that missing sheep! In our weakness Jesus is there ready to save!

Date: ________________

Popular Opinion

Bible Reading: Luke 4 - 5

Focus Word: Reliable

I wrestle with the idea of being liked and being right.

People pleasers be careful!

I find the ability to lead, motivate and inspire to be fun. Often our gage for good leadership is how many are following behind. Big numbers excite us. We hope to amaze others with our wisdom and the great choices we make.

I believe we have to pay attention to this metric. Ideas cannot take hold without advocates. Organizations, from companies to churches, will not make headway without a certain mass of followers to get the job done. Growth often means positive feedback.

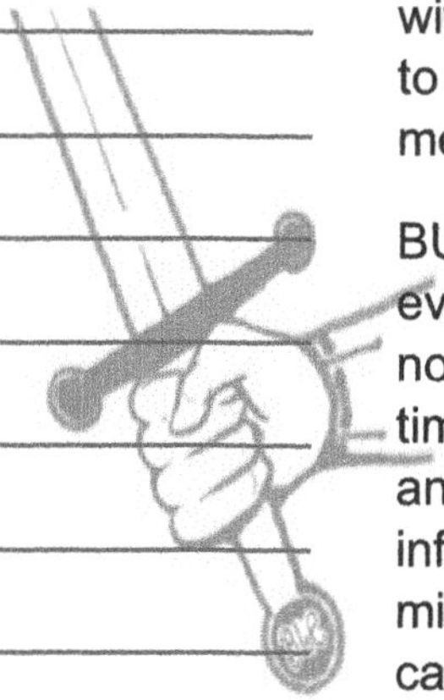

BUT!!! Numbers are not everything! Popular opinion does not have the final say! There were times when Jesus amazed people and there were times when He infuriated them. He was rejected, misunderstood and hated. Be careful to check your motivations!

Date: ________________

Teacher/Mentor

Bible Reading: Luke 6 - 7

Focus Word: Denial Of Self

One more step on yesterday's thought on motivating and inspiring the masses.

Good teachers need to motivate and inspire.

We need good teachers in our lives. Sometimes these are people, but I think we could include books, movies, and the things that we pay attention to that have huge influence in who we are and how we live.

We also need to consider our influence in the lives of others. Are we being the good role model, wisdom seeker, thoughtful, loving person that positively impacts those around us?

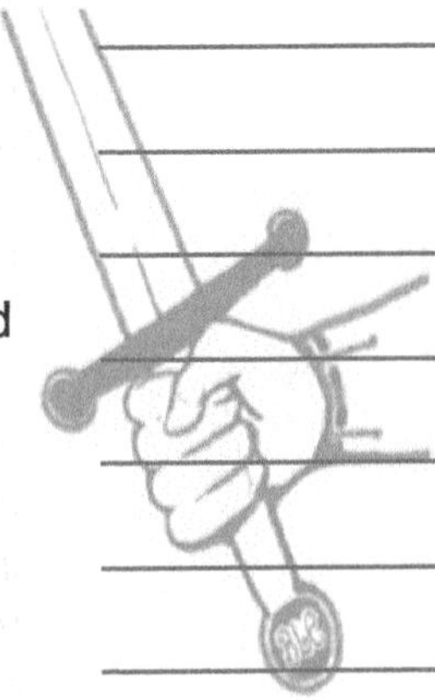

Let me just say to those who are parents, put your kids around good teachers because Luke 6:40 is powerful!

"...Everyone who is fully trained will be like their teacher." (NIV)

Week 13

Date: _______________

Worldliness 101

Bible Reading: Deuteronomy 21 - 28

Focus Word: Trust

In the Old Testament God often made it clear that the nation of Israel was not to associate with the nonbelievers who lived all around them. They were to be careful about who they married and in what traditions they got mixed up. God had set them apart.

There are certainly Biblical interpretation issues to sort out, but the idea of "in the world but not of the world" can get very complicated and filled with differences of opinion and conviction.

Have you ever visited an Amish community? Maybe they have it figured out!

Legalism and thinking ourselves better than others can be an issue, but I wonder if our greater problem is that anything and everything is fair game. We can rationalize every behavior and activity! We are so quick to adopt the ways of the world! What are these worldly entanglements doing to us?

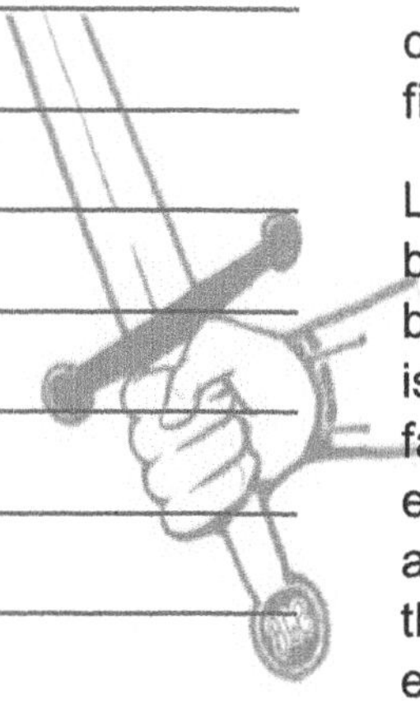

Date: ________________

Encourage Others

Bible Reading: Deuteronomy 29-34

Focus Word: Confession

I keep a file of notes and cards that have encouraged me in the past. I even write down encouraging statements that I have received. These statements can provide a bit of strength when difficult times inevitably come.

One of the greatest compliments I have received was from a teacher leaving my school who said that I had a way of "speaking life" to them.

Aren't I amazing!?

Sorry, just wanted to throw that in (with sarcasm), but that was kind!

Moses tells the people to choose life and with this good and abundant life will come blessings.

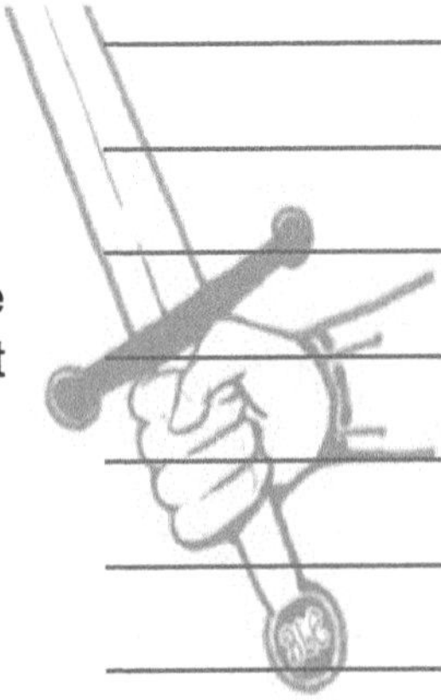

Remind people around you that life is filled with responsibilities and yet it is fun, joyful, and good. Sometimes it will be hard but keep perspective and be grateful. Encourage others! We all need it!

Date: ________________

Praise Him

Bible Reading: Psalms 61 - 66

Focus Word: Repentance

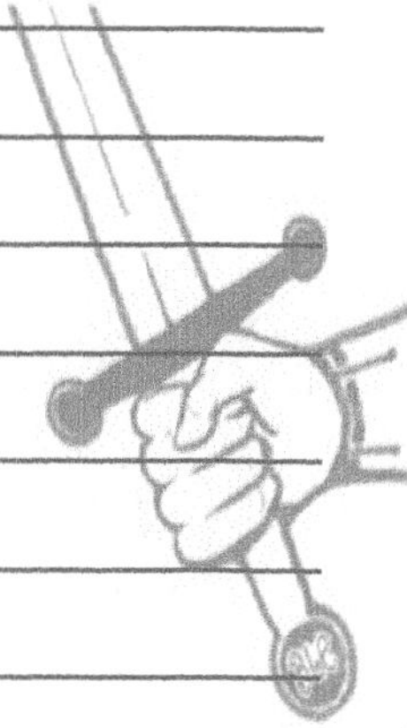

Okay, so I am a young baby boomer, but I like praise songs way more than I like hymns!

And my favorite hymns are those set to modern praise and worship music!

But I know there are lots of people, both young and old, who would disagree with me!

There are so many differences in the body of Christ! We each bring our unique perspectives and experiences as we seek to honor God. And that is a good thing! Let's not let our differences get in the way of serving our God!

This section of scripture is filled with Praise song lines! Reminds me of a ditty from when I was a kid:

Praise Him, Praise Him, all you little children, God is love, God is Love!!

Use the psalms to help; figure out a way to praise Him today!

Date: ________________

Genius/Idiot

Bible Reading: Luke 8 - 9

Focus Word: Submission

In the education world we are constantly trying to teach, improve understanding, and help kids sort out issues with wisdom. Then we are always in search of the best way to measure that they retained what we were trying to teach!

We like to talk about high test scores and National Merit scholars.

So how does Peter go from a genius in Luke 9:20 to an idiot in verse 33!? Peter goes from answering tough questions to jabbering without even knowing what he was saying in just 13 verses!

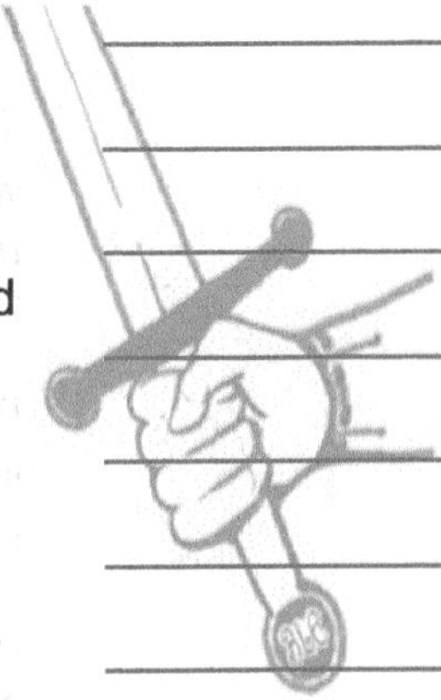

How is Jesus, His Word, His principles helping you to achieve more than your IQ would suggest you are capable? How do you and I tap into God's wisdom and allow God to use us in places we would be completely lost without Him?

Or consider how we can be exposed as idiots when we do our own thing, with our worldly minds, and stammer nonsense like Peter.

Date: ________________

Harvesting

Bible Reading: Luke 10 - 11

Focus Word: Teachability

There is a lot of work to do out there. Are you doing the right thing? Just being busy cannot be the measure of success. Everyone seems to think they are busy!

God has big results in mind; there is much to do for His kingdom. The fruit is ripe, it is time to harvest! Are you participating?

Jesus says it another way, something like this, if you are not gathering then you are scattering! If you are not participating in the right things then you are against Him!

Be part of the solution, not part of the problem!

Back to Teaching 101 for a second. Learning levels start with simple memorization, but at the highest levels of learning comprehension is…

Problem solving! Using what we know to explain, disentangle, and create! Let's go get it done! Let's participate in God's harvest!

Music With Meaning

Music can be so powerful for your worship, edification, encouragement!

I have listed some music you can find online that really delivers a message that I think justifies and establishes the power and importance of your journal work.

1. History, Matthew West
2. Write your Story, Francesca Battistelli
3. Lead me to the Cross
4. Forgiveness, Matthew West
5. Do Something, Matthew West
6. My Story, Big Daddy Weave
7. Do Life Big, Jamie Grace
8. Strong Enough, Matthew West
9. Come thy Fount
10. Day One, Matthew West
11. If We're Honest, Francesca Battistelli
12. World Changers, Matthew West
13. The Story of your Life, Matthew West
14. Family Tree, Matthew West

Week 14

Date: ________________

Leading

Bible Reading: Joshua 1- 8

Focus Word: Patience

I love to think and learn about leadership. I think we are all leaders at different stages. I also believe we can find ways to lead better.

I suppose leadership often sounds like something for the driven and the ambitious. I certainly hope you have some of those qualities, but I think leadership is for all of us because we want to walk with Jesus. Each one of us have to consider how God has called us to lead.

One of my favorite verses is the Joshua 1:6 because it speaks of courage in leadership!

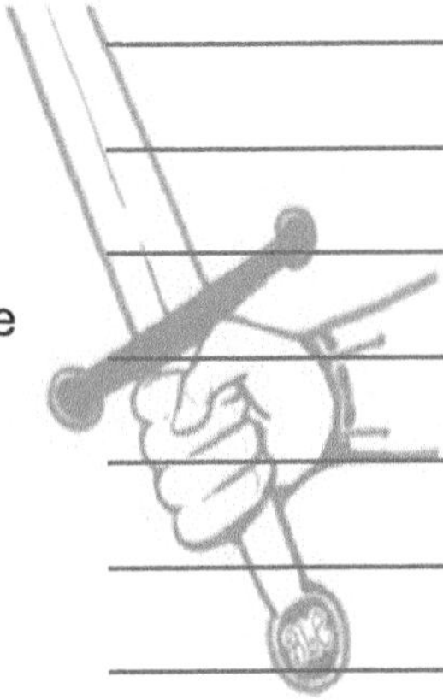

I pray you are courageous!

Good leadership needs guidance from God! Continue through verse 9 and see how God's Word is key to everything we do!

Love "The Law"!

Date: ________________

Leader Power

Bible Reading: Joshua 9 - 15

Focus Word: Unity

Here on earth leadership requires cooperation, delegation, hierarchy, titles, pay differences, and followers.

I believe leadership works best when it fits into the Body of Christ. The Body of Christ requires unity.

Folks are typically willing to follow people they respect, people they admire, people they trust. The masses want someone they have confidence in, someone with purpose.

I think you will see that Joshua was good at what he did and that God blessed him. He inspired confidence and he brought unity.

Try not to rush through these stories, these battles, without considering all the leadership issues that had to be navigated.

Is it still possible for Christians to have an impact? To be influential?

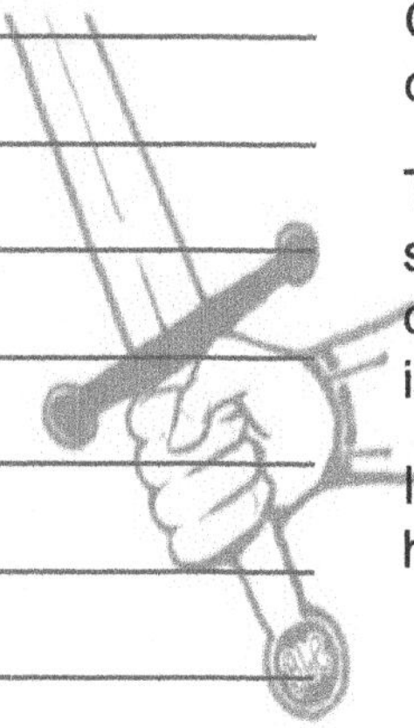

Date: ________________

Good News/Bad News

Bible Reading: Psalms 67 - 70

Focus Word: Restoration

Life is rarely simple.

There are so many reasons to praise the Lord and we need to do it much more than we do!

That said we cannot escape the fact that life can be hard. Sometimes we just do not know what to do next.

Sometimes we feel ripped off, forgotten, and so discouraged.

Our daily walk with God is filled with good news and some bad news. Peaks and valleys.

Lord help me to handle the combination of blessings and curses that come in this life!

Help me to live in victory regardless of my circumstances!

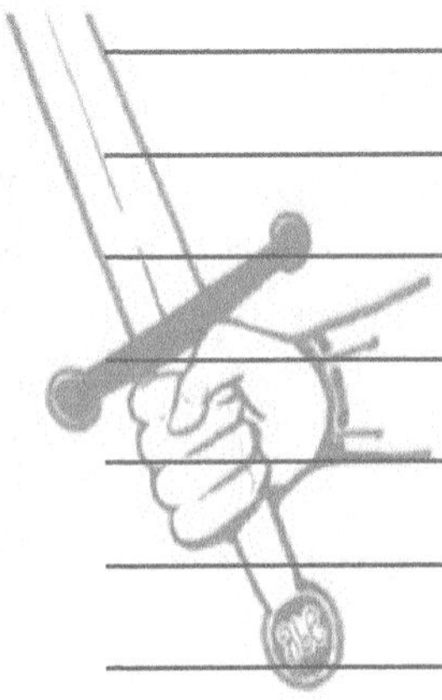

Date: ________________

Anxious for Nothing

Bible Reading: Luke 12 -13

Focus Word: Authority

Remember that God is in charge. You are not God and you are not in charge.

So yes, there is a lot to do. Yes, it can feel stressful and the pressure at times is unbearable.

So where do we put our concerns? How do we handle our time commitments? What do we do when things do not make sense?

Think about how much God knows you and loves you. The Bible assures us again and again that God knows our hearts and has our back!

"Every hair on your head!"

"Even the Birds…"

Lord, help me to have the right perspective!

I can do all things through Him who gives me strength (NIV)

Date: ____________________

Payment

Bible Reading: Luke 14 -15

Focus Word: Generosity

My pastor says that every time we say "yes" to something we by implication have to say "no" to something else.

As I hear that, I assure myself that somehow I have figured out ways to produce more quality "yes's" than most! Hear that pride coming though!?

Finishing a task is good! Helping others is honorable! Accomplishing a lot of things is great!

There is a cost involved. Are you and I willing to pay? What parts of your life are being neglected?

Schedule for success and stick with your plan.

Why wouldn't we give it our very best?

Truth is, we are the lost coin. We are the lost sheep. We are the lost son, both of them.

Choice Theory says there is a cost or a consequence to our decisions.

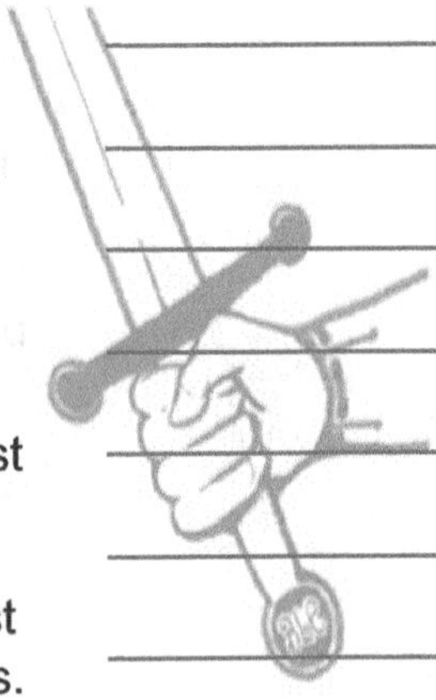

Christian Growth

I love the beginning of the school year each fall. It always seems like the kids grow so much from the first of June to the middle of August.

Luke 2:52 tells us that Jesus grew. He grew in wisdom, stature, and in favor with both God and man.

In I Samuel 2:26 we read that Samuel grew much the same way.

Acts 9:22 tells us that Paul gets saved as an adult but takes off on a growth process that made him an effective evangelist.

I Peter 2:1-2 talks about the need to grow up spiritually in our salvation.

Brain research is proving what our grandmothers already knew! Kids develop, or grow up, in stages. There is a certain period of time during adolescence, that the brain is not fully developed.

How do we teach our children to love God and relate to the people they come into contact with?

Positive relationship foundations, guidance and direction are imperative during this time of development. What a blessing it is to have teachers and coaches supporting parents and saying the same basic things that kids hear at home during this vulnerable, fragile, growing up time period!

How did you navigate the teen years?

What relationships were key for you growing up?

Who do you rely on for the support needed to see you, or your kids, become wise, strong, and maintain a walk with the Lord during this crucial stage of life?

Week 15

Date: ______________

The Price of Sin

Bible Reading: Joshua 16 - 23

Focus Word: Contentment

Check out the story on Achan in Joshua chapter 7.

Achan gets greedy and takes what he was not suppose to take.

Not only is he in big trouble, but his whole family suffers because of his sin.

How many of us would be furious if the system that applied to Achan was applied to us!? If we were held accountable for the sins of others?

What is the impact of my sin on my family and friends?

It is so easy to get way too comfortable with sin. Confess, repent, and make it right! You are sure to hurt those around you with your guilty actions and poor choices!

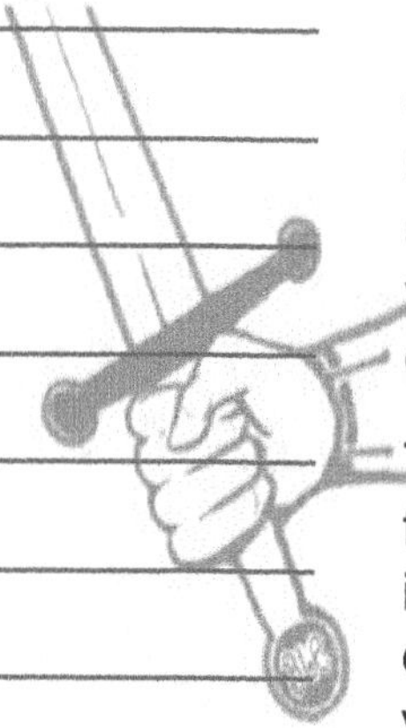

The good news is that God will forgive us, but we have to move into right decisions, and have a change of behavior. Throw off your sin and be like Him!

Date: _______________

Decide and Follow Through

Bible Reading: Joshua 24

Focus Word: Creativity

Joshua makes his big statement here, "I can't decide for you, but as for me...I am going to follow God and His Word!"

He also takes responsibility for his family.

I think you will find a lot of scripture that gives the impression that your life has a huge impact on others.

It is not just a me, myself, and I situation.

You have been designed to be an impact player and make a difference.

Realize that the way God has called you to make a difference can be way different than how He seems to be using everybody else. We were each created to be unique and made in the image of God!

A key aspect of being an image bearer is to be creative! Embrace the call of God in your life!

Date: ________________

Fight for Optimism

Bible Reading: Psalms 71 - 73

Focus Word: Dependability

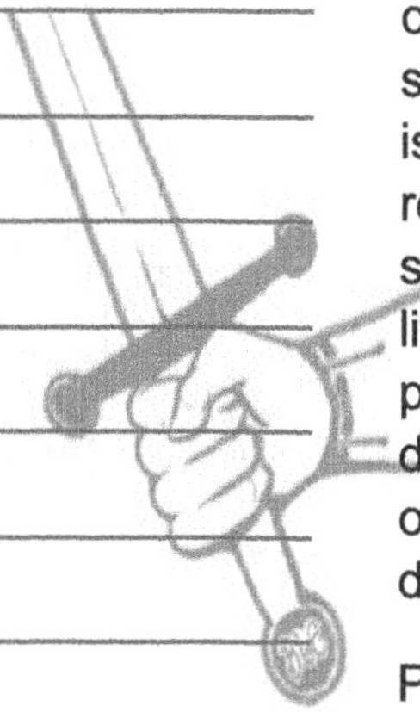

I like movies; at least I like good movies! I seem to watch many movies that are terrible with the hope to find just a few that are great.

One idea for the index pages in your book could be all the movies you watch this year with a little summary and what they were trying to get you to do or think. Movies, books, and TV shows are powerful as media can subtly change the way we think.

Quick Example: There is a movie called "Me before You." Let me tell you, it is horrible! The producers clearly want you to buy into situation ethics. When your hope is down, when you feel you have received the shorter end of the stick, go ahead—take your own life. It is not worth living! The producers tried to romantically devalue life and especially the life of those who are physically disabled.

Pay attention to the message the world dishes out. Be discerning and choose the hope of Christ!

Date: ________________

Being Good

Bible Reading: Luke 16 -17

Focus Word: Diligence

Being a good person, the kind of guy or girl that others enjoy being around, can generally be summed up in a few lines of advice:

Work hard! Make the most of your opportunities. Be good at what you do. Give it your best.

And when success comes your way, remember the grace that was given to you. Remember the people who were there for you, and that God gifted you in special ways.

Fight off the idea that you are better than others. Give grace, be patient, be kind, and show love to those around you.

On your way up the ladder, take a few people with you. Be a part of a team where everybody gets better and everyone gets credit! Love surely does cover a multitude of our weaknesses.

Not only is this stuff Biblical but it puts you on a path for success here on earth!

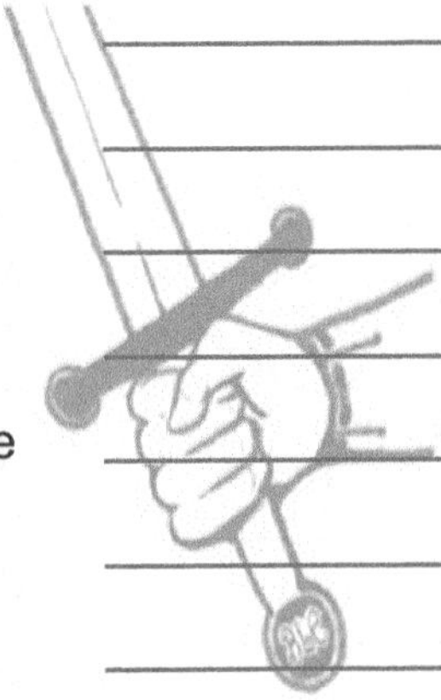

Date: ________________

Stay Humble

Bible Reading: Luke 18 -19

Focus Word: Enthusiasm

Life can be difficult.

You have probably felt it. Do you also take time to notice the difficulties that others have to work through?

Sometimes the best medicine for our own troubles is to step into the shoes of another and work to bless them and hold them up in their time of need.

This practice can also help us avoid getting cocky or arrogant when things seem to be going our way.

God is the giver of every good gift. Invest in people. Celebrate the victories of those around you.

Especially take time to celebrate the work of Christ in another. Salvation is so awesome because it totally changes the trajectory of a life!

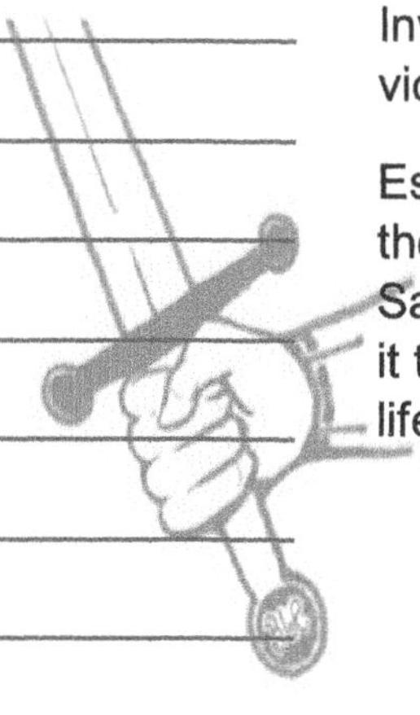

Week 16

Date: ________________

Unaware

Bible Reading: Judges 1 - 5

Focus Word: Gentleness

I believe journaling helps you to be aware, pay attention, consider issues, stay thoughtful, and be introspective about life.

I have mentioned it before, but here it is now, the WORST verse in the Bible, Judges 2:10.

These are people that were given a godly heritage and yet became sidetracked not realizing they were lost and in trouble!

One compromise after another and we are so far from where we should be; it is crazy!

A quick related reminder, the focus words printed under the verses are just little reminders about our character conditions. Are we strong in these areas, or do we need to realign and get focused in a spot we have become lax?

Tweaks along the way are easier than total overhauls! Let's not allow Judges 2:10 to play out in our own families!

Date: ______________

Friendship

Bible Reading: Judges 6 - 9

Focus Word: Humility

Friendship is wonderful. The value and strengths of friends are powerful.

Bless your friends. Be an encouragement to them.

As you journal consider the power of your friends on you.

We find ourselves liking what our friends like, talking about things they talk about, even believing the things they believe!

Be a friend to others. Love outsiders, love people, love and work with those who are different than you!

Yet consider differences of belief. Consider how influence works and be mindful of who you hang around and what has become important to you.

By the way—What can you learn from Gideon?

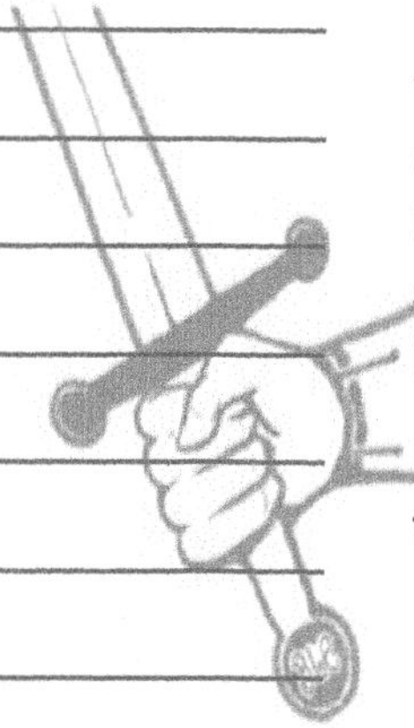

Date: ________________

Education Again

Bible Reading: Psalms 74 - 78

Focus Word: Loyalty

If every problem is a nail, then every solution requires a hammer.

Sounds good but I am pretty sure that makes no sense!

If I am an educator (and I am) then every problem has some educational application.

Guilty!

But how can you not see the power of a culture and the principles of passing good things in the culture from one generation to another through strong families and quality Biblical focuses, and worldview sensitive education?

I think we Christian are messing up the ideas behind Psalm 78 with all kinds of crazy rationalizations.

Learn and grow God's way. Invest in the Body of Christ!

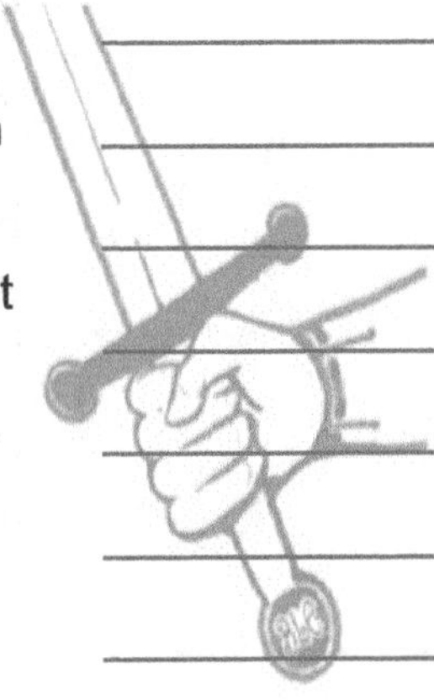

Date: ________________

Amazed and Astonished

Bible Reading: Luke 20

Focus Word: Resourcefulness

People were amazed and astonished by what Jesus did and by what He taught.

Jesus was able to combine the mind, spirit, and soul in a way that touches our hearts.

This is deeper than just a lesson to the brain. The system of learning that God employs goes beyond the limitations of the human brain. Jesus can touch those who struggle with schooling or memorization because the learning issues of the world are small hurdles in comparison to the mighty resources Jesus has at His disposal.

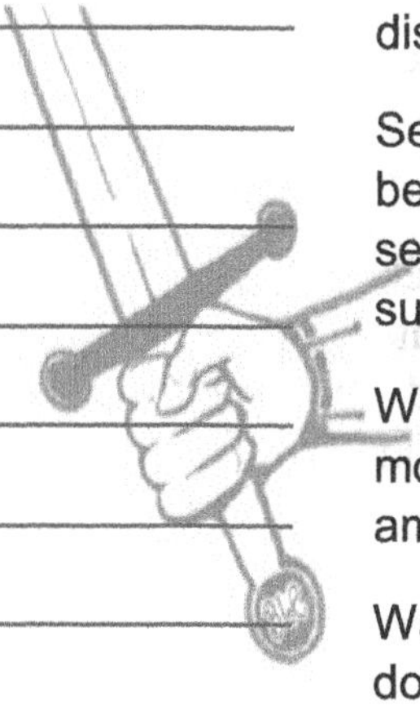

Search for God's truth! It may only be noticed by those with eyes that see, really see, with some supernatural depth.

When we finally get it, that "aha" moment, then we are absolutely amazed.

Walk with God and see what He does!

Date: ________________

Prayer

Bible Reading: Luke 21 - 22

Focus Word: Responsibility

Prayer is talking to God.

Tell Him what you are thinking. Ask Him questions. Let Him know when you don't get it and things seem to make no sense.

Ask Him for help. Tell Him you know He is amazing and all powerful, but sometimes your finite brain just doesn't understand.

Often times your prayer will be answered in your Bible reading. Sometimes it will be answered in circumstances. Sometime His answer comes from a friend or family member.

Sometimes the answer is to wait or you receive no answer at all.

Write out your prayers and pay attention for the answers. Go back to these pages later and marvel at the way things have changed and life is different. Be fully engaged in your prayer life! Journaling can help!

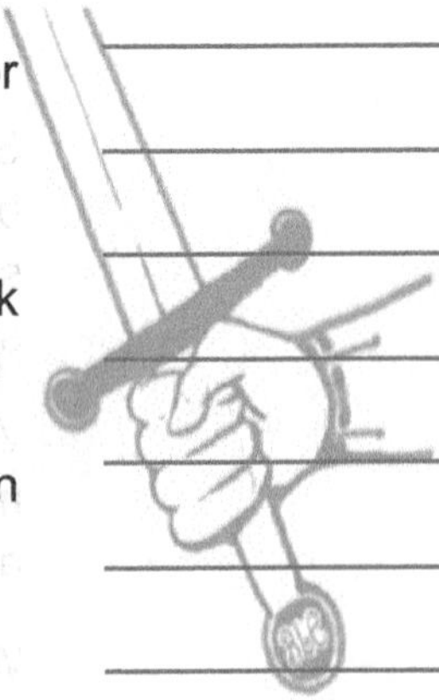

Resilience: Bouncing Back!

There is a lot of research that tells us that people who are resilient and tough are going to make it through life better than those who are fragile and weak. A very interesting study by Dr. Steven Southwick and Dr. Dennis Charney called *Resilience: The Science of Mastering Life's Greatest Challenges* explains that resilience is a set of skills that help people not only to get through hard times but to thrive through difficult circumstances.

Resilience is more than simply having a certain kind of personality that appears to cope with difficulty well. It is a learned ability! You get better with practice, training and the right kind of focus! That is very good news for a society and culture that is often stressed out! There is no doubt that each of us will have times of trouble (yes, it is scriptural), and life can be very hard!.

Dr. Charney notes the value of a tight knit community, stable role models, and one's belief in their ability to problem solve while also explaining the complicated brain pathway ruts that worrying actually creates leading to many health problems.

Charney summarizes ways we can overcome the negative consequences of stress. The list includes 1) develop a core set of beliefs that nothing can shake, 2) find meaning in your trauma, 3) stay positive, 4) watch and model resilient people, 6) lean on others, 7) exercise, 8) don't dwell on the past, and 9) think about your unique strengths and find confidence.

Sometimes I wonder if my introspection makes me overthink or sabotage my goal to be resilient and strong? Another reminder of my need for prayer and scripture!

My piece of advice is to know life can be tough and not to be surprised or undone by the crazy situation you are in. How cool when I stumbled onto my Bible reading for the day, II Corinthians 4:16 through chapter 6 and it said not to lose heart! Do you think Paul knew about tough times? He went through beatings, ship wrecks, sleepless nights, and talked about having nothing and yet had everything in Christ. Wow!

Lord help me to be resilient and bounce back when things are tough!

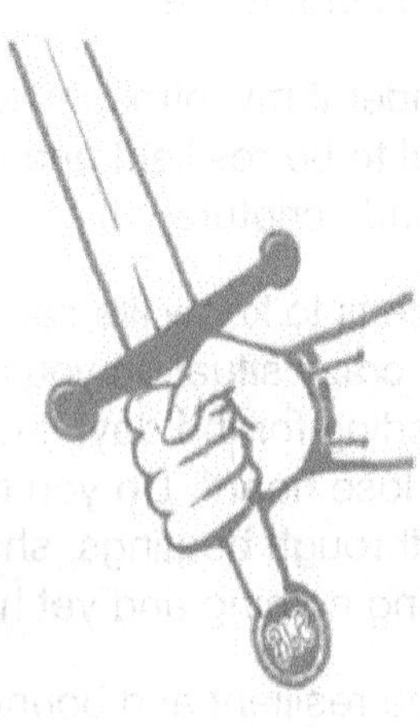

Week 17

Date: ________________

Crazy Stuff

Bible Reading: Judges 10 - 16

Focus Word: Truthfulness

How many times have you had crazy stuff happen to you?

Have you ever experienced something that you are pretty sure has never happened to anyone else?

Ecclesiastes 1:9 states that there is nothing new under the sun.

Now my challenge for you is to find something worthwhile in the two judges Jephthah and Samson. These were two men in positions of power who made big mistakes! Their stories are filled with crazy stuff!

There really are great people in the Bible, heroes of faith, but there are also stories of other men and women that leave us wondering how God wove them into the picture.

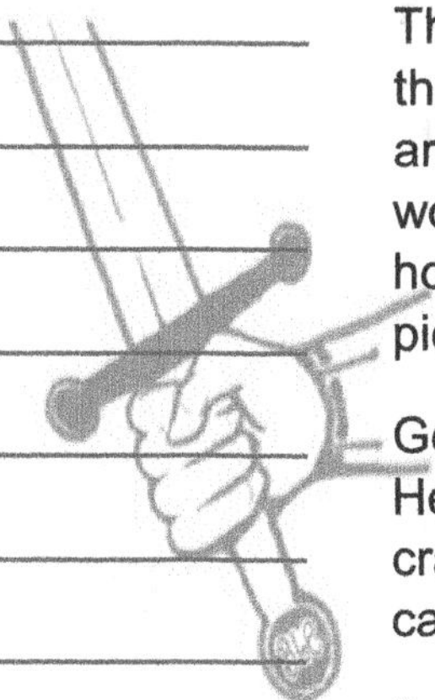

God used them despite their flaws. He used them in the midst of the craziness! And the good news, He can use you and me too!

Don't let the crazy stuff get you down!

Date: ________________

The American Dream

Bible Reading: Judges 17 - 21

Focus Word: Spirit-filled

Work hard and give everything you do your very best!

Self-improvement and success can be wonderful benefits to hard work and the Lord will certainly use you.

Unfortunately I believe the American dream has created a big problem.

People in America believe they can do whatever they want. Not just the "you can do it" encouragement, but no boundaries, no rules, "I am my own boss" kind of thinking.

The issue we read about in Judges is that people did whatever they thought best and they left God out.

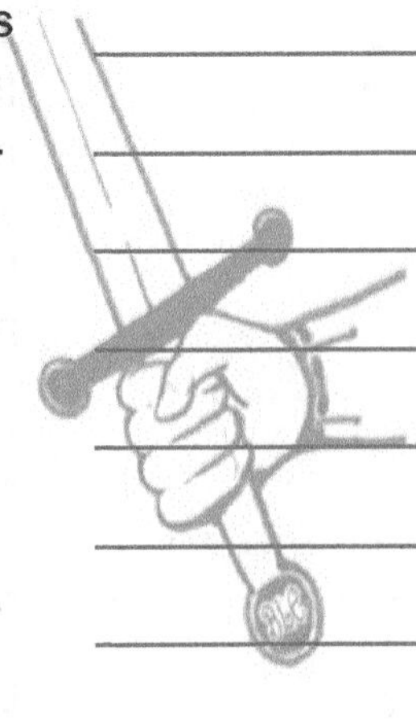

It is a scary world when people have no absolutes, no authority, and no basis for right and wrong.

How do you fall to this trap? Do you have blind spots that have been created by our culture?

Date: ________________

Parenting Habits

Bible Reading: Psalms 79 - 82

Focus Word: Thoughtful

My wife and I did a cool thing with our boys when they were little and it was time for bed. We sang them a song.

Part of the song comes from Psalm 80:29 and part comes from Numbers 6:24.

"The Lord Bless you and Keep you. The Lord shine His face upon you, and give you peace, and give you peace, and give you peace forever."

We did it together and it was an important habit that happened every night. It was one more small way to make sure our sons grew up thinking about God every day.

Think through the child rearing process carefully, it goes by so fast. The consequences are eternal and multi-generational!

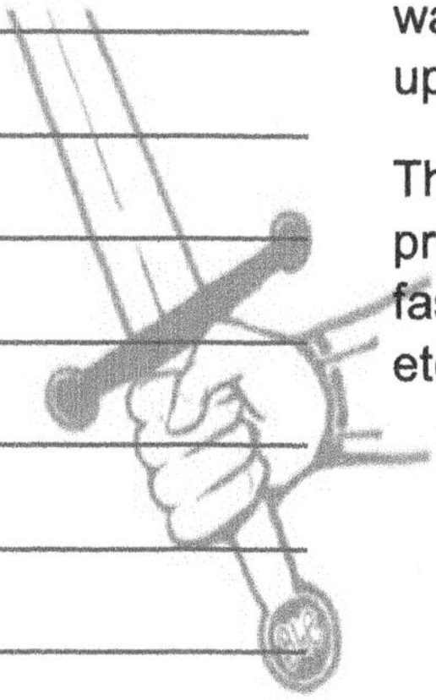

Date: ______________

Heart Burn

Bible Reading: Luke 23 - 24

Focus Word: Carefulness

Heartburn usually does not sound like a good thing!

I love the road to Emmaus story.

The risen Jesus catches up with some guys who are recounting the crucifixion. They do not recognize them.

He tells them about Moses and the prophets and explains how it all pointed to Himself.

Must have been a great lecture and an incredible discussion, but when the travelers turn around Jesus is gone.

Their eyes were opened! Praise the Lord when our eyes supernaturally can see!

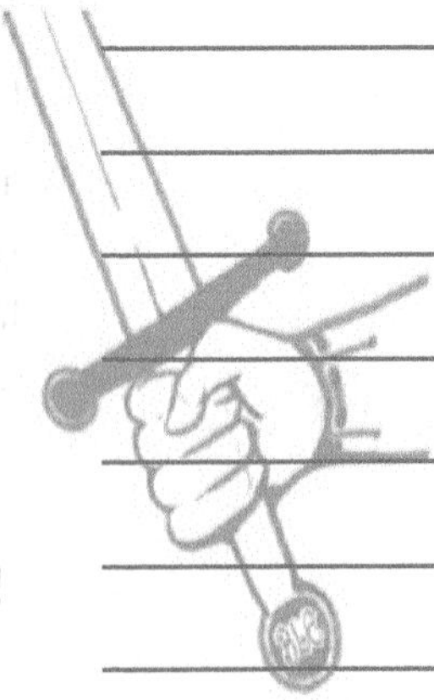

As they thought about His teaching, they realized something was going on in their hearts and the best way to describe it was "it burned."

Seek truth and let your *heart burn*!

Date: ________________

Bible Scholar

Bible Reading: John 1

Focus Word: Forgiveness

There is so much about scripture I do not understand, but I believe God gave us His word to teach us.

I want to be smart, dig deep, and figure out the intricacies of scripture.

Unfortunately, I am not smart enough to comprehend all that God has set before us in His Word!

While I do not understand it all, I am so thankful that God had a plan to communicate, teach, and relate to us through the written word!

Think about His supernatural plan to save the world. Think about the people who He calls together as disciples. A friend of mine told me there is no plan B with God!

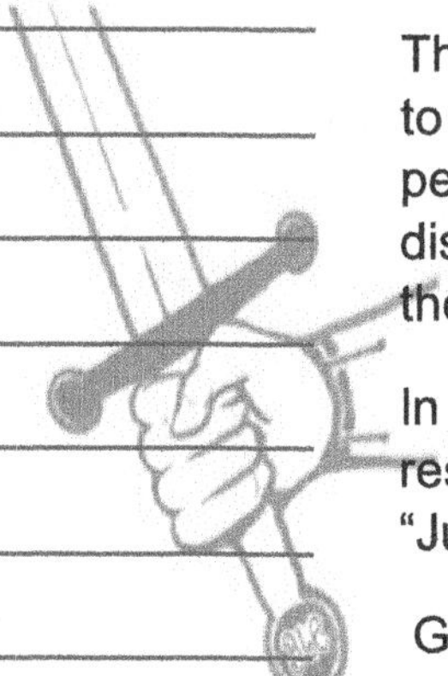

In John 1 when Phillip gets some resistance, I love what he says: "Just come and see for yourself!"

Go to the Bible and see for yourself!

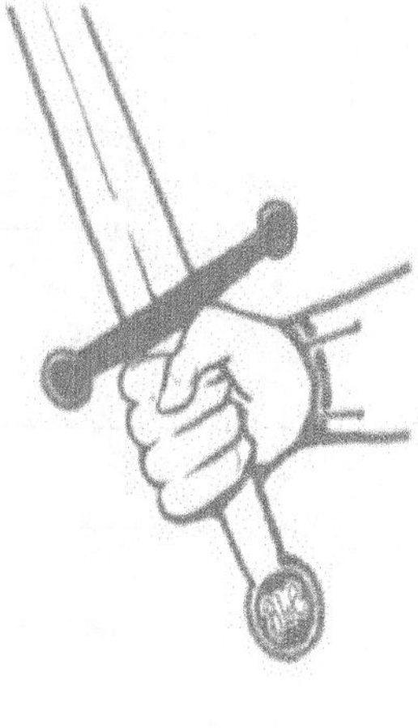

Week 18

Date: ________________

Love Story

Bible Reading: Ruth 1 - 4

Focus Word: Friendliness

You will see love demonstrated in several different ways in the short book of Ruth.

Marrying my wife was one of the greatest, biggest, and best decisions I ever made.

It is also a decision I keep making everyday. I get so many benefits for loving her and serving her with all my heart.

The commitment Ruth gives to her mother-in law Naomi is often repeated at weddings:

"Where you go I will go, and where you stay I will stay. Your people will be my people and your God my God." (NIV)

The book of Ruth is filled with role models for us to consider and follow! What a love story!

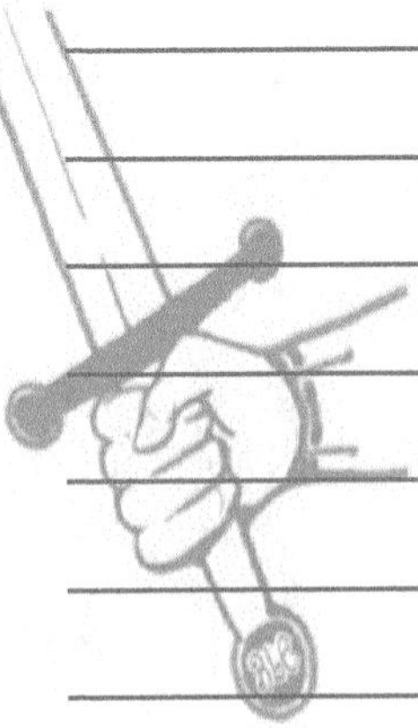

Date: ________________

Come on Parents!

Bible Reading: I Samuel 1 - 8

Focus Word: Generosity

Many of us grew up with a dream to be parents! I am thankful that God makes a way through natural parenting, adoption, and other opportunities to have an impact on the next generation!

Parenting is both a blessing and a big responsibility.

Sometimes I get irritated when I see poor parenting. 1 Samuel 2 is a prime example, as good of a guy as Eli may have been, he was a terrible parent! He reaped some terrible consequences in his family!

By the way, Samuel was no better as a parent (1 Samuel 8)!

Maybe this is where the bad reputation for pastor's kids began?

Love God, love your spouse, and say "no" once in a while to your kids!

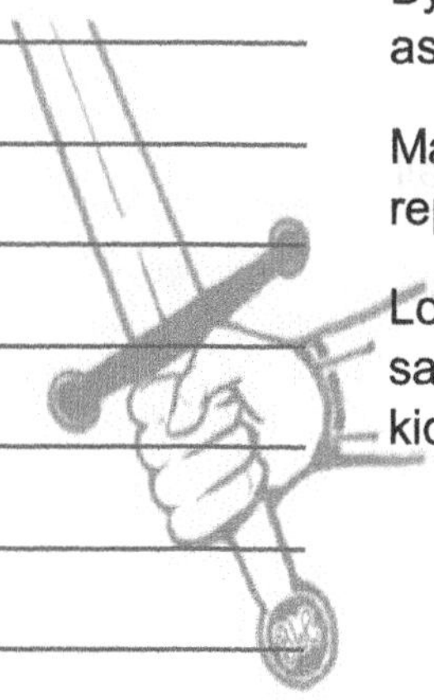

Date: ________________

Commit to Your Church

Bible Reading: Psalms 83 - 88

Focus Word: Helpfulness

I love the Body of Christ!

We need to participate in the Body and that may mean activities in church and a lot of other places!

I hope you are able to find a great church! And remember, that churches and pastors are not perfect.

It is a huge blessing to be in a church where you are known, loved, and taught. It is wonderful to be part of a Christian community.

It is magnificent to praise the Lord through singing.

Get plugged into your church! Work on the idea of worship; we all need it! Be part of a local Christian community! It feeds our soul and makes us stronger and more content.

Love your church!

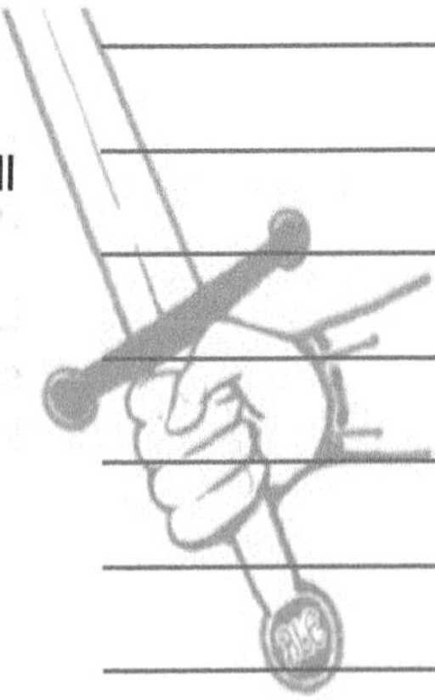

Date: ________________

Salvation

Bible Reading: John 2-3

Focus Word: Honesty

When did you get saved?

What is your testimony?

No games, no charades, are you a Christian?

Do you practice a deep kind of belief that has absolutely changed your life?

It is a supernatural thing!

We cannot work our way into it. It is not some scale that tips towards the idea we are more good than we are bad!

Salvation is about God's grace.

We just come to Jesus and say this is who I am, a sinner. I need help, I cannot do it, would you cleanse me of who I am and make me new!?

God loves honest prayers!

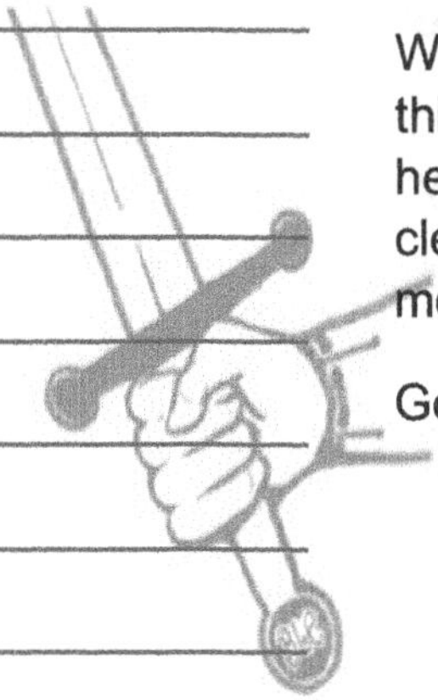

Date: ____________

Bad People Getting Saved

Bible Reading: John 4

Focus Word: Honor

It is so cool to hear a testimony of someone who was going in the wrong direction when Jesus got a hold of them in some fantastic way and wham, bam, everything changes and they end up an on-fire Christian!

Have you ever found yourself angry or ticked off at bad people?

The list of evildoers spreading destruction today seems never ending! ISIS and terrorism! Abortion advocates! Murderers, rapist, drug dealers, and human traffickers.

There is a lot of bad stuff out there!

Here is one way to think about these people in a more loving way: Think of "bad people" as sinners, as casualties of war. Satan has them and they are his prisoners.

They need the freedom that only Jesus can give.

He can turn a life upside down!

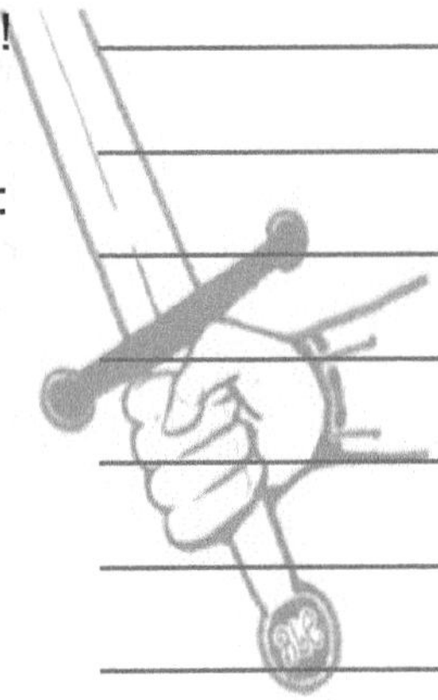

Week 19

Date: ______________

Finish Well

Bible Reading: I Samuel 9 - 15

Focus Word: Initiative

I heard some crazy statistic about the number of pastors who do not finish well.

You know how 90% of all statistics are made up, right?

We do know that a pastor's life is tough. The issues that go on in the Body of Christ can really make church leaders second guess and wonder what they are doing!

Finishing well takes a lot of work! A commitment to staying close to the Lord, keeping in His Word, being honest about personal struggles and keeping accountable. There are many other issues, of course (I hate to over-simplify), that factor into our ability to finish strong.

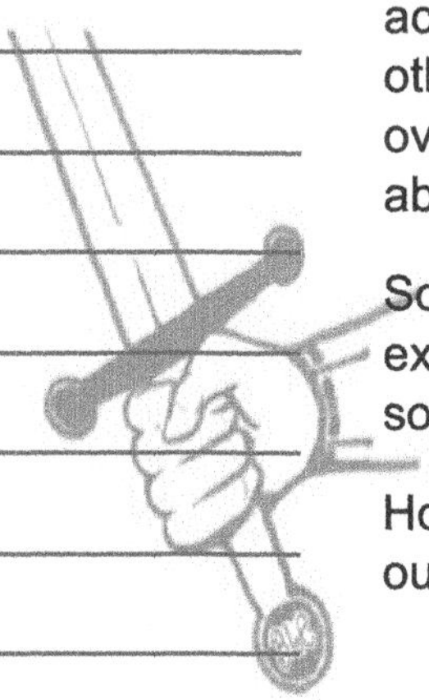

Sorry for another negative example, but King Saul did not do so well in the long run.

How can we reverse engineer the outcomes of Saul?

Date: ________________

The Confidence of David

Bible Reading: I Samuel 16 - 22

Focus Word: Meekness

David saw this terrible guy named Goliath taunting the Israelites and making fun of God. David was moved to action.

His confidence was incredible. It certainly seemed a bit cocky to his brothers that David would even think that he could take down a giant.

So where did David get this confidence?

He practiced on a lion and a bear. He had smaller tests that increased is competence and belief in what he and God could do.

Stay close to the Lord as you make big, risky decisions. Do not forget how God has helped you before.

Think about your training, the curriculum that has prepared you to do even bigger things.

The combination of a willing, trained, disciplined person is powerful! It inspires confidence!

Date: ________________

Poetry Touches the Soul

Bible Reading: Psalms 89 - 91

Focus Word: Promptness

I hope the Bible reading portion of your journal is going well. There may be times when you question the value of your reading or at least struggle to understand what you are reading. Press on!

Today's verses have the ability to touch you in a special way with poetic verse. Don't miss the beauty of God's Word in the Psalms!

Another thought: Take a moment to think about time management. Time flies when you are having fun! I would say it even flies when you are not! Be sure to make the most of your time.

We put a lot of time into our jobs and our career, make it count!

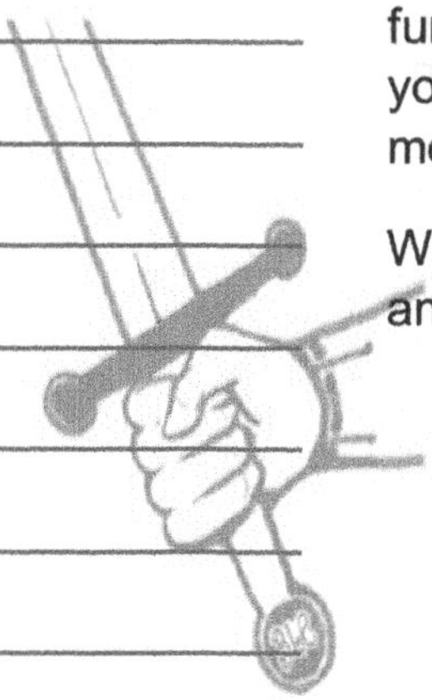

Date: ____________________

You Decide

Bible Reading: John 5 - 6

Focus Word: Respect

You are in the driver's seat of your life.

Life can be hard, but you are not a victim. You decide the path you want to take. Problem solve and quit blaming everyone else.

The answers are at your finger tips. Not deciding sometimes is the worst decision you can make!

Use God's Words, the stories and parables in front of you to navigate life and make sense out of the things you are up against.

The Bible offers encouragement and direction that is far more than hollow phrases. Apply this stuff to your own life and decisions!

Be humble, get help, figure it out, and get it done!

Date: ________________

Beauty Out of Ashes

Bible Reading: John 7

Focus Word: Self-Control

There is a song out there about how God can take the difficulties of life and make them into something beautiful and wonderful.

Life was certainly difficult for Jesus on the way to the cross. So many people were unwilling to follow Jesus during those last days of His ministry.

Even while some plotted to kill Jesus, verse 31 says that "many in the crowd put their faith in Him."

Somewhere in the crowds of those last days Nicodemus appears to be realizing how amazing Jesus is.

No matter the circumstances, no matter your current level of success, streams of living water flow through the believer! You never know when God is going to use the struggles in your life to bring others to Him!

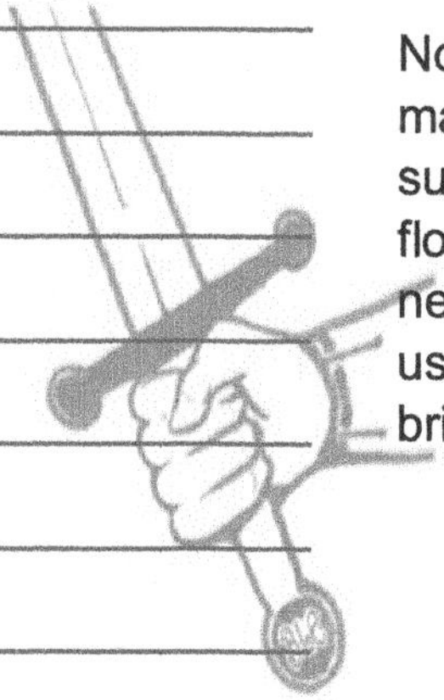

Week 20

Date: ________________

Tough Day

Bible Reading: I Samuel 23 - 31

Focus Word: Tactfulness

David had a huge ordeal with Saul even after Samuel had clearly anointed David to be the next king of Israel.

One particular situation involved Saul army destroying David's towns and the wives of his warriors being taken captive!

The men David was fighting with became distressed. They had been on the move and nothing was easy, but now this!

David's men were so bitter they talked about stoning David.

Yikes! What next? The situation just went from bad to worse!

But check out 1 Samuel 30:6—David found strength in the Lord.

From that point on David started moving, making decisions, and planning with purpose. Leading! Fighting! Focused!

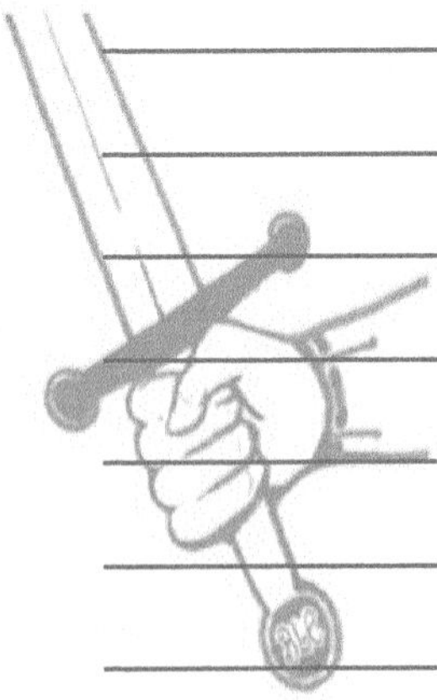

Date: ________________

Conflict

Bible Reading: II Samuel 1 - 8

Focus Word: Thankfulness

Joab and Abner had been mighty warriors and leaders for their king for a long time.

But Saul was now dead. How would David unite the kingdom?

Dealing with conflict. You can't help but run into conflict. You are either in the middle of it, or you are watching it.

Prayer was key to David uniting the kingdom. God provided him with competence and victory.

God's favor was obvious and yet David was humble along the way.

Joab was a piece of work! He was not always easy to deal with but he was very loyal to David.

Conflict is normal. Work through it.

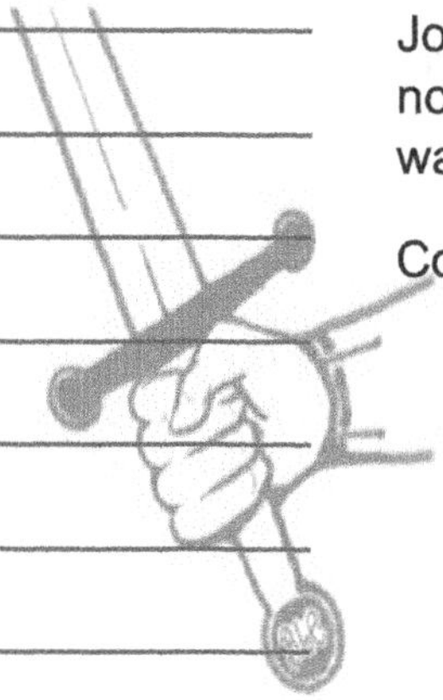

Date: ________________

Know Your Place

Bible Reading: Psalms 92 - 97

Focus Word: Self-Confidence

Life! You are good at some things, but you are not so good at other stuff.

You have places where you need to grow. You have been given responsibility and you need to pull it off.

The Lord can help you. He can equip you. He can prepare you, but you have to start with humility and know where you stand before the Lord.

The Psalms help us to know who we are before an amazing, awesome all powerful God.

A humble combination of ambition and self-confidence can be a powerful tool in the hand of God.

Pray for the right perspective.

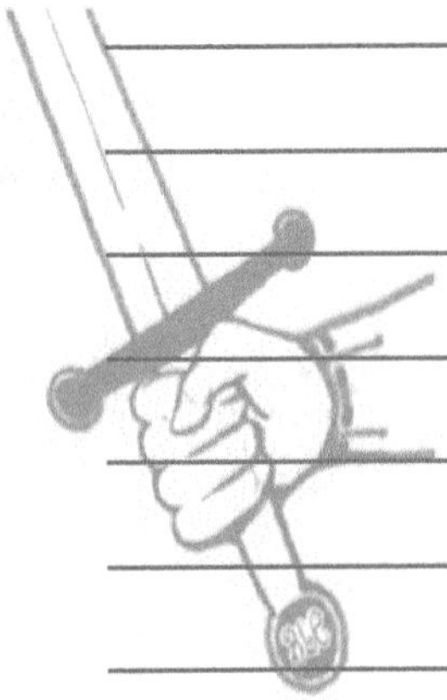

Date: ________________

Jesus the Messiah

Bible Reading: John 8

Focus Word: Thoroughness

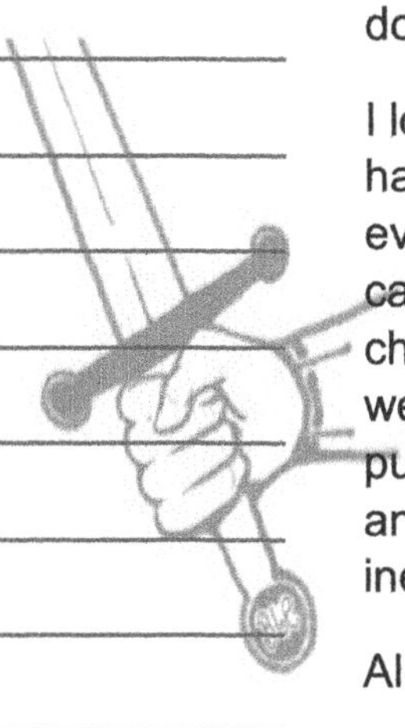

Jesus makes it clear who He was and is.

He is not just a great teacher. He is not just a really smart and influential man.

Sometimes we have to decide what are we going to do with the idea of not compromising on issues such as salvation, heaven, hell, and truth.

Don't be a offensive to others about it, but realize, these issues change everything!

What about your friends? Where does Jesus fit for them?

I love the word integration. We have to integrate God into everything we do! I believe we can do just about anything we choose and still serve Jesus, but we have to be focused and purposeful or life will get in the way and we will find ourselves ineffective.

Align yourself with Jesus!

Date: ____________________

Blindness

Bible Reading: John 9 - 10

Focus Word: Focus!

This blind guy really takes a beating from everybody.

First everyone wants to blame him and his family for his blindness. Then once he is healed no one believes him.

He experienced the love and power of God. He was a simple man, he was a thankful man, and to him it was very clear, everyone needs to get to know Jesus!

The insults just kept coming.

In exasperation all the formerly blind man can say is that "**this is remarkable**!" The doubts and discussion the Pharisees were having was ridiculous! To him it was obvious, "I was blind but now I see!"

Thank the Lord for miracles and good eyesight!

How is your eyesight?

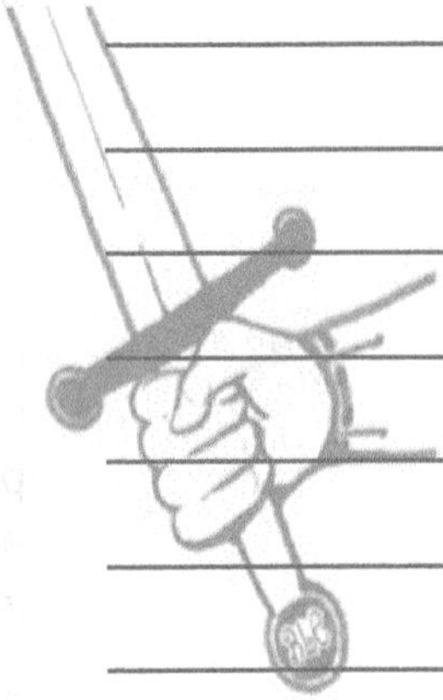

Image Bearer

You know the biblical doctrine of being created in the image of God, but do your children? I have another message for the parents who may be reading this. All of us are designed to do something special and amazing. We are all beautifully and wonderfully made. We each have huge potential.

Read Genesis 1:26-31 and Psalms 139:13-17

What a precious thought it is to realize that our specialness comes from God, the creator. It is amazing to consider how creative humanity has been in history while at the same time claiming dominion over the earth the Lord has given us.

When we watch TV or spend 4-6+ hours a day on the internet, we are certainly not living up to our potential. Sometimes our kids are asked to do too little. What does it mean to be designed to do the work that God has prepared for us to do?

Read Ephesians 2:8-10 and Matthew 25:14-30

Biblical education helps students to identify and invest in their talents. Anything we strive to be good at, math, basketball, art, etc...has to be developed through learning. There comes a time when a student's base of knowledge becomes so strong that they are no longer just adding to their knowledge, but multiplying it. Progression becomes geometric not linear.

We have to teach our kids to be responsible and to be stewards of the gifts and talents they have. When we use our talents God's way He multiplies them! It is called talent math, and it doesn't work like "regular math!" As your child develops, are they living up to their potential? Can anyone really be at their full potential without using Jesus' principles?

Image bearing requires purposeful training and curriculum!

Week 21

Date: ________________

Going From Bad to Worse

Bible Reading: II Samuel 9 - 16

Focus Word: Virtue

David was so strong. He was so smart. He was the perfect leader.

Not sure how this all works out, but while most kings were fighting, his own men were off in a war, he was home, in a place where his weaknesses were going to be exposed.

I once hired some help to fix a leaky roof at my school. We had water damage on walls and were trying to figure out where the problem was coming from.

One contractor told me that water finds the weak spots of your structure and it seeps through.

I suppose sin is like water in this case.

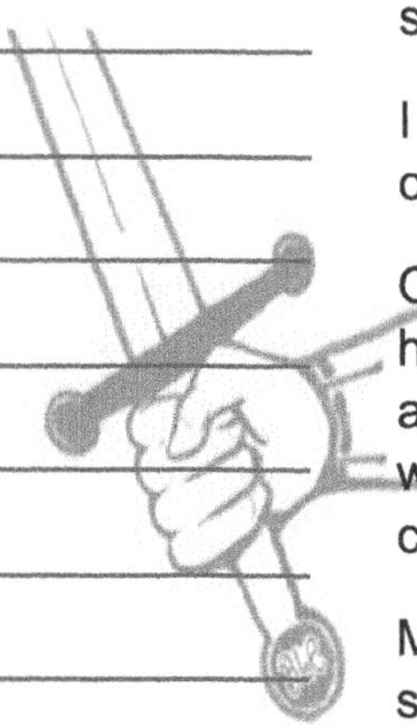

Our success in other areas cannot hide our flaws! In fact we may actually have a gap that sin has a way of revealing and a weakness can become even worse!

Maybe you have heard that certain strengths have certain weaknesses???
We all need grace!

Date: ________________

Oxymoron

Bible Reading: II Samuel 17 - 22

Focus Word: Tactical

Some of our favorite everyday phrases seem to be contradictions when you take a moment to think about them. An oxymoron is a figure of speech that combines terms that would usually be contradictory. Check these out:

Pretty ugly

Terribly good

Once again

Bad luck

Do nothing

Honest politicians

The fun goes on and on!

You will see some contradictions in the life of David.

How are you full of contradictions?

Consider Justice and Grace!

Date: ________________

Wonderful Words

Bible Reading: Psalms 98 - 102

Focus Word: Courtesy

Philip Bliss wrote the following hymn in 1874:

Sing them over again to me, wonderful words of life, let me more of their beauty see, wonderful words of life: Words of life and beauty teach me faith and duty.

Beautiful words, wonderful word, wonderful words of life.

Truth. Strength, power, encouragement, inspiration, motivate, God's words, the psalms, think about these things!

There is so much we can do with our time, but sometimes I choose poorly!

There is so much I can read and learn, but again, sometimes I choose poorly!

Today choose to choose well!

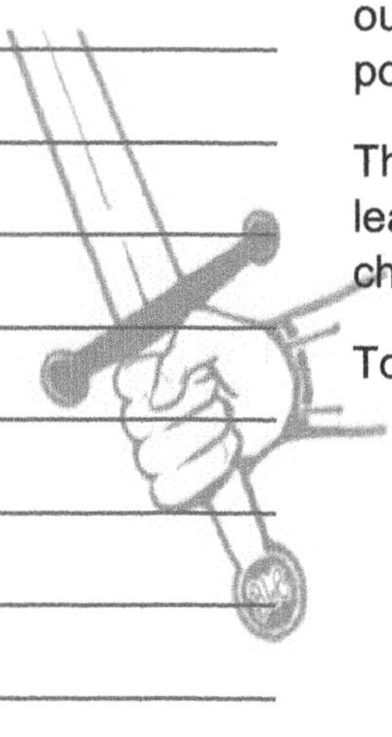

Date: ________________

Worship like Mary

Bible Reading: John 11 - 12

Focus Word: Worship

Mary the sister of Lazarus really knew how to worship.

She had so many experiences with Jesus, He was her friend, He had saved her from some big messes. Mary knew firsthand just how amazing and wise Jesus was.

I can have moments of understanding and implementing worship the right way, but I fear these moments are few and far between.

I hope as you read these accounts of Jesus, you can find diverse and beautiful ways to consistently worship Him!

It really is an act of grace that we can see, understand, and pursue Jesus.

I am thankful for your passion to know God and follow him!

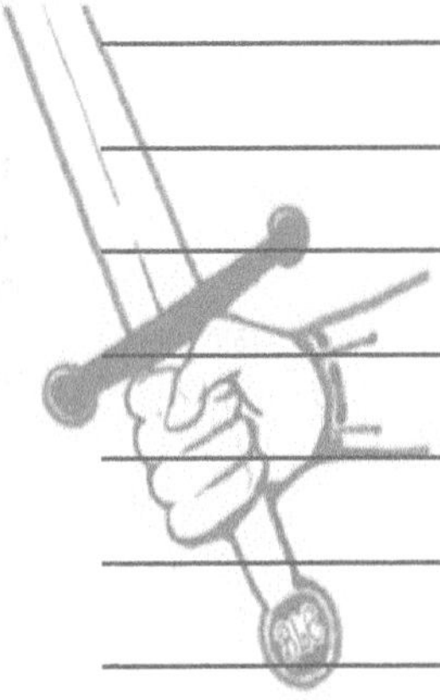

Date: ________________

Hard Times are Typical

Bible Reading: John 13 - 14

Focus Word: Diligence

Do not be troubled when life offers its seemingly endless challenges.

I am not sure who told me this, but one Sunday morning at church I wrote in the margin of my Bible these four things (John 14).

1. God is real!
2. Heaven is real!
3. Jesus is the way!
4. Don't be afraid!

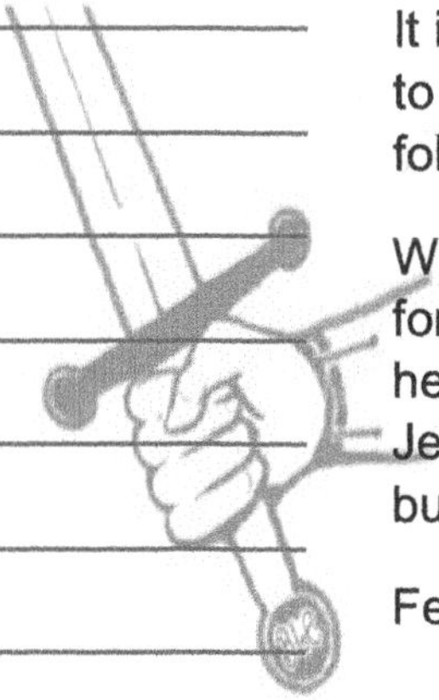

It is crazy to me that people want to do their own stuff and refuse to follow Jesus.

We need to have a broken heart for the things that break God's heart. We need to think like Jesus. The hard times will come but rest in these four truths.

Fear is not from God!

Week 22

Date: ________________

Hodgepodge

Bible Reading: II Samuel 23 - 24

Focus Word: Eagerness

The challenge of a project like this is to think about how life connects with scripture.

When you read as many as eight to ten pages in the Old Testament you will find so many issues and topics that could be addressed!

So today, I threw together several assorted words that stuck out to me as I read these passages in II Samuel.

Leadership

Mighty Men

Teammates

My sin's effect on others

Costly sacrifices

Legacy

Continue to ask God to guide you, direct you, and show you how the study of His word is meant to transform your life!

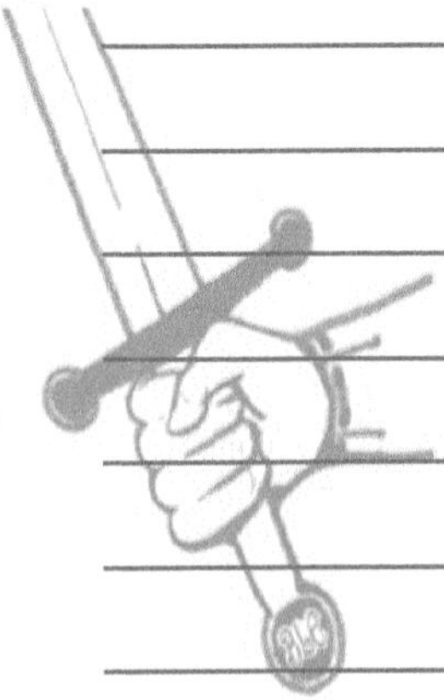

Date: ________________

Solomon Asks for Wisdom

Bible Reading: I Kings 1 - 9

Focus Word: Understanding

This is a pretty long reading on the life of Solomon.

I love that he asked for wisdom.

What is the difference between wisdom and intelligence?

Is it possible that we can be wise at one point, or in some season of life, and let it go in another season? It sure seems that while Solomon was wise he made a few poor decisions!

It appears that Solomon led very well! He impressed many people around him! He had a lot of success!

I would like to think that success can often be a great validation on God's blessing and your application of God's principles in your life.

God's ways work!

If we get infatuated with our own success it can actually lead us away from God. Did that happen to Solomon? Ponder this thought.

Date: ________________

Praise Him

Bible Reading: Psalms 103 - 105

Focus Word: Knowledge

Powerful verses in the Psalms!

I love Keith and Kristyn Getty. They have written some amazing hymns/praise songs.

One of my favorites is *Speak, Oh Lord.* Check it out on YouTube.

I love to turn on my iTunes or the video on YouTube and just listen to the words and allow them to move me to desire Christ.

Speak to me Lord through the people around me, your Word, my pastor, and the situations you put me through!

Teach me!

Help me to notice the important stuff.

Renew my mind, because it often gets messed up!

Fulfill in us your glory!

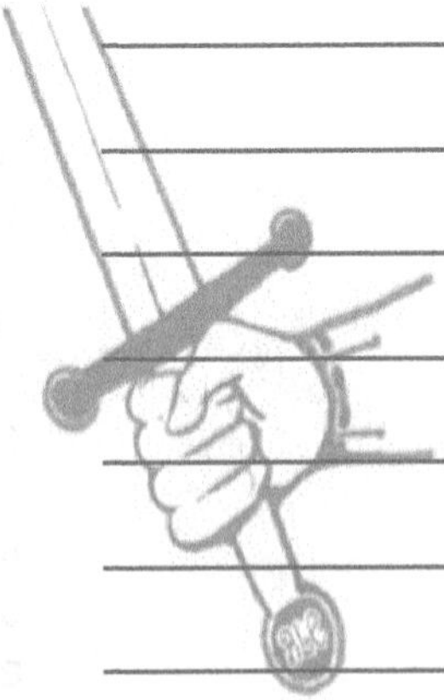

Date: ______________

My Goals or God's?

Bible Reading: John 15 - 16

Focus Word: Thoughtful

We like motivated people. I like it when someone has a goal, sets out to accomplish something big or hard, and gets it done!

But how do we know when it is my goal and not God's goal I am chasing? Is this just some worldly thing that is not really benefitting the kingdom of Christ?

To me this is a life long struggle and a tension that you will always have to think through and pray about.

I am struck by the passage in John 15:5 concerning the vine and the branches. The summary statement that without Christ, without Jesus, without His Holy Spirit guidance and direction, you and I can do NOTHING!

Chase the things of God!

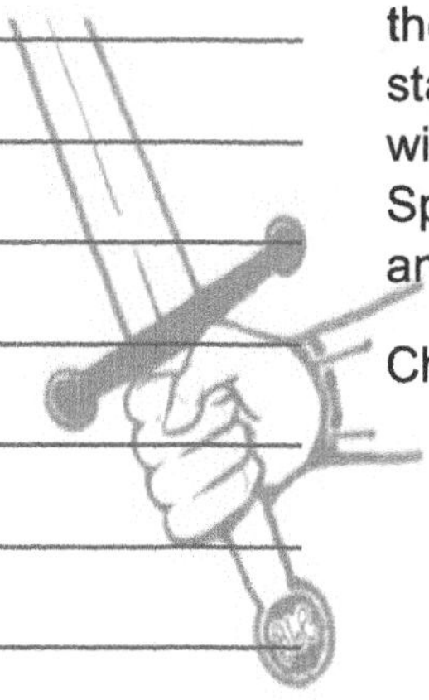

Date: ________________

Jesus Prays For You

Bible Reading: John 17 - 18

Focus Word: Fortitude

Yes, that is right, Jesus prays for you.

God's system of salvation, the Church, ministry, relationships, truth, all of it was set up more than 2000 years ago through Jesus, our Savior.

Notice how Jesus prays for His disciples and the people they will reach. That means you! Mind blowing, I know!

Don't you just love Peter!? He was so willing, but just like me; he seems to blow it a lot!

Be strong through the ups and downs of life. Be willing to get back up, try again, start over, when you have made a mess of things!

Thank you Jesus for your work in my life! Thank you for thinking about me from the beginning!

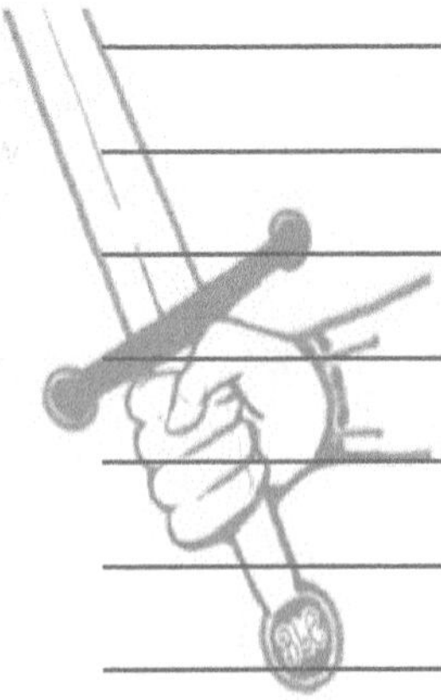

Week 23

Date: ______________

Wisdom Part 2

Bible Reading: I Kings 10 - 15

Focus Word: Piety

Remember how Solomon asked for wisdom a few chapters back?

How was it wise to have 700 wives and 300 concubines???

Yet, the Queen of Sheba was very impressed. Notice her comments to Solomon.

As I think about leadership I often am overwhelmed. So much to think about, so many pressures, so many problems, and so many different points of views and interests.

As Rehoboam is thinking about how to lead, he rejects real wisdom and listens to the wrong voices.

Here is some simple leadership advice:

Serve people, love people and work will be accomplished while relationships are created and prioritized!

The power of loving people!

Date: ________________

Elijah Rocks!

Bible Reading: I Kings 16 - 22

Focus Word: Fear of the Lord

I have my favorite Bible characters! Peter was crazy. John the Baptist was so committed. Moses was an amazing leader. Daniel was so smart. Paul was relentless.

We named our four boys Josiah, Isaiah, Noah and Micah—now there is a good group!

But check out Elijah here, what a powerful guy he was!

You could talk forever about this guy and his commitment to God. Notice the cool transition to another man of God, Elisha.

Let's consider God's sovereignty for a bit.

A prophet tells Ahab some bad news. So Ahab decides to trick God and the prophet while believing he can overcome the prophecy.

No chance! A warrior randomly shoots a bow into no where land, and it just happens to kill Ahab, just like the prophet said.

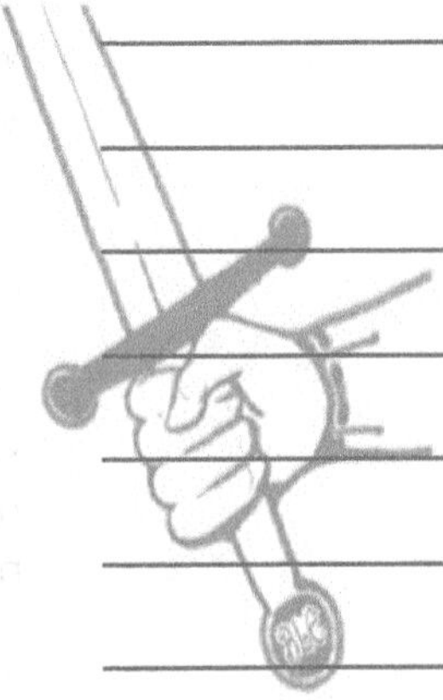

Date: ________________

Cause and Effect

Bible Reading: Psalms 106 - 108

Focus Word: Miracles

When are we going to stop going our own way and finally just pause, listen, and pay attention?

God is trying to tell us, trying to warn us, trying to help us, but so often we just do not get it!

Silly people! Silly you and silly me!

Throw this saying in for free from the Navy, "Loose lips sink ships."

Reminds me of Psalm 106:33. We all need to think about our words and their effect!

Date: ____________

Jesus Crucified

Bible Reading: John 19 - 20

Focus Word: Healing

A huge stumbling block here for many people. Jesus crucified. He died for you and me.

The Messiah sacrificed His life so that you and I might have eternal life.

CS Lewis talks about this. Jesus said he was the Messiah and so we need to see him as either a madman, crazy wacko, or believe him and worship him.

But don't you dare call him some nice teacher, or just interesting, or someone who doesn't effect me! That's not who Jesus is!

You either take Him at face value or you reject Him.

I suppose another way of saying it is that if you take Jesus only with all your conditions, all your selfish priorities, are you really in fact just rejecting him!?

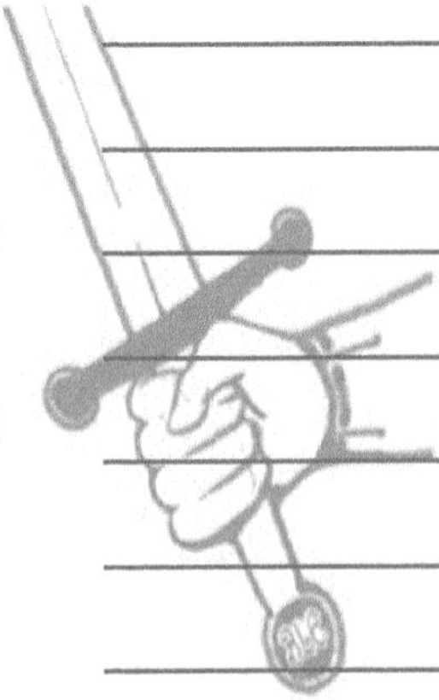

Date: ________________

The Empty Tomb

Bible Reading: John 21

Focus Word: Prophecy

Josh McDowell and others have written about the "proof" of Jesus and His resurrection.

One piece of evidence that really intrigues me has to do with how the disciples believed it!

They changed their life from that point on and most of them died martyrs for the cause of Christ.

People do not live and die for a lie, for a trick.

The grave was empty and they never found the body. The disciples saw Jesus after He died, and they were there when He ascended into the clouds.

I know, it is still an act of faith, but your faith is based on solid evidence!

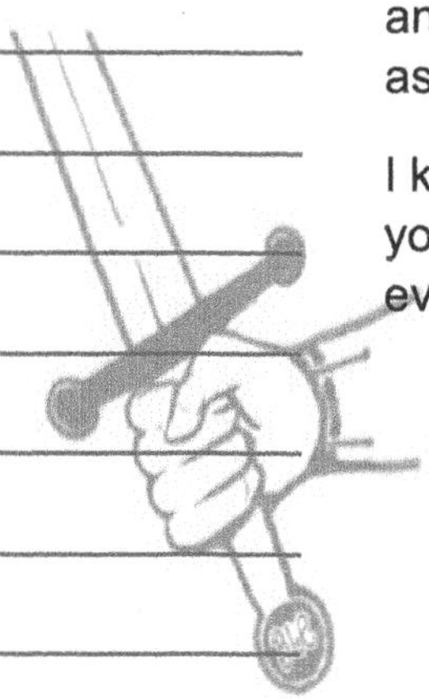

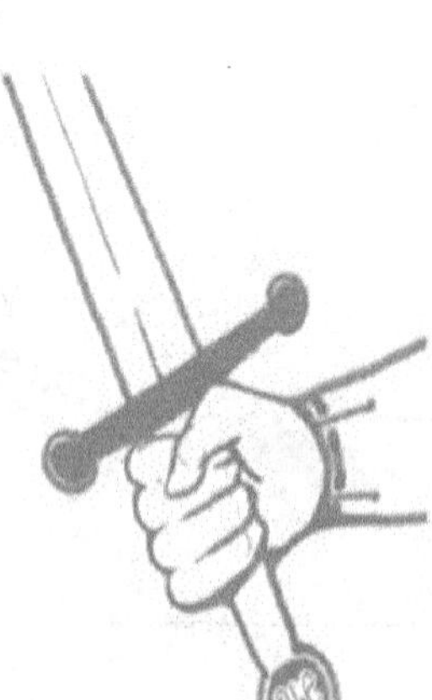

Week 24

Date: ________________

Bible Times Versus Modern Times

Bible Reading: II Kings 1 - 7

Focus Word: Peace

Elisha—what can we learn from this prophet?

How does Gehazi get all mixed up in a mess that doesn't turn out so well for him? Again, sometimes we are our own worst enemy!

What is it about the story of Naaman that resonates with you?

Reading about awful diseases and bathing in a river makes me glad I get to live in this modern time period! Very thankful for the cool things God has allowed mankind to pull off over time.

But are there tradeoffs to living in the 21st century? Comparing the benefits of the modern age to the "old days" what do you see as the downside? What problems do we have that our favorite Bible characters would not have experienced?

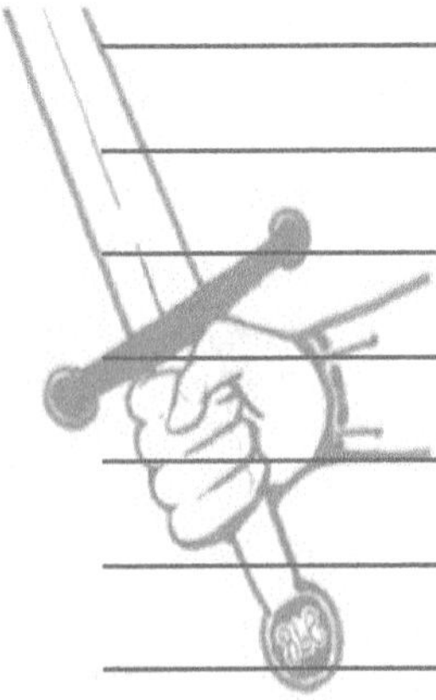

Date: ________________

Deception

Bible Reading: II Kings 8 - 15

Focus Word: Goodness

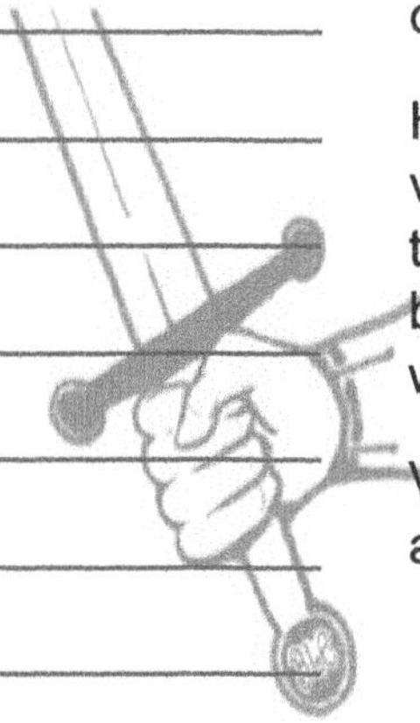

I understand it was Sir Walter Scott who said, “oh what a tangled web we weave when first we practice to deceive!”

Some of our favorite movies like to deal with deceptions and manipulations whether in business or in personal life.

A well-made film can actually manipulate the audience such that the “good guy,” the one you feel empathy for, the one you want to end up on top, is actually the one doing all the shenanigans.

Our quest to get what we want can often lead to short term victory.

Have you ever heard of a pyrrhic victory? It is a Roman/Greek term that is used when a victory is won but at too great a cost to be worthwhile!

Victories won through deception are often pyrrhic victories!

Date: ________________

Ponder

Bible Reading: Psalms 109 - 115

Focus Word: Chastity

Does anyone use the word ponder anymore?

It means to think, consider, wonder at length about some issue before you.

Maybe we should ponder things that amaze us. Or maybe we should ponder something that makes no sense.

The Psalmist sure seemed to spend his time pondering God. Think about a few of these statements:

Great are the works of the Lord.

Blessed is the man who fears the Lord.

The fear of the Lord is the beginning of wisdom.

You are the steward of the earth.

The love of God is powerful.

Ponder the things of God!

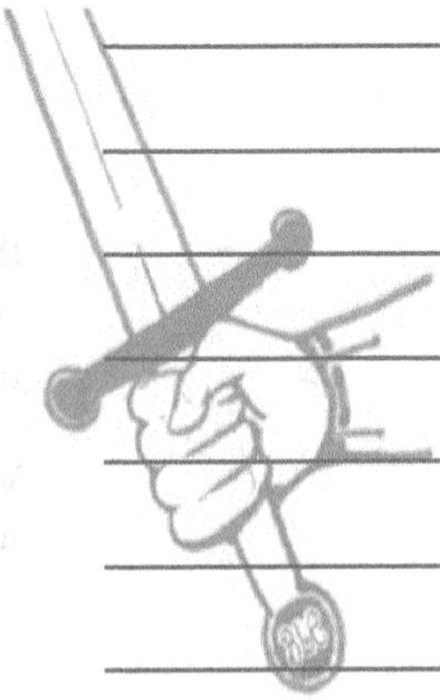

Date: ________________

Now What?

Bible Reading: Acts 1 - 2

Focus Word: Modesty

So Jesus left and passed the job of spreading the good news over to the disciples.

Now what?

There is work to do!

So these disciples, and you and me, are really the plan for the spread of the gospel?

Where does the Holy Spirit fit in? How has this mission changed today?

In Acts 2 people hear the good news, recognize their sin, and next is a most beautiful phrase: “they were cut to the heart.”

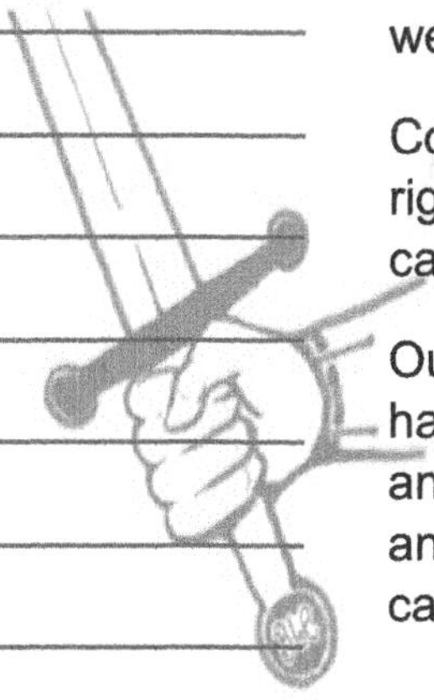

Confess, repent, and move in the right direction. That is what God calls us to do.

Out of thankfulness to the one who has saved you, use your passion and calling to go problem solve and fix as many things as you can .

Date: ________________

Take it to the Next Level!

Bible Reading: Acts 3 - 5

Focus Word: Love

Quick Hits from Acts 3-5:

- Peter sure does step it up! He came a long way from his low point denying Christ!

- Nothing like times of refreshment! Boy that feels good!

- Look at what normal, ordinary, unschooled people can accomplish with God's help! I still believe you should do everything possible to train and prepare yourself as God can use you in ways you cannot imagine!

- Powerful prayers! Prayer paired with a willingness to do the hard things is strong stuff.

- Nice introduction to Barnabas, a man full of encouragement. Be an encourager today!

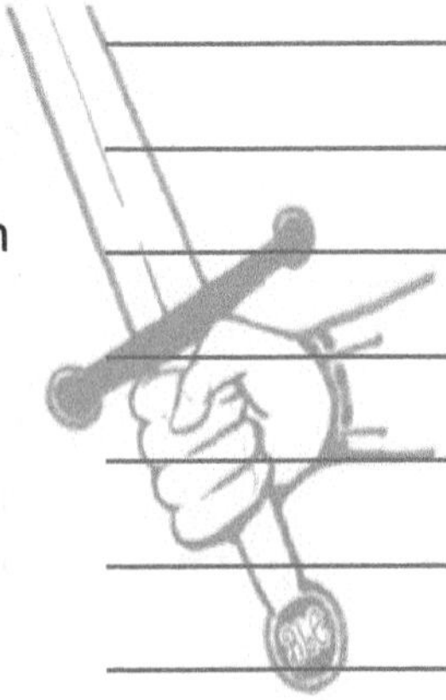

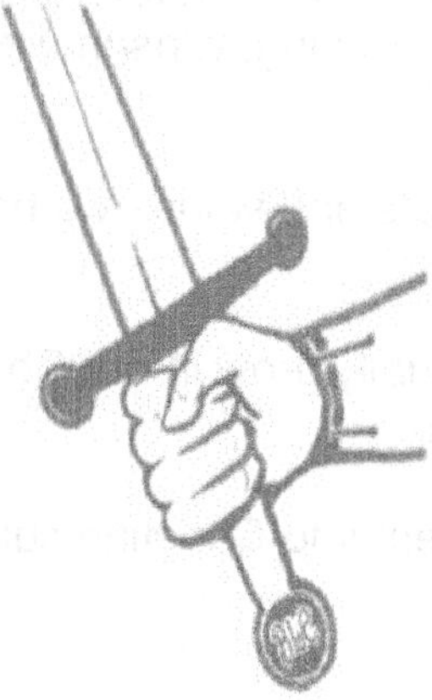

Investments

I used to be in awe of investment advisors. They looked so smart, so rich! They would speak with such authority telling people to buy low and sell high. Then came the market crash of 2008.

What are you investing in? Something that offers an earthly reward or an eternal reward?

I have known men who invested a whole life into their dream retirement. Ever met someone who hated their work, but loved the money?

Read II Corinthians 9:7-14 and Luke 12:13-21

How much fun is it to participate in something that is going well, something that is making a difference?

What is the difference between an owner and a hired hand?

Read John 10: 1-18

Who is responsible for the education of the next generation? Is that something we should be investing in?

What kind of returns can we expect from an investment in Biblical education? An investment should expect a return. If we invest in Biblical education, will we get what we paid for? Will our output be strong, well adjusted, Bible believing, winsome adults ready to make an impact on the culture?

Can we salvage the strong beliefs and values we have against the moral slide of our nation?

Can we, the Body of Christ, actually grow in our Christian beliefs and convictions?

How can you make an investment into Christian culture and the next generation?

Week 25

Date: ________________

The Good King

Bible Reading: II Kings 16 - 22

Focus Word: Joy

The divided nation of Israel ends on a bit of an upswing with Hezekiah.

Unfortunately it was not enough.

I hate the thought that we as Christians may now live in a society where what we do for Christ is not considered good, normal, or even acceptable. It is crazy to me to think that a country like the United States of America could turn into a place where Christianity is counter-cultural and squeezed out!

Unfortunately, Christians often just don't make sense to the outside world! We may do everything right and still feel like we are getting no where.

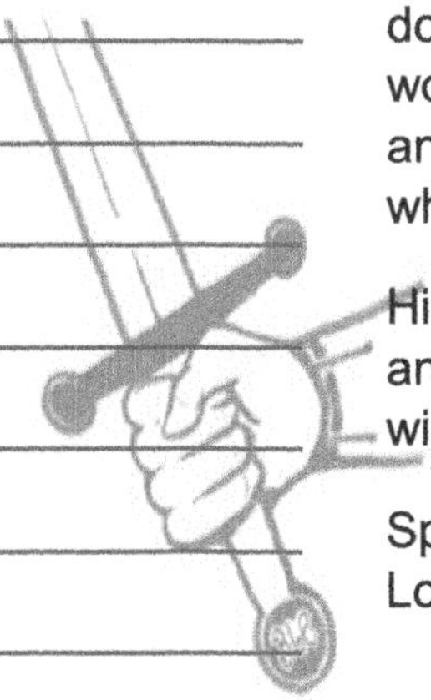

History is filled with tough times and the good guys do not always win (at least here on earth).

Spread your issues before the Lord and pray for our country!

Date: ________________

Boy Wonder—Josiah

Bible Reading: II Kings 23 - I Chronicles 2

Focus Word: Peace

Josiah started young, in the face of a culture that no longer valued the things of God, and made a difference.

He was not perfect but he finished strong.

I love the words of II Kings 23:25. Moses used similar words in Deuteronomy, and Jesus repeated them in the gospels. Here is the Biblical description of Josiah:

"Neither before nor after Josiah was there a king like him who turned to the Lord as he did—with all his heart and with all his soul and with all his strength, in accordance with all the Law of Moses." (NIV)

He did his very, very best! What a legacy!

Do not lose heart. Keep up the good work!

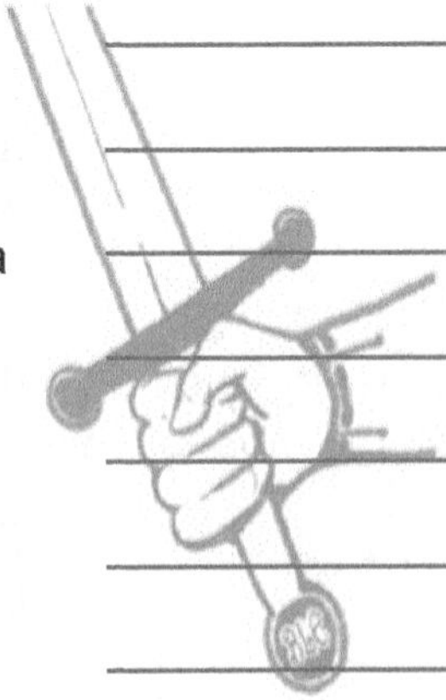

Date: ________________

Death

Bible Reading: Psalms 116 - 119:40

Focus Word: Long Suffering

I am not sure where the idea of "booing" comes from. If we do not like something we boo it! People boo at football games or when they spot politicians they do not like. Not very nice!

But I say "boo" to sickness and death. I do not like them one bit! We have all felt the pain and sting of death.

Death is a 100% situation. Everyone dies eventually.

BOO! It stinks!

But what????

So live well, because Psalm 116:15 proclaims that God holds precious the sight of saints who die.

Life is short! It's not over until God says it's over! But some day it will be over! Use it for Him!

Date: ________________

Death of Stephen

Bible Reading: Acts 6 - 7

Focus Word: Kindness

Here we go, another hero!

Get to know Stephen's story. He is an amazing example of personal sacrifice for the glory of God.

What was the point of his sermon?

Why didn't the folks see it, understand, confess, repent, make it right, and move towards truth?

Doing the right thing does not always give you good, successful, prosperous results! Ugh!

But notice that guy named Saul standing there watching the madness? Hmmm...maybe even in Stephen's death, God had a bigger plan!

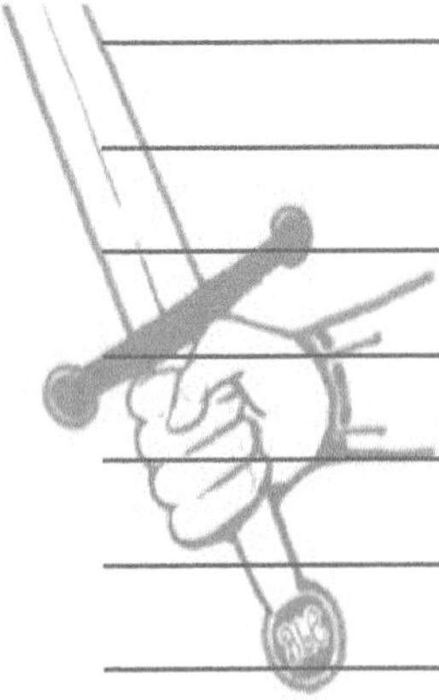

Date: ________________

Salvation Story

Bible Reading: Acts 8 - 9

Focus Word: Goodness

The man once know as Saul became Paul. Talk about an amazing salvation story!

Have you ever heard someone talk about a "Damascus road salvation story?" It means a big turn around— a life spiraling out of control turns to God's grace—the miracle of miracles!

Paul is going to be a big part of your New Testament readings from now on!

So what is your testimony? Take time to find out about other people's testimonies.

Celebrate God's grace!

Week 26

Date: ____________________

Jabez Prayer

Bible Reading: I Chronicles 3 - 7

Focus Word: Faithfulness

The Jabez prayer just kind of sticks out in the middle of less than exciting information about clans and families (genealogy).

Bruce Wilkerson wrote a little book about Jabez that I think is great.

Check out your version, but it goes something like this, "Lord bless me and enlarge my territory. Have your hand on my life, keep me from harm and help me not to cause pain in other people."

Not sure how this worked out in the particulars, but God granted his request!

Think through the Jabez prayer and live out its principles.

Now that is a great testimony! Cool stuff!

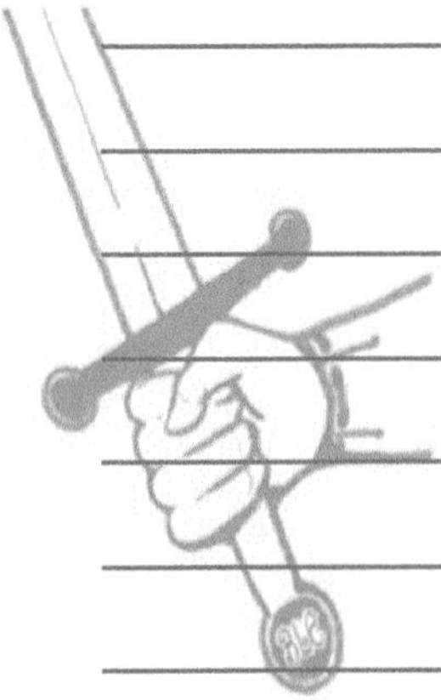

Date: ________________

Understand the Times

Bible Reading: I Chronicles 8 - 15

Focus Word: Fix it!

This might be a section where you can read fast. But be sure to slow down for a couple spots along the way!

So some guys hear about David's desire for Bethlehem water, they put their life on the line to get it, and he pours it out!

What is that about!?

I Chronicles 12:32 tells us there was something special about the men of Issachar.

Why? Simple phrase…

Because *they understood the times* and knew what their nation should do.

What a powerful statement!

Do you understand the times? What kind of learning and commitment is it going to take to get to that point?

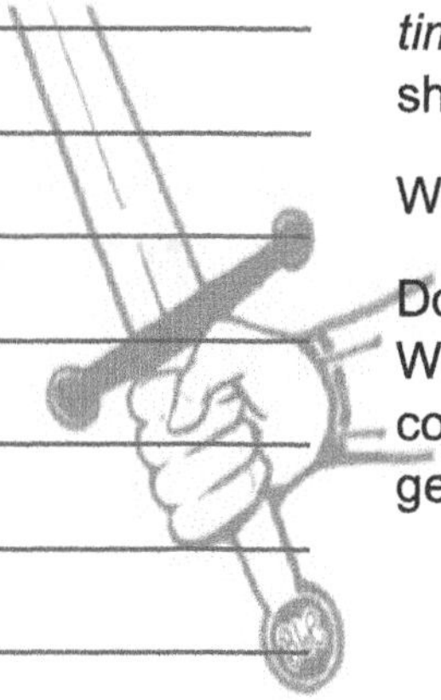

Date: ________________

Bible Focus

Bible Reading: Psalms 119:41 - 119:176

Focus Word: Self-control

Wow, Psalm 119 is a long chapter!

Verse 11 is a great reminder of the value of hiding God's Word into your heart.

God's Word is like a lamp for your feet and light for your path. What a metaphor!

Lord help me with discernment! Discernment is great word for such a time as this! We can only have discernment when we are using God's Word as a light for the path ahead!

Why would I look anywhere else but God's Word for the light I need!?

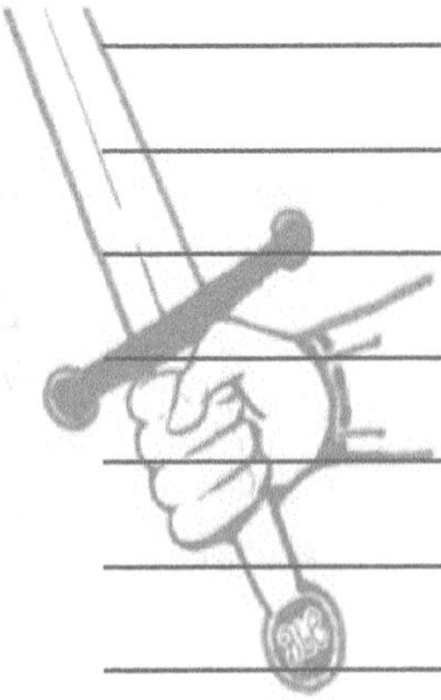

Date: ______________

From Jews to Gentiles

Bible Reading: Acts 10 - 11

Focus Word: Stewardship

Peter goes through a big "aha" moment.

What is the big deal about eating pork?

We will continue to see a theme of legalism and grace and how to sort all this out as we continue throughout the New Testament.

Here in Acts we find the first group of people that are called Christians. Isn't it cool that you are a part of that lineage!?

You, ________________ (your name) are a Christian! You are part of a long line of believers dating back to the time of Christ!

What does the term Christian mean to those around us today? What can we do to uphold the name of Christ in our communities?

How has being called a Christian become a joke or aligned with some extremist Isis or cult?

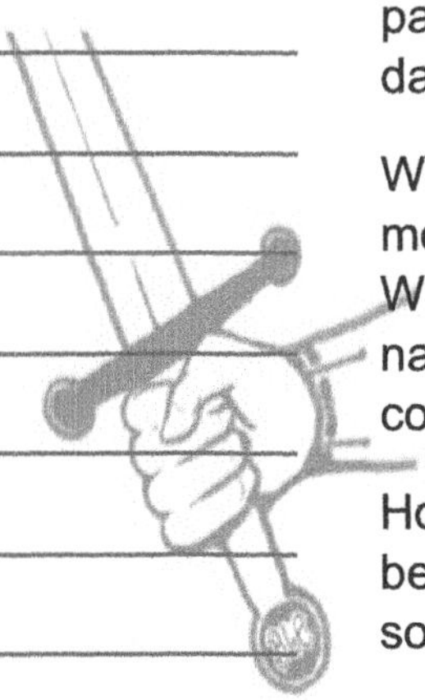

Date: ________________

Spreading the Gospel

Bible Reading: Acts 12 - 13

Focus Word: Progress

Quick Hits from Acts 12-13:

- Peter's amazing story continues.

- Herod is awful!

- Paul and Barnabas are off to the races in the realm of reaching people.

- Do you have a heart for people?

- What is your part in spreading the gospel?

- How can you relate to shaking the dust off your feet and moving on?

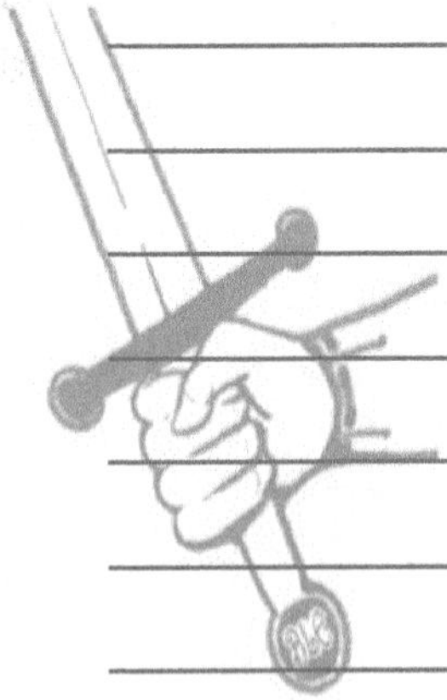

Week 27

Date: ________________

David's Team

Bible Reading: I Chronicles 16 - 23

Focus Word: Prepared

David is called a man after God's heart.

With that kind of title you will be surprised to learn of his many failures, weaknesses, and sins. But pay attention to his passion, his leadership, his organization, and his walk with God.

Take note of the good guys, the team, that David has around him. There were some remarkable people devoted to David's team!

David's general Joab gave a speech just before going into battle that really impressed me:

"Be strong and let us fight bravely for our people and the cities of our God. The Lord will do what is good in his sight."
II Samuel 10:12 (NIV)

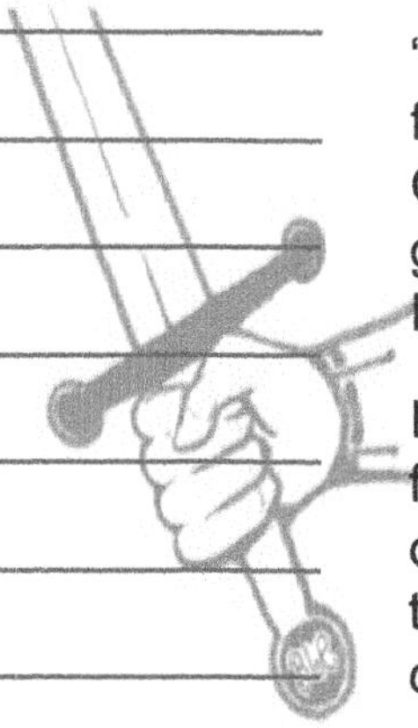

It appears that everyone is in the fight together. There is a reliance on God and a commitment to the team that is infectious! Can we create that kind of team today?

Date: ________________

The Body of Christ

Bible Reading: I Chronicles 24 - 29

Focus Word: Mentor

In the Body of Christ we are all so different.

We look different from one another. We have different dispositions and attitudes. We laugh at different jokes. Our abilities and skill sets are different. What drives us, our passions, are different.

Some are leaders and some are faithful followers. Some are musical and some are mechanical. Some are intellectual and some are just not.

We have different temptations and weaknesses. Different blind spots. We need each other.

Appreciate the differences in others and in yourself!

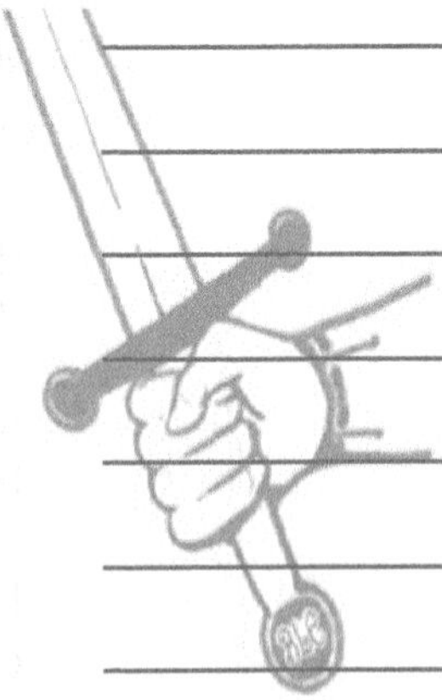

Date: ______________

Go Boys!!

Bible Reading: Psalms 120 - 129

Focus Word: Disciple

I am very blessed to have four boys. I love my sons. It is fun to see them grow and do incredible things.

So Psalms 127 is my psalm!

We all want to be part of building a heritage. Think about more than my boys and more than your kids (although our children are certainly key to building a legacy).

Think about the fruit and the blessing of a life lived well. Think about having an impact for Christ!

It feels good! There is joy in doing the right things. There is a pay-off for doing things God's way.

You cannot earn your way into heaven, but you can make life more abundant and satisfying.

May the Lord bless you and keep you!

I am not perfect and my boys are not perfect, but I have seen God work in me and I am now seeing God work in Josiah, Isaiah, Noah, and Micah! Praise the Lord!

Date: ____________________

Even Christians Disagree

Bible Reading: Acts 14 - 16

Focus Word: Equipped

Have you ever been ticked off, upset?

Have you ever been angry at someone you love, that you are close to?

Have you been surprised by the treatment you get from another believer, someone who is a part of the church, someone who you thought was a Christian and should be treating you better?

Matthew 18 is a good place to sort out conflicts.

Here in Acts you will find that Paul and Barnabas have a disagreement. Two of our Biblical role models could not seem to agree!

Conflicts are not necessarily bad, but they need to be handled well and good things can result.

This sharp disagreement between Paul and Barnabas ended up doubling the missionary effect. God used their issues for His plan.

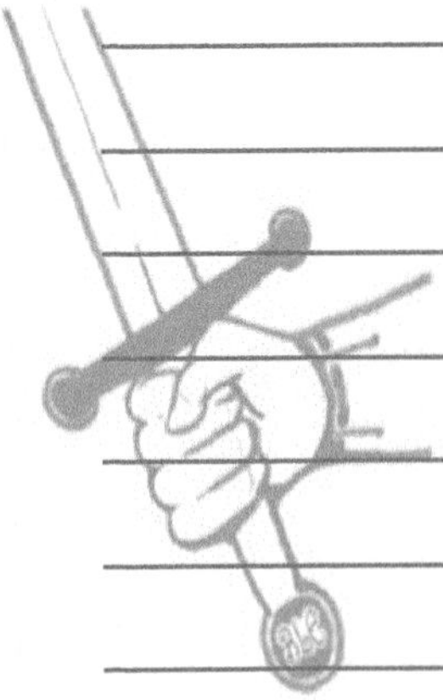

Date: ________________

The Bereans

Bible Reading: Acts 17 - 19

Focus Word: Transformed

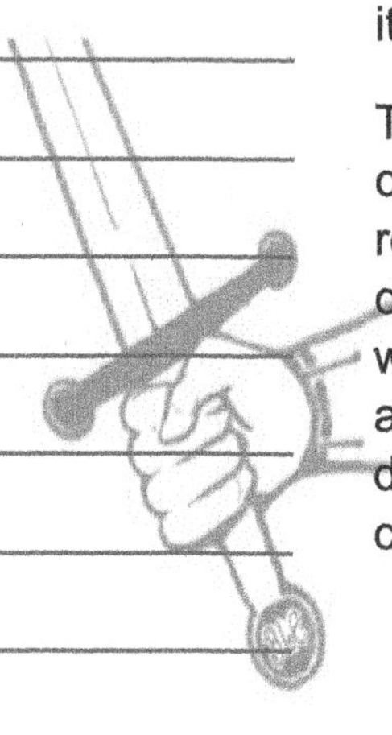

I have been waiting for this scripture in Acts 17. It is one you just have to know and follow.

Be like the Bereans!

This journal is for Bereans! People who are committed to studying the scripture and applying it to life!

Filter everyone, every message, every movie, every book through the ideas you learn in the Bible.

I have some history friends who write "Berean articles" about politics and other culture news items.

This group of people were of noble character. They were eager to receive the message and then check it against scripture. They were open to wisdom and curious about the things of God! And they did this every day! That is commitment!

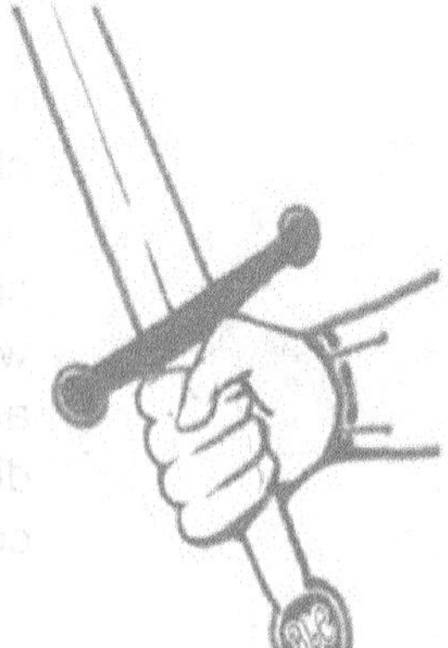

God and the Bible

Have you heard of the Westminster Confession of Faith? It was created by "Church fathers" in the mid-1600's. Here are three questions of the Shorter Catechism:

Q. 1. What is the chief end of man?
A. Man's chief end is to glorify God and to enjoy him forever.

Q. 2. What rule hath God given to direct us how we may glorify and enjoy him?
A. The word of God, which is contained in the scriptures of the Old and New Testaments, is the only rule to direct us how we may glorify and enjoy him.

Q. 3. What do the scriptures principally teach?
A. The scriptures principally teach what man is to believe concerning God, and what duty God requires of man.

Read the following:

I Peter 1:24-25 Hebrews 4:12 II Corinthians 10:4-5

How important should the Bible be in the education of children today? Is it something that can be easily dismissed or regulated to Sunday only?

Did you know that the Supreme Court ruled that the Bible was to be outside of the public school system in 1963?
Check out *Abington School District v. Schempp.*

How important is the Bible to our modern day culture? What has to happen for the Bible to be a part of our thinking and the basis for our daily decisions?

Week 28

Date: ________________

Am I Wise?

Bible Reading: II Chronicles 1 - 10

Focus Word: Powerful

Here in II Chronicles we will be reviewing the life of Solomon again.

How is Solomon wise? How do you personally need to be better in the wisdom area?

How do you overcome the times when you were opposite of wisdom? When do you make decisions that are foolish or stupid?

How can you correct that?

Who are the people in your life that you believe are bringing wisdom to the real world?

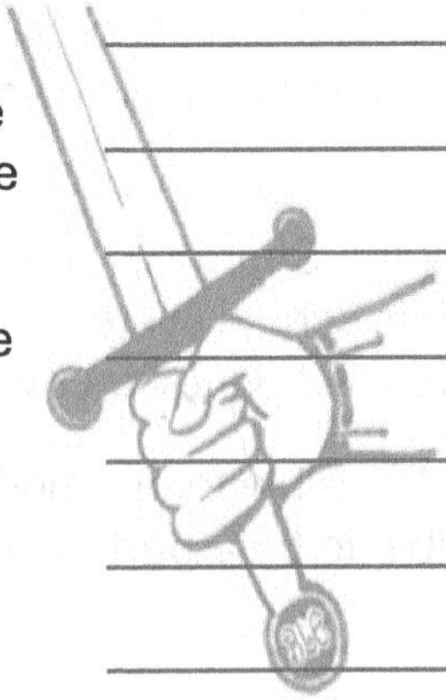

Have you changed concerning the value of wisdom? How do you see it differently than you used to?

Do you have big decisions that are going to require a little wisdom coming up in your life?

Could you use some wisdom today?

Date: ____________________

Just Do It

Bible Reading: II Chronicles 11 - 18

Focus Word: Grace

There is nothing you can do to earn God's love! It is all about grace!

There is no to-do list that will put you on the path to being great, amazing, and heaven bound.

Some people in your life may have made you feel that you have to complete certain list and behave in certain ways to merit their love. I am sorry about that! That is not the way God works!

But I also believe there are things we must do! Not to earn something from God, but just to be the best we can be and enjoy the life God has given us.

Inaction and paralysis are not helping us! Go forward in God's grace!

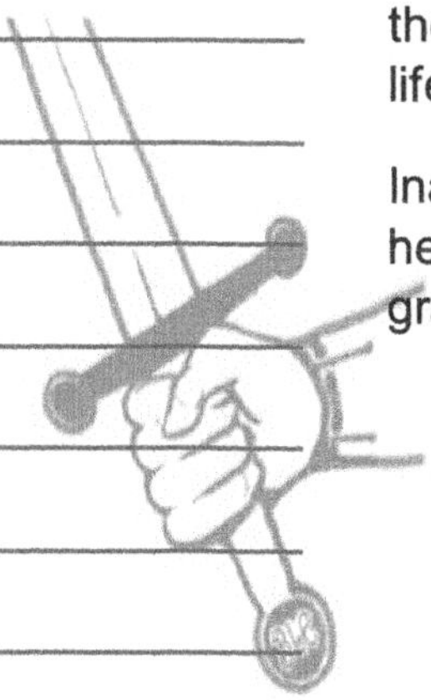

Date: ________________

Generations

Bible Reading: Psalms 130 - 136

Focus Word: Unity

Do you value the people who came before you? The people that made your life possible?

Sure, your parents and your grandparents, but what about the people before that?

What do you know about your heritage? Have you ever looked into your family tree?

Many of our heroes in the Bible were in it for the long game. They sought the blessing of God on future generations they would never meet and strove to leave their country and descendants in a better place. Have we lost that desire in self-centered America?

You are an important part of that family tree. And you will have an effect on others that will come after you. In fact you might be the beginning of a new family tree! What is the heritage you are leaving these people you do not even know?

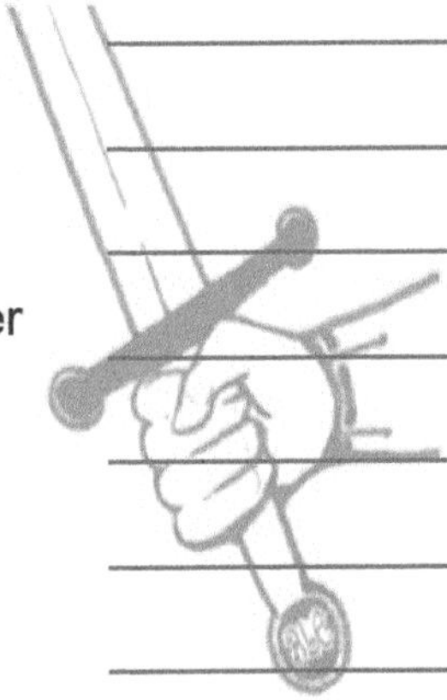

Date: ________________

Don't Fall Asleep!

Bible Reading: Acts 20 - 21

Focus Word: Ambassador

I have had a few occasions where I have overslept. It is terrible! To blow an appointment is the worst!

Have you ever fought sleep while driving? Again, the worst. I have opened windows, even splashed water in my eyes while driving. I know, not good, not safe.

Wait until you read about Eutychus!!

Don't fall asleep on life and wake up lost or in trouble! Pay attention!

Who do you know who needs a wake up call?

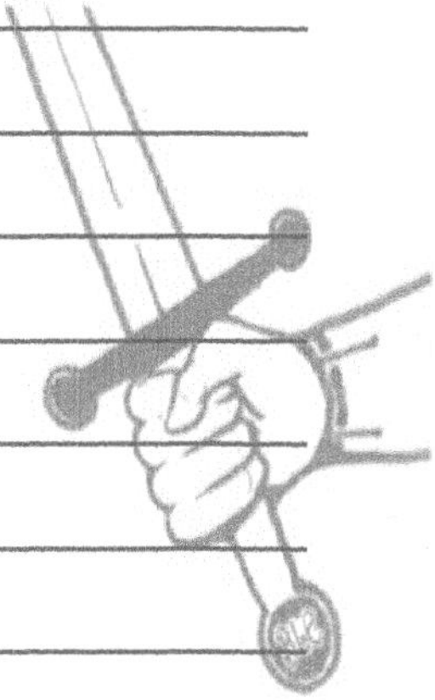

Date: ____________________

Paul's Battles

Bible Reading: Acts 22 - 23

Focus Word: Tenacious

American Christians have had it pretty easy over the years. But there is still persecution out there!

What persecution have you gone through? Do you have friends who have been persecuted?

Sometimes I have know people to get persecuted and I felt that they brought it on to themselves, it did not have to be that way. Am I strong enough to stand up for truth?

Will I be ready for persecution?

Maybe I am too tolerant, so people would not think to persecute such an accommodating guy. Think about that.

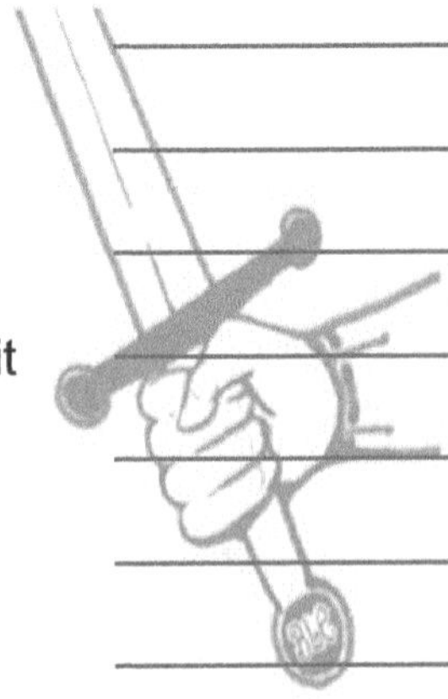

Interesting how the Lord spoke to Paul one night, basically saying hang tough, it is not over, in fact, it is just getting started! The plot thickens for sure!

"Never, never, never, give up!!"

Winston Churchill

Week 29

Date: ________________

Another Hodgepodge

Bible Reading: II Chronicles 19 - 27

Focus Word: Humble

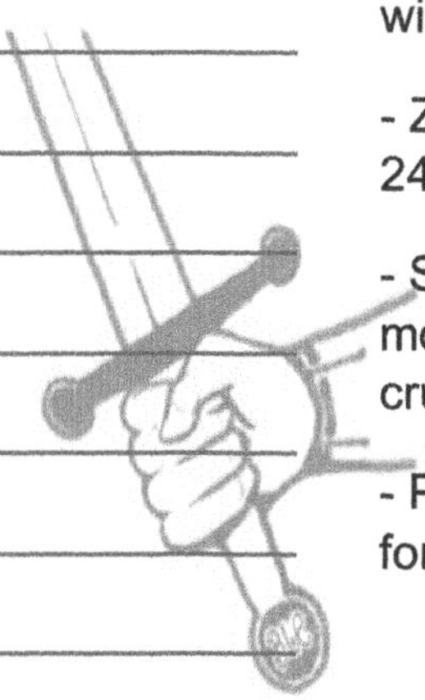

Quick Hits from
II Chronicles 19-27:

- A cool mention about family shows up in chapter 20 verse 13. The power of a family! The commitment of a dad to their mom and the "little ones!"

- Otherwise we see a lot of messes.

- Kings die and no one regrets it! No legacy there.

- Kings following advisors who lead them astray, the opposite of those who walk with the wise grow wiser!

- Zechariah is a bright spot in 24:20, but then they kill him!

- Strength, power and skill have moments of success only to be crushed by pride.

- Pride goes before the fall; watch for it!

Date: ________________

Reform and Revival

Bible Reading: II Chronicles 28 - 34

Focus Word: Purity

Keep praying for it! Yes, it can happen: Reform and Revival are possible.

Check out what Hezekiah was able to be a part of in II Chronicles.

No matter how bad things can get, some will stand up, some will see the truth and a remnant will hold the mess, the church, the community or the organization together.

You may be picked to do some holding together. Seek God and work whole heartedly in the mess!

People will gain confidence and grow in courage thanks to strong leadership. Hopefully, you and I can get off the roller coaster and be consistent in our walk with God! Reform and revival are possible!

Date: ________________

Don't Forget!

Bible Reading: Psalms 137 - 142

Focus Word: Purposeful

Psalm 139! One of my favorite, most poetic, most wow-God-really-loves-me psalms!

If you ever get down and depressed, camp out on this psalm.

If God knows us this well, why wouldn't we want to get in sync with him and know ourselves, be honest and move to the places where God can guide us, direct us, help us the most!

How can we waiver on our stance on abortion and at what point life begins when we hear about God's plan for each life?

How are you doing in the tests of life? Are you remembering God and His plan for you? Be encouraged! Ask God to lead you "in the way everlasting!"

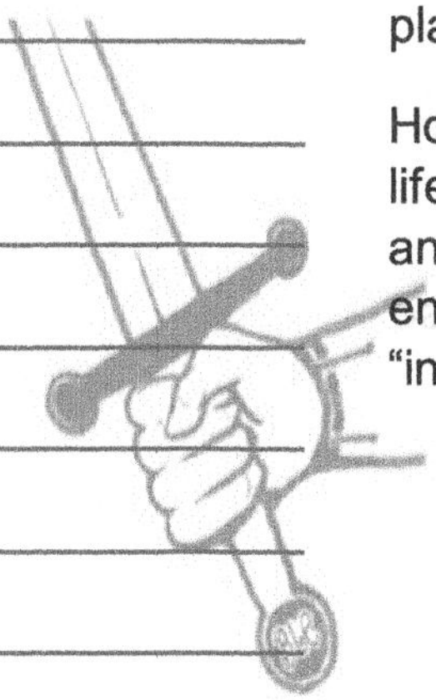

Date: ________________

You Never Know

Bible Reading: Acts 24 - 26

Focus Word: Commitment

Life does not always look so hot. It was very difficult for Paul, but look at who he was talking to! He was before the big shots of his culture telling them about Jesus!

You just never know how God will use your circumstances to orchestrate His plan.

The challenges are going to be there. I know I have been in some work situations that were unbelievable crazy and hard.

But what some meant for evil, God turns for good! If everything was going so perfectly and you were happy with every situation, you might not lean on Jesus as you should.

So, thank you Lord for the hard times. Who can know where these experiences are taking you!?

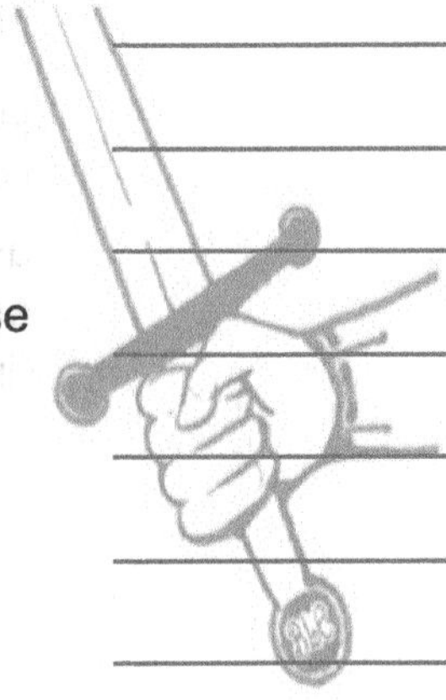

Date: ________________

Chapter 29

Bible Reading: Acts 27 - 28

Focus Word: Great Commission

You might have guessed by now but I love the learning process!

I love the phrase that Festus says to Paul, "You are out of your mind Paul! he shouted. Your great learning is driving you insane!" Acts 26:24 (NIV)

Isaiah 55:8 does tell us that God's thoughts and our thoughts do not always match up. But isn't it cool that we can become more like Jesus in our words, thoughts and actions?!

Maybe we will look a little crazy. I hope there are a few times we look extra smart too!

The title is a trick. Did you catch it? There is no chapter 29 in Acts!

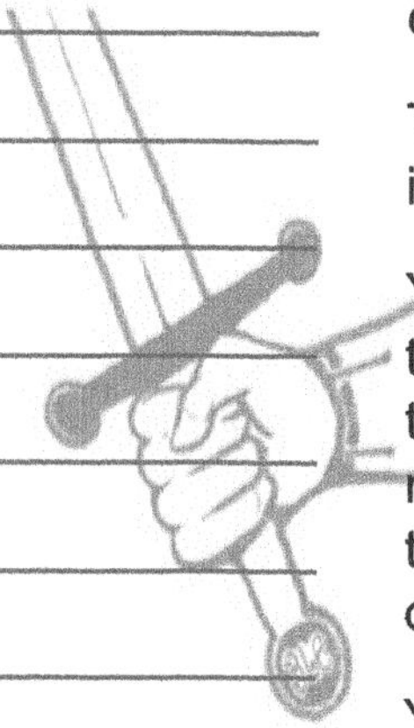

You are the one called to spread the gospel. You are the growth of the Church. You are the plan to move beyond the work of Paul and the rest of the apostles in the book of Acts.

You are chapter 29!

Week 30

Date: ________________

Pledge

Bible Reading: II Chronicles 35 - Ezra 5

Focus Word: Diligent

The pledge of allegiance to the American flag.

Does that still take place in your schools and in your places of work? What is a pledge? Is this a good habit for America?

A pledge is meant to be powerful. Are we still willing to pledge allegiance to anything in this country?

I think Daniel was onto something in Daniel 1:8 when he said he resolved not to defile himself. Resolve! I love that word.

Do we have the perseverance and tenacity to stick to something no matter what?

How about the word covenant? A covenant is like a contract but more.

Making a pledge or covenant is important but the follow through is the most important part!

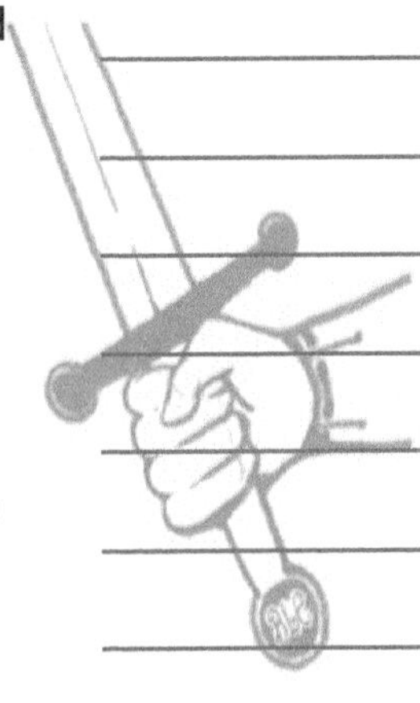

Date: ________________

God's Guy in a Secular World

Bible Reading: Ezra 6 - 10

Focus Word: Servant

Ezra figured out how to live for God in a world controlled by pagans.

You will not realize it here, but he was a contemporary of Nehemiah who you will read about in the next Old Testament book.

I like how Chapter 7 deals with his calling and purpose. He was focused on the work God had asked him to do. He did his work with excellence!

An Old Testament theme that keeps reappearing is what I will call sowing and reaping. You could also call it "cause and effect."

How do we benefit from this principle? Or how do we fall short? Yes, there are days I am simply thankful for grace!

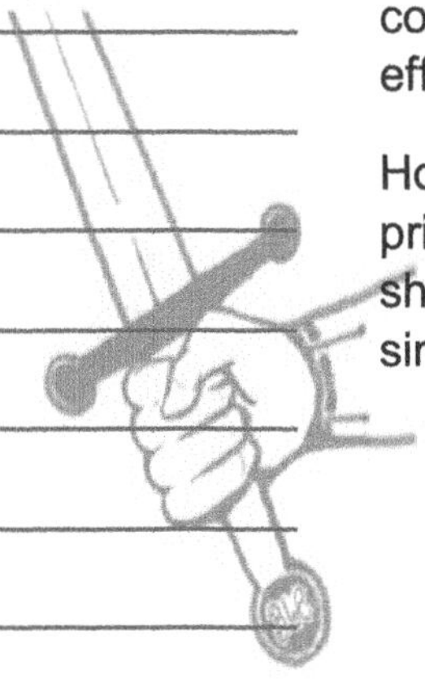

Date: ________________

Praise Him!

Bible Reading: Psalms 143 - 147

Focus Word: Consistency

Notice words like remember and meditate! Notice the love and care the Lord demonstrates to you.

Consider how fast life goes by; the days move very fast.

Think about how things come and go, how knowledge and culture are transferred from one generation to another.

The Lord is acting on our behalf, are we taking the time to notice?

Pay attention!

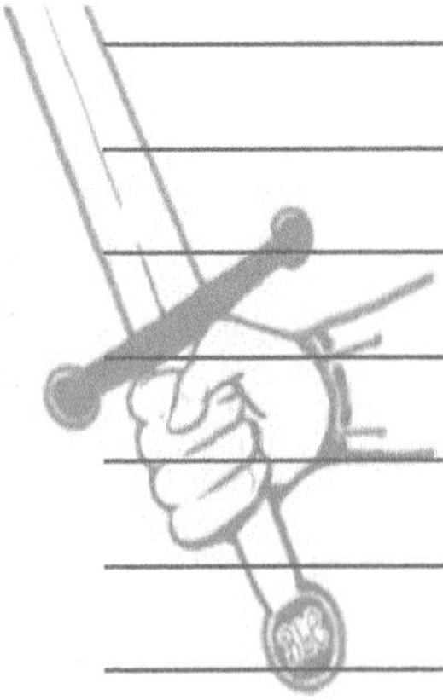

Date: ________________

Deep Stuff

Bible Reading: Romans 1 - 2

Focus Word: Broken

Romans! Roll up your sleeves, you are now jumping into theology.

Sin nature.

Judgment.

A Righteous God.

Law and Grace.

Circumcision is weird but it signifies an adherence to law/ rules.

I like rules. There is certainly a place for rules. I do not think you should throw them all out, but remember just following rules is not how to get close to Jesus or enter into heaven.

Keep reading, and maybe re-reading. The book of Romans is not for the faint of heart!

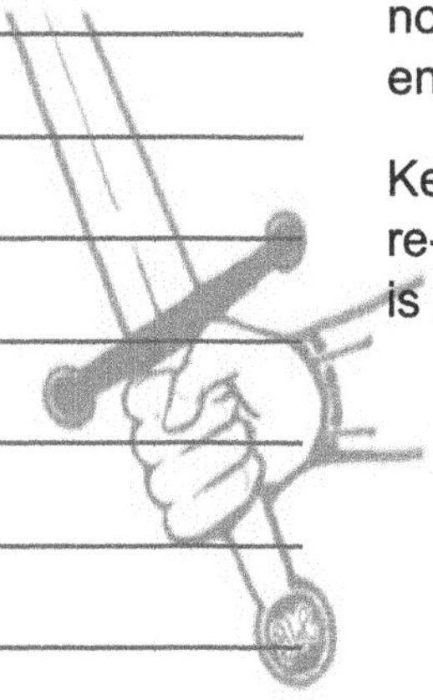

Date: ________________

Faith

Bible Reading: Romans 3 - 4

Focus Word: Assurance

For all have fallen short, no one is blameless. You and I are sinners.

We need a savior.

Abraham is a great illustration of faith. Faith is not a mind game, but an act. Abraham certainly had to act!

If you really believe your chair will hold you up, you act on that belief by taking a seat. Your faith becomes action.

What activities do you need to start or get involved in to prove your faith?

Tithing/giving away money is a great place to exercise faith. If done out of obedience and for the right reasons you may be surprised by the results...try it.

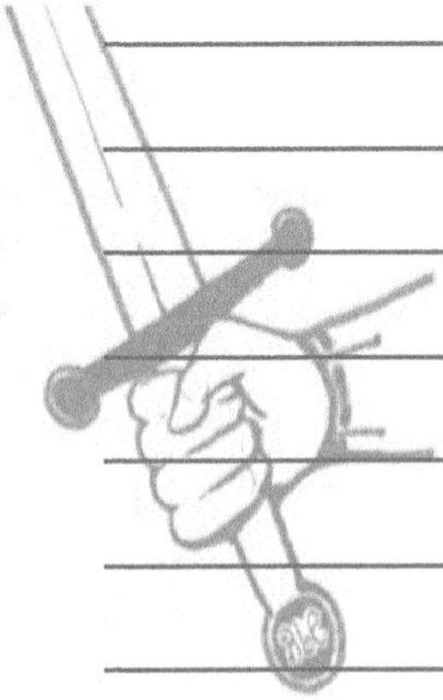

Kingdom Courage!

Sometimes even the most fundamental acts of obedience can put us at odds with the prevailing worldview and practices.

Read the following:

I Thessalonians 1:9 | John 7:24

II Corinthians 10:3-5 | II Timothy 2:24-26

Colossians 4:6

Did these Christians understand that life as a Christian requires believers to oppose the spirit of the age in crucial and perhaps even dangerous ways? Consider how false deities today, things like wealth, sex, power, and prestige, must be exposed, carefully noticed and dealt with using discernment. Parents filled with "Kingdom Courage" do not hesitate to oppose the *status quo* when the salvation and growth of their children is at stake.

Paul argued gently and reverently with those he sought to persuade. Even if his conversation sounded like judgment, it was at least seasoned with grace and therefore more likely than not to be heard and pondered.

Are our kids equipped to think like this?

Educating for the Kingdom of God will find us opposing the standard beliefs and practices of the day. We will be isolated, vilified, challenged, and perhaps even threatened, for such is the way of people who feel their world being threatened.

But we must stand our ground, graciously, and reasonably insisting on the rightness of truth, and backing up our arguments with lives that demonstrate the reality of an education focused on the truth and love that we proclaim.

How might an army of such "truth bearers" change the world?

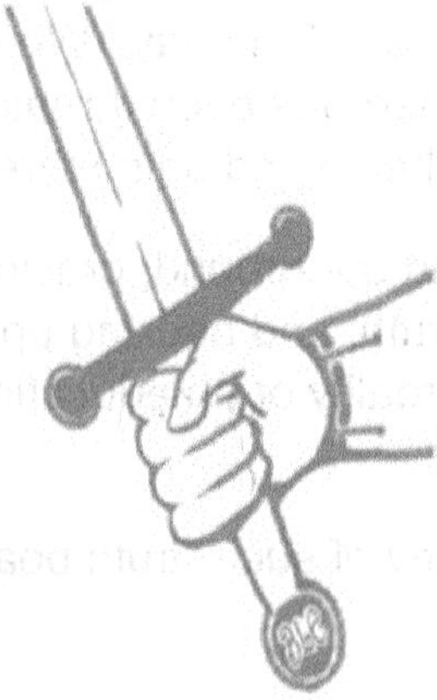

Week 31

Date: ________________

Nehemiah and Leadership

Bible Reading: Nehemiah 1 - 8

Focus Word: Available

The book of Nehemiah is a great treatise on leadership.

I have heard that many times leadership is just about showing up and fighting the fight each and every day.

Nehemiah starts with a concern for his people and a desire to make a bad situation right. He prays. He talks to all the right people. He raises money and takes responsibility. What a beautiful picture of moving from an idea, to goals, and then on to implementation.

Nehemiah gets the job done in fifty- some days.

Be inspired and stay hopeful that you can do what God asks you to do!

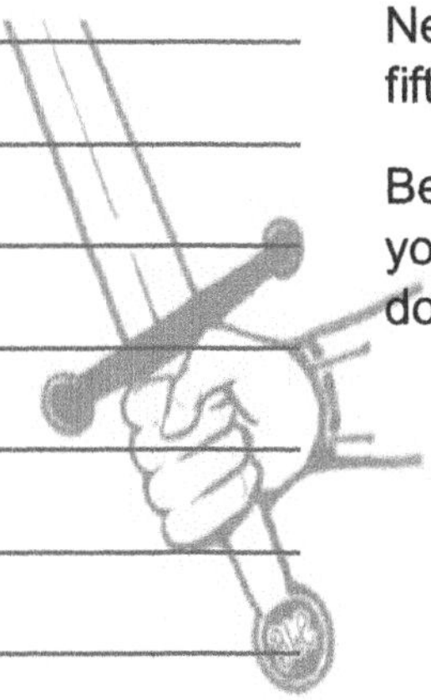

Date: ________________

Opposition

Bible Reading: Nehemiah 9 - 13

Focus Word: Responsive

I do not actually believe in luck.

But there is a bit of a "draw" or what feels like "luck" based on what God has in store for you. Our situation might feel random at times.

But remember, He is not surprised!

We are often surprised to find ourselves facing opposition. Things will be going along well and then it seems like all the wheels fall off. You are doing something to benefit a group and then suddenly your hard work is taken for granted or actively opposed by those who you had hoped to serve! It happens!

Consider this, anything you do in line with God and His principles may create a counter attack by Satan and his evil forces.

Yes, it is difficult to accomplish big endeavors! Go forward anyway!

Date: ________________

Breath

Bible Reading: Psalms 148 - 150

Focus Word: Compassion

Dancing has long been controversial in the American church. But realize that in some context it can be a part of praising the Lord!

Dancing as worship!

But let's not stop there…

Just breathing can be a part of worship.

Some day, at some moment, we will breathe our last breath—so until then, every breath is a gift from God.

Inhale—praise Him!

Exhale—praise Him!!

God makes the heart beat and fills our lungs with oxygen.

Live your life in praise!

Date: ____________________

Priesthood of Believers

Bible Reading: Romans 5 - 6

Focus Word: Maturing

This is a good time to review the idea of the Priesthood of Believers.

As a Christian you have the ability to read God's Word, His message to you and figure out what it says. You do not need a priest to figure this out for you.

But...

You need to keep digging. You might need some help. There are many study methods and techniques that can give you so much more insight.

It's exciting that you can know something and be right! But also be willing to be humble and realize the times that you do not get it, and you need to read, research, and ask questions diligently.

I believe God will continue to give you insight on tough passages. Keep reading.

Date: ________________

Tough Passages

Bible Reading: Romans 7 - 8

Focus Word: Holiness

Here in Romans may be one of the most difficult passages to understand.

The idea of sin, what it is, how it works us over, and what we need to do about it is all here.

Can we overcome sin?

Two steps forward and then one step back? A transformed mind is key to success.

Check out chapter 8 verse 6.

A mind controlled by the Spirit produces life and peace. Living by the natural desires is hostile to God. The difference is life and death!

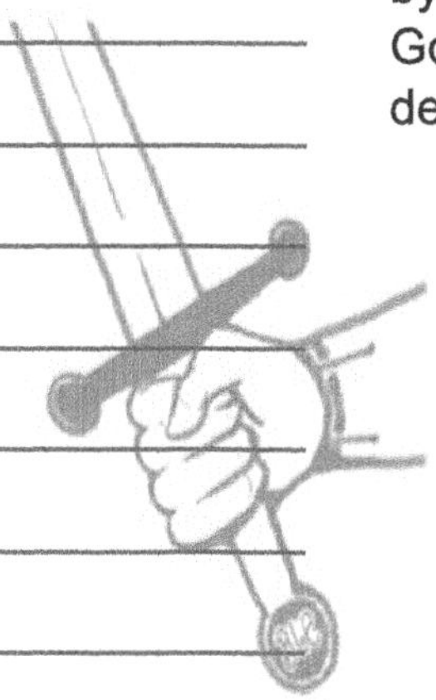

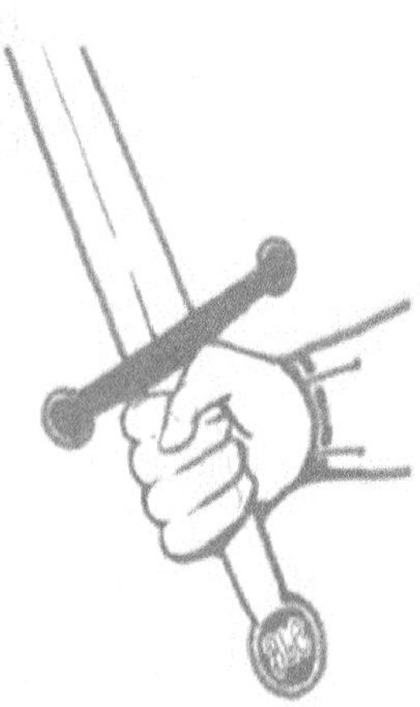

Week 32

Date: ________________

For Such a Time As...

Bible Reading: Esther 1 - 10

Focus Word: Reliable

Isn't the story of Esther great?! So many twists and turns along the way. In the end God used Esther and others to do His will and save the Jews! Mordecai comes through with big-time wisdom when He tells Esther that all that has transpired has set her up to make a difference for the Jewish people.

"Who knows if perhaps you were made queen for just such a time as this?" Esther 4:14 (NLT)

Have you had those times in your life where it seemed that everything is riding on the way you chose to handle a difficult situation? Situations where your career or the lives of each member of your family seemed to hang in the balance? Trust God in the big decisions as well as the smaller ones and take comfort in the fact that His plan will prevail no matter what you choose!

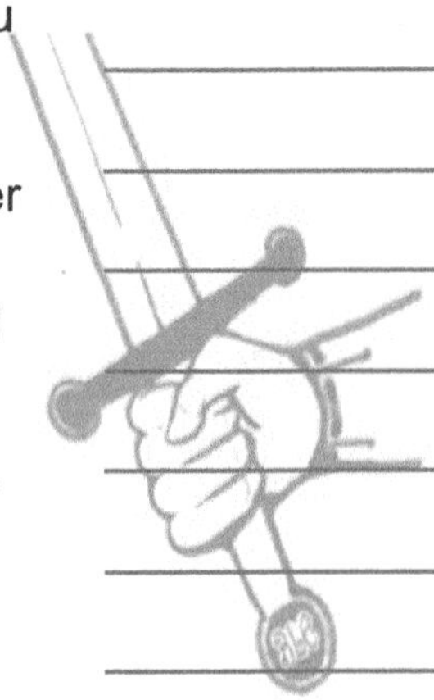

Date: ______________

The Problem of Pain

Bible Reading: Job 1 - 12

Focus Word: Revelation

CS Lewis wrote a great philosophical book that centers on dealing with pain. I appreciate the perspective Lewis provides on the human condition.

What does the story of Job tell us about the problem of pain and the impact of Satan on our world?

I Peter 5:8 tells us that Satan is alive and well! He is ready to mess with your life! It's a fight to the finish that ends with God on top.

If II Chronicles 16:9 is about God looking to bless those of us who want to please Him the reality is also that Satan is out there looking to destroy us.

We may never suffer the physical destruction and death that Job experienced, but Satan can be very destructive in our lives nevertheless!

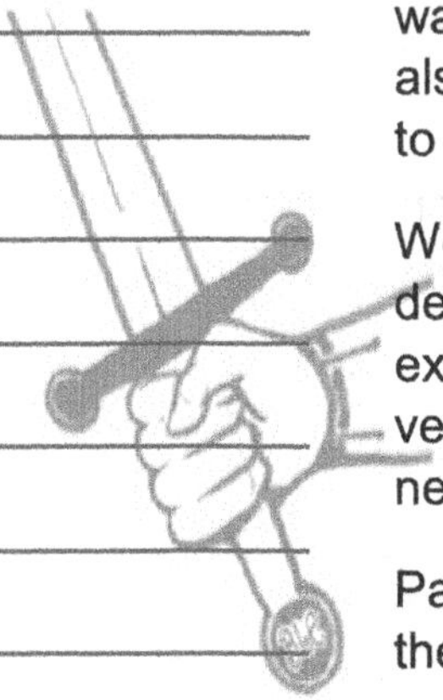

Pain is a part of life. Turn to God in the hard times.

Date: ____________________

Trust Him

Bible Reading: Proverbs 1 - 3

Focus Word: Confidence

You will love Proverbs.

Small bite size words of wisdom to help you negotiate the issues of life. Take your time and really think about what is being said.

How many favorites verses can one person have? This section is definitely up there!

Proverbs 3:3—Trust in the Lord with all your heart!

Don't lean on what you think, that will often lead you astray!

But as you acknowledge Him and learn from His Word, wrestle with the issues, He will reveal Himself and help you to make sense of it!

I believe I am more confident when I apply truth and His Word!

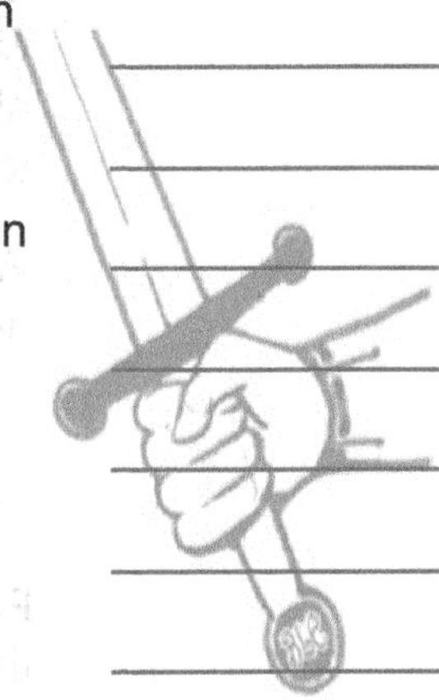

Date: ________________

Who is in Charge?

Bible Reading: Romans 9 - 10

Focus Word: Sacrifice

Who is in charge? This is something we have to think about and sort out often.

I know I like being in charge, leading, moving and shaking as I go through life. But I often don't have as much control as I like to think I do!

How many times has God gotten my attention and told me: "No, you are not in charge."

The creator, sustainer, God of heaven and earth, does not need me to help Him out! He doesn't need to check in with me as he rules the world! Some 7 billion people on the earth today and countless billions that have come before us are all in His hand!

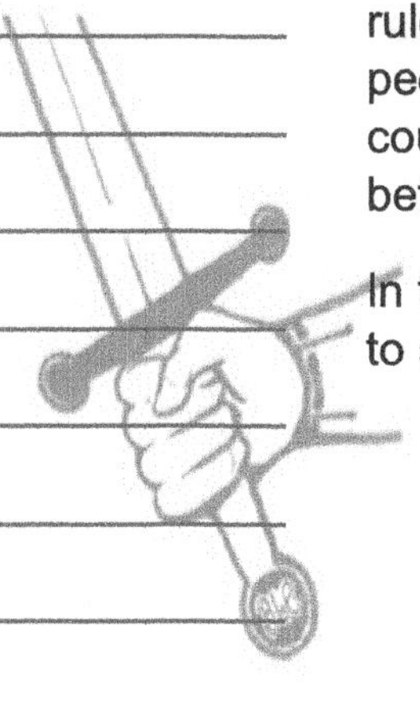

In the end it's about God. I need to step back and let Him lead me!

Date: ________________

Love

Bible Reading: Romans 11 - 12

Focus Word: Integrity

This section of Romans is packed full!

Stop acting like the world, that will get you nowhere! Instead, be transformed by a way, a practice that only God can orchestrate and get on the path of renewing your mind!

I know this theme keeps showing up, but hey, I am an educator. This mind renewal and strengthening is the key to what we do!

Who wouldn't want a renewed, transformed mind? I will say it again, how can we get the most out of our education without Jesus and His Word and principles ingrained in our training?!

Add God's love to the equation and you are powerful!

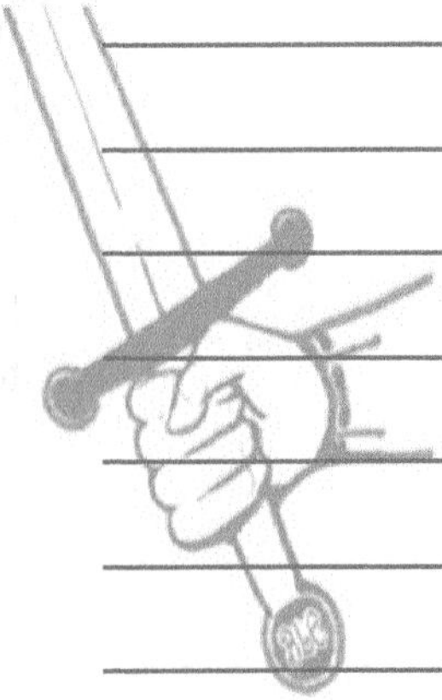

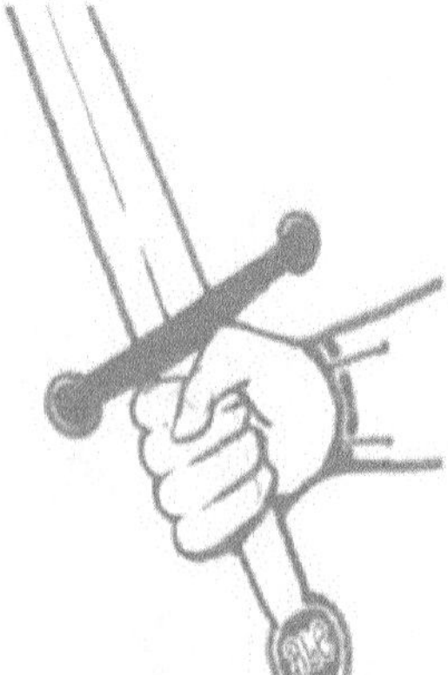

Week 33

Date: ________________

From Bad to Worse

Bible Reading: Job 13 - 21

Focus Word: Confess

Poor Job!

The pain and loss just doesn't let up! And then, after all the bad, his friends come by to tell him he deserved it all!

What an amazing example and trust, conviction, and walking with God. In the midst of it all Job said: "though He slay me, I will trust in God."

Take this as a challenge to be a better friend than Job's friends were! Walk with others, side by side, as they face hardships. Encourage, offer a shoulder, and stand with them in the hurt and in the chaos.

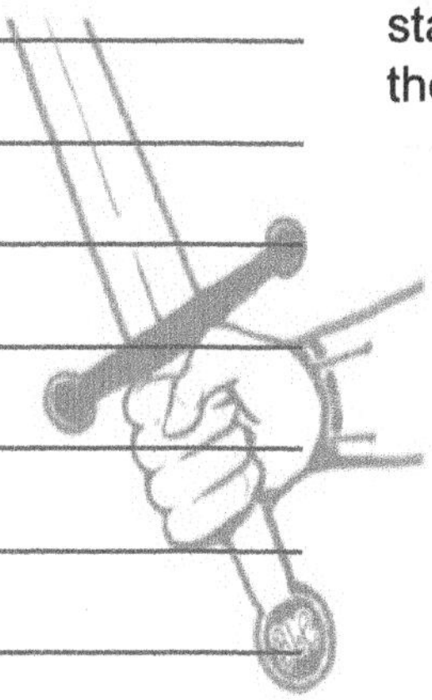

Date: ________________

Fight for Righteousness

Bible Reading: Job 22 - 31

Focus Word: Submit

Every once in a while you will see wisdom from Job and his friends, but the real challenge is to discern Godly talk from simple human perspective.

We need to slow our reading down as we walk through chapter 31.

This is a great covenant to make! A covenant with your eyes not to lust. The options and temptations are so great today. In our hyper sexualized culture immodesty and even nakedness is no big deal. We are encouraged to take what we want and treat others as objects to be exploited for our own satisfaction.

Marriages and ministries are being hurt because of pornography.

Problem solve this one! Work on winning!

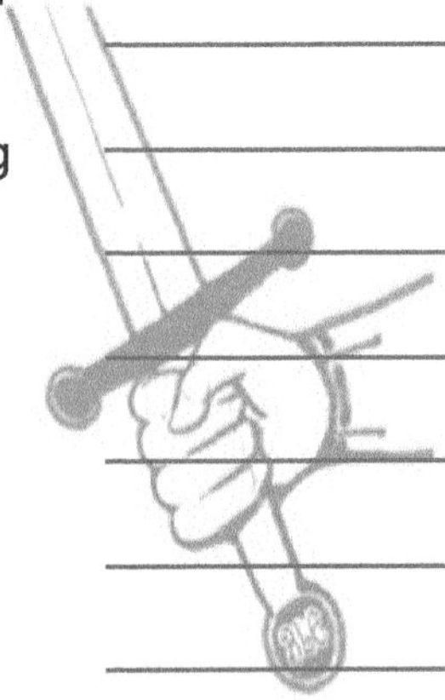

Date: ________________

Guard Your Heart

Bible Reading: Proverbs 4 - 6

Focus Word: Protect

Guard your heart!

The heart is the control center of who you are. It seems to be some combination of mind, spirit, and soul.

There is a thought process that is bigger, deeper than just brain activity. This is that mysterious part where God comes in and makes us wiser and smarter than the world can fathom.

Guarding your heart allows for an abundant life that is wonderful and rich. A life in step with God.

Parents—do not miss this as you raise your children! Guard their hearts, teach them to be discerning! Give them the Bible as a moral compass.

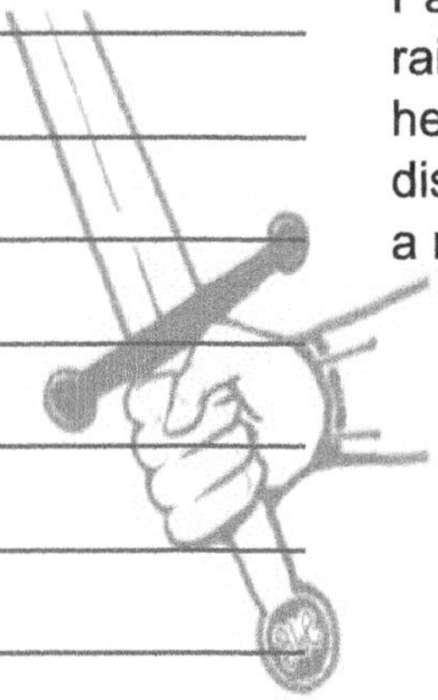

Date: ________________

Government

Bible Reading: Romans 13 - 14

Focus Word: Teachable

Pray for the leaders in your life. Submit to the governing authorities.

In God's plan, good, great, and even not-so-great leaders, have been established by Him.

Our leaders are often the consequences of our actions and our beliefs as a country. We often seem to get what we deserve. We elected them!

If we are headed for trouble as a country it may be exactly what we need to look to Jesus, repent, and get serious about our love for Him and our need to depend on Him.

A day may be coming where we cannot submit to our leaders. At that point we must be ready and willing to pay the price.

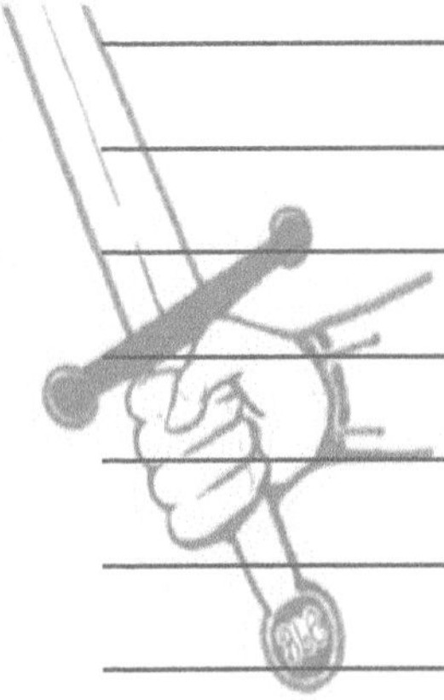

Date: ____________________

History

Bible Reading: Romans 15 - 16

Focus Word: Patient

I love to read. I especially love biographies and autobiographies. History is so full of excitement and plot twists that even Shakespeare would have a hard time dreaming it all up!

Romans 15:4 tells us that the things we read from the past (including His Word) are there to teach us.

Sure, we can learn a lot from our experiences (both good and bad). But do not miss out on the wealth of knowledge you can get from other people's experiences! It's interesting and way less painful!

Learn from the exercise of writing out your story, your personal history. See this journal as an attempt to learn a few things in less painful ways.

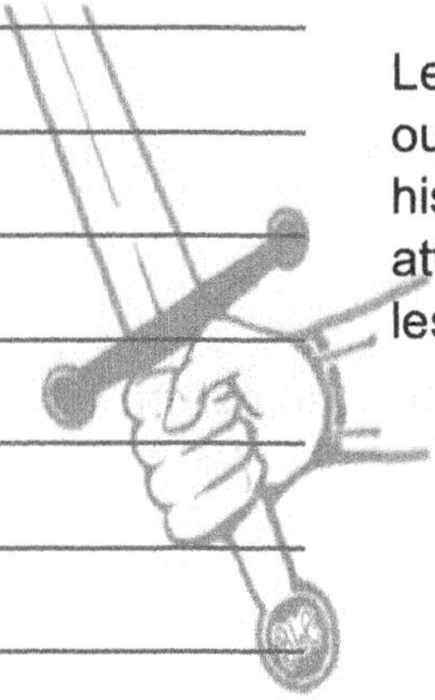

History is Bunk!?

I have had discipline issues to solve with many kids over the years in my schools. Getting the facts right, who did what, when, and how, are all crucial pieces of the puzzle that must be sorted out!

I find little guys want to become revisionist historians. They want to re-write history. What we find is that those who control the information deemed historical can control what and how we think!

Read the following passages:

Joshua 4:1-7	Acts 4:27-28
Galatians 4:4-5	1 Kings 22:8-38
Deuteronomy 8 and 15:9	Isaiah 46:8-11

Sometimes we must remember the things God expects us to remember and forget the things God expects us to forget! Have you ever forgotten the wrong thing or remembered something you would have been better off forgetting?

The right view of history allows us to be properly connected. A right view of history gives us a sense of community, the ability to recognize our place in the story, and allows us to determine what is worth fighting for. A Godly view of history should give us a sense of responsibility!

What activities are children involved in today that teach them a proper sense of the importance of the past?

Why would God tell us so many times in the Old Testament to "remember"?

How might revising history hurt Christian culture?

Week 34

Date: ________________

Who Do You Think You Are?

Bible Reading: Job 32 - 42

Focus Word: Unified

A lot of back and forth between Job and his friends here, but by the end of the book God has something to say!

Remember Isaiah 55:8?

My ways are not your ways!

Do you really think your "pea brain" is going to figure all this out and make things right for God (or better than God)?!

The book of Job helps us to put our life, our goals, our dreams into perspective.

I want to do well! I want to live the abundant life! But in many cases, I do not really even know what that means!

Let's stay humble and say to our Lord, "Use me, put me to work, I deserve nothing, I will follow you and worship you."

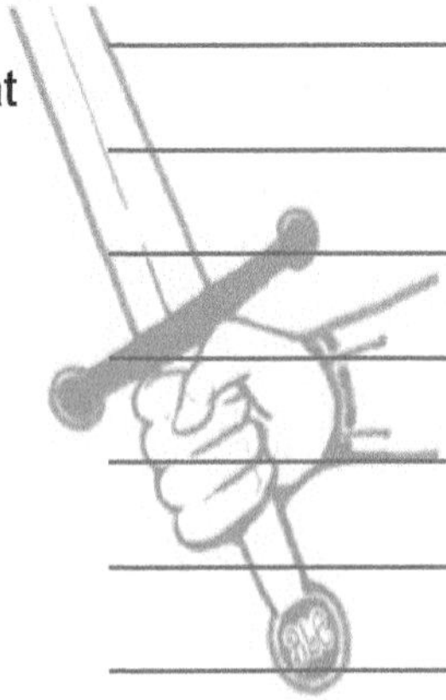

Date: ________________

Here I Am, Send Me.

Bible Reading: Isaiah 1 - 8

Focus Word: Restored

Isaiah was one of the prophets during the divided kingdom of Israel. His service was during some really dark days in the life of the Jewish people.

His willingness to be a servant, a prophet for the Lord as explained in chapter 6, is a beautiful willingness to do and be what God asks.

We Americans love to be free, but in God's kingdom we are unworthy servants who must be ready to do as He pleases. That is way easier to write than to do!

And for you smart "heady" types, check out Isaiah 1:18 where we are called to "reason" together.

Let's put the best of our thinking to the work of the Lord and the dominion He calls us to in Genesis 1 and 2, just like Isaiah did.

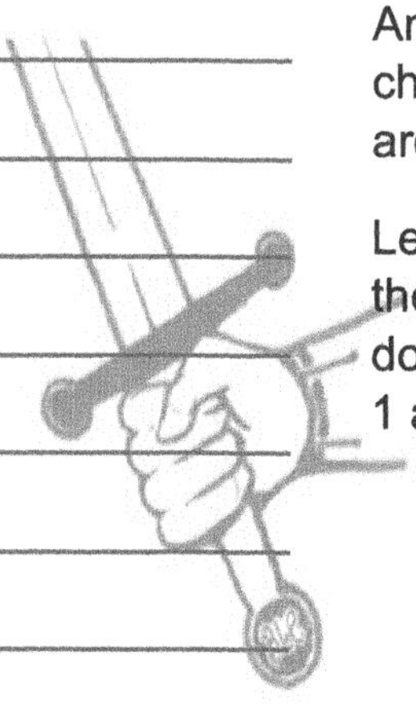

Date: ________________

Fear/Wisdom

Bible Reading: Proverbs 7 - 9

Focus Word: Authority

The fear of the Lord is the beginning of wisdom.

This phrase is found in several different places in the Bible. How do you see fear and wisdom being linked?

I have seen God portrayed as some nice grandfatherly guy who just wants to make things good, better, nice for us all. Probably too simplistic and selfish for how it really works.

Wisdom is such a key ingredient to a life well lived for God. What is the Lord doing in your life to grow your wisdom quotient?

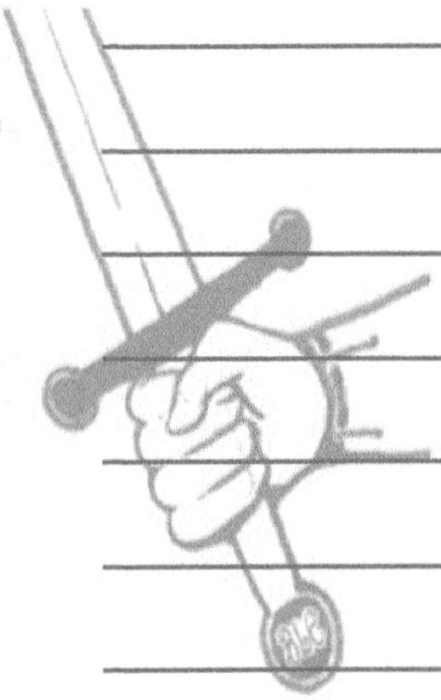

Date: ________________

Foolishness

Bible Reading: I Corinthians 1 - 3

Focus Word: Persistent

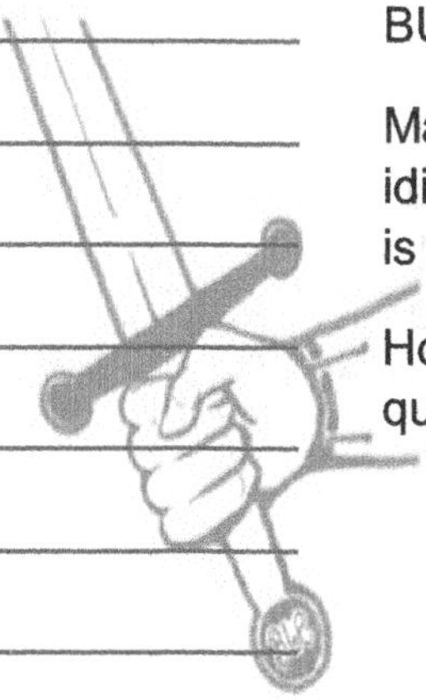

You have been reading through Proverbs and the focus seems to be on wisdom. Now we land on a passage that proclaims the message of the cross is foolishness!? (I Cor. 1:18)

What can possibly be attractive about foolishness?

I am so sure that when the Body of Christ is rolling we are just going to have everyone wanting to join us! It will just make so much sense and why not, we are such nice, good, productive, successful people!!

BUT WAIT! Reality check!

Many people will think we are idiots! The message of the cross is foolishness to the nonbeliever

How best do we handle this quandary?

Date: ________________

Working Together

Bible Reading: I Corinthians 4 - 6

Focus Word: Competent

I have heard that rarely do you find people getting fired or frustrated because they cannot do their job. Most of the issues in work and in life are people problems!

Sorting out conflicts is not easy. In this passage you will see that Paul has to deal with many of them!

I do not want to oversimplify because the issues before you are a big deal, but a reminder here may be in order...

Love covers a multitude of sins!

Yes, sin is irritating, but start seeing the folks that drive you crazy as casualties of war, then work together with gentleness and kindness. Conflict is not fun but it doesn't have to mean the end of a relationship and it certainly does not signal that God is done working!

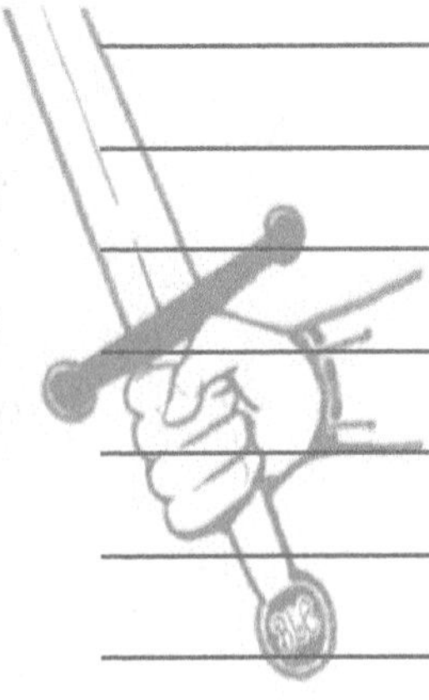

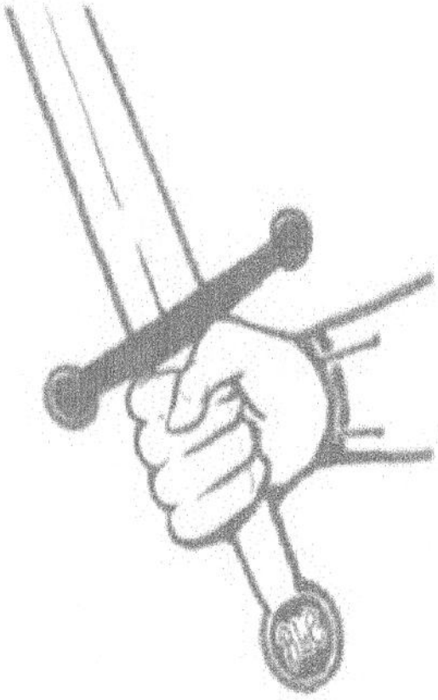

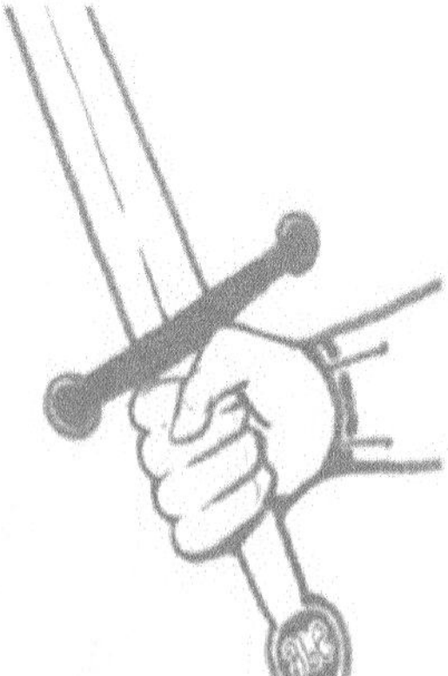

Week 35

Date: ________________

Jesus Foretold

Bible Reading: Isaiah 9 - 24

Focus Word: Reverence

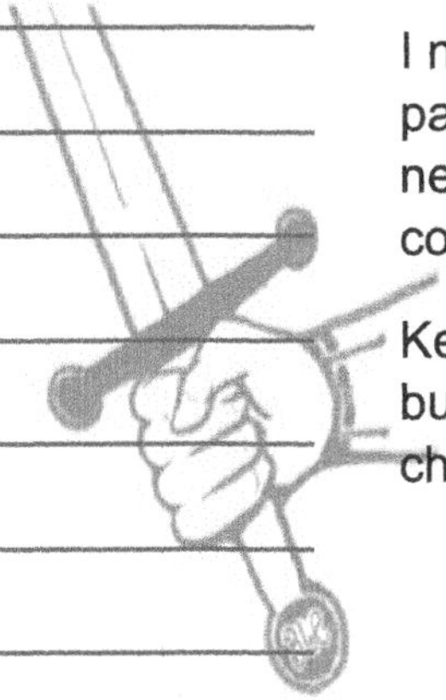

I hope you are hanging in there on the Bible reading.

I have taken the approach that you read through the ten or so pages of Old Testament material a little faster than the wisdom and poetry sections or the New Testament.

Isaiah is fascinating as He shares things that will come to pass 500 or more years into the future. Take a moment to notice how chapter 11 describes Jesus.

You will also notice talk of a future time, a heavenly time that is hard to imagine.

I notice that every time I read a passage, I learn more, something new. I gain an insight I had not considered before.

Keep it up! Slow down at times, but it is also okay to skim a few chapters if you need to.

Date: ________________

Heart Focus

Bible Reading: Isaiah 25 - 31

Focus Word: Authenticity

Make sure you walk the walk if you are going to talk the talk.

That is a lot of pressure and I do not want you to think you have to be perfect to share the work of the gospel. So talk it up even if you are still a little nervous about the walk! Just keep working on the walk!

Isaiah 29:13 deals with the heart. That is where we align our thinking and our actions. It is a the heart level we find our true motivations.

Yes, we will blow it! Yes, we will make mistakes! Repent, confess, and let's go for it again! And again!

And again!

And again!

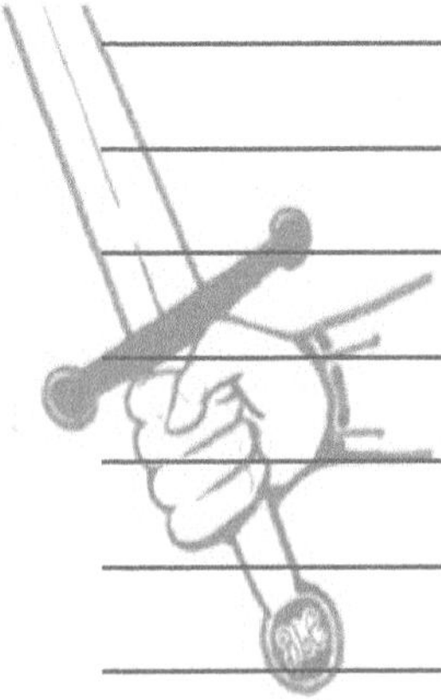

Date: ______________

Self Improvement 101

Bible Reading: Proverbs 10 - 12

Focus Word: Alert

Proverbs just pummels us with good ideas, things to do, ways to improve.

Today you will be loaded up with pithy statements that really can make your life better.

It is tough to memorize them all or to make them stick, but try focusing on a couple today!

It really is like pulling a needle out of a haystack, but one of my favorites is a reminder in Proverbs 11:25 that he who refreshes others will himself be refreshed!

When I am needy it may sound counterintuitive to serve and help others, but that may be when God will give us energy, perspective, and focus that we could not have received any other way.

Let the refreshment begin!

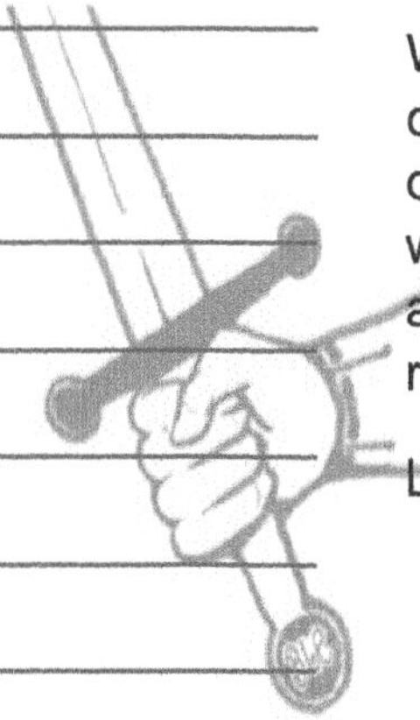

Date: ________________

Run the Race

Bible Reading: I Corinthians 7 - 9

Focus Word: Grateful

Small note to a mixed crowd that includes male and female, young and old, and married and unmarried people…

Do the sex thing right!!

It is a wonderful amazing thing that has been messed up in our culture.

No more time for that, but you sure can write about it in your journal entry for the day!!

What I want to focus on is running the race! Giving it all you've got for God! What a great metaphor and a real honor for those of us who are runners to know we are being used to teach all you folks a lesson!

Hey, maybe you should pick up running; it helps you understand the apostle Paul better!

I mentioned earlier an idea to use the Index pages to chart your exercise plan. How is it going?

Date: ________________

History

Bible Reading: I Corinthians 10 - 11

Focus Word: Hopeful

Do you ever find yourself getting tired of all the messes and problems we read about in the Old Testament? I find this especially true after the kingdom divides. And Judges tells us one bad story after another.

In I Corinthians chapter 10 that is explained!

We can learn from history and that includes learning from negative examples. Are you learning from your own history? Are you learning from your own experiences, both the good ones and the bad?

What can I do right now to swing a little positive force and momentum into my future?

When things have you down and discouraged....

Think and innovate.

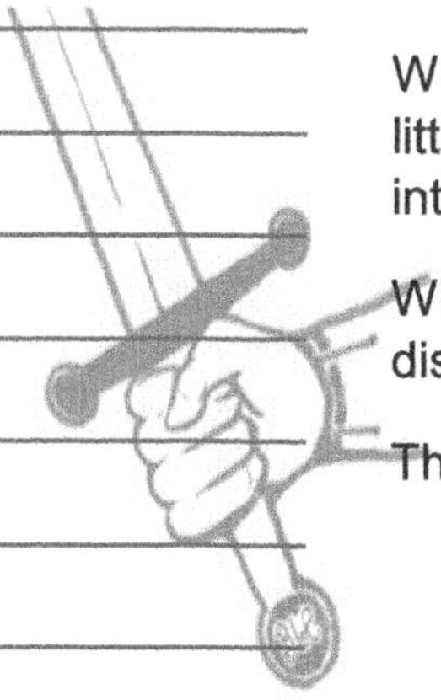

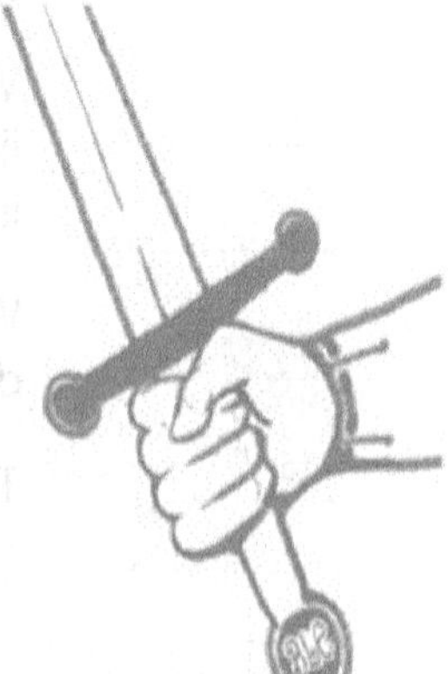

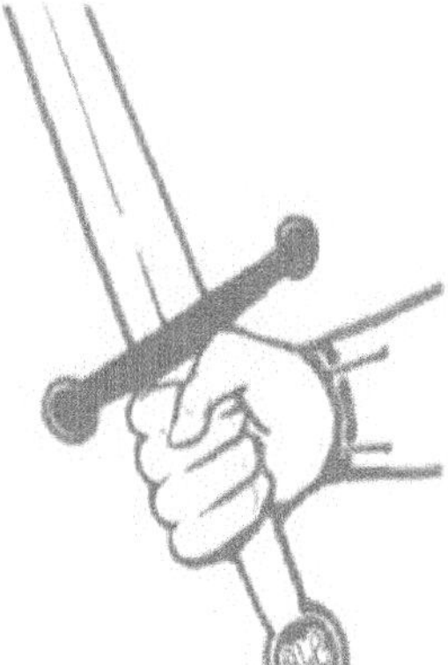

Week 36

Date: ________________

Grit

Bible Reading: Isaiah 32 - 39

Focus Word: Accountable

Isaiah had to go through a lot of messes.

In chapter 33 you can just feel him saying, "Hang in there!" to the people of Israel, even when things are looking bad.

Trust the Lord for long term outcomes because sometimes things do not go our way in the short term.

There have been studies trying to figure out what kind of people "make it" in a tough military special operations group.

You can look at grades, recommendations, sports accomplishments, family background and the predictors are almost always wrong.

The ones who make it have some combinations of behavior and persistence that is often called "grit."

So, do you have grit today?

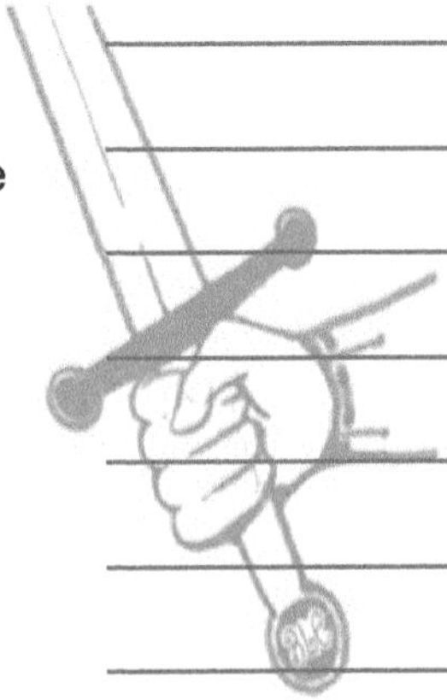

Date: ________________

The Everlasting God!

Bible Reading: Isaiah 40 - 45

Focus Word: Contentment

As you read through Isaiah you will find a Psalm-like quality of worship and encouragement. That is especially true when you read chapter 40.

If you ever get a chance, go see the "The Ark" in Williamstown, Kentucky. Ken Ham and the Back to Genesis organization have done a tremendous job showing off the amazingness of Biblical stories. What a feat Noah and his family pulled off!

But don't stop with how amazing Noah was. As is obvious, what an amazing God we serve and worship! It was this amazing God who had to teach and provide all the resources that Noah needed.

Isaiah reminds us here that the Lord is able, and that it is God who we serve.

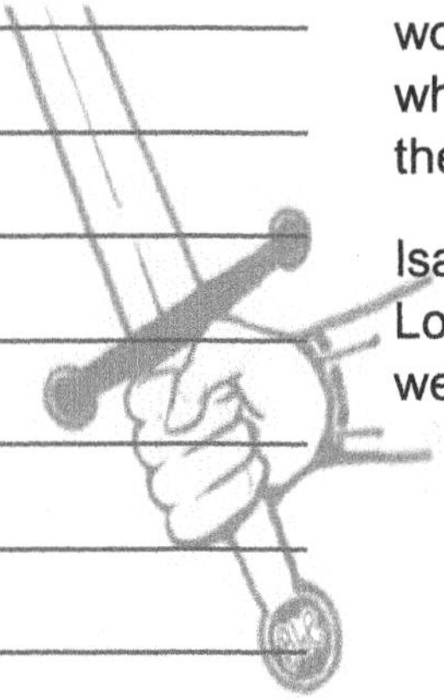

Date: ________________

Hope Comes with Risk

Bible Reading: Proverbs 13 - 15

Focus Word: Boldness

Take your time when you read through Proverbs! It is full of wisdom and truth to reflect on and consider.

I love hope!

I like to believe we can make things better. But there is the possibility that our great hopes and ambitions will fail and we will not realize the outcome we so desired.

Check out Proverbs 14:4 and consider that verse this way. There are many benefits, especially in the Bible days of agrarian societies, to the owners of oxen. But having an ox also means cleaning up its messes. The farmer is always busy because he constantly has to clean up after his animals!

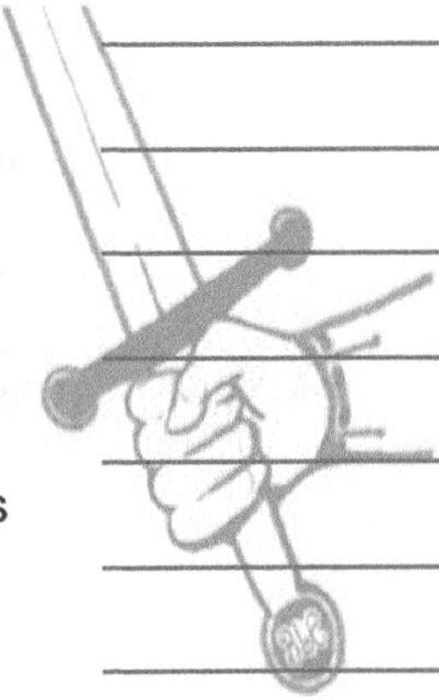

Putting yourself out there and making this world a better place is good, right, and helpful, but it does come with risks! Sometimes you have to do the dirty work that others refuse to do!

Date: ________________

You are Gifted

Bible Reading: I Corinthians 12 - 13

Focus Word: Creative

You will find a beautiful picture of the Body of Christ and how the different parts function uniquely and yet in harmony to make our efforts more effective and powerful.

How are you alike and different from those you are close to? What sets you apart from your family members? What do you do well?

Do you see where you fit in? What are your gifts? Where is the best place for you to make your most valuable contribution?

In the end, what is the goal for the body of Christ? How can you be part of that?

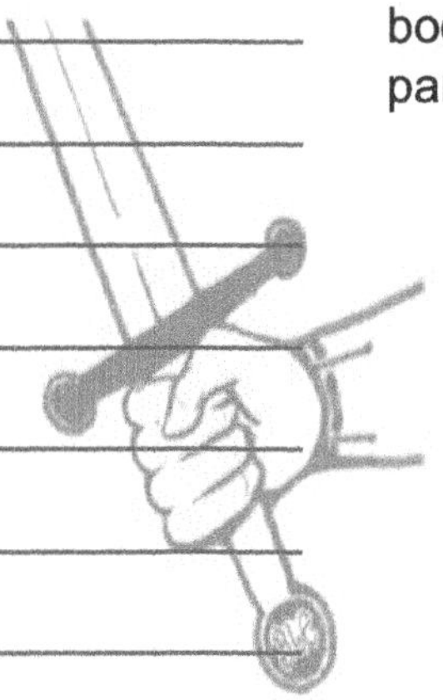

Date: ________________

The Mind

Bible Reading: I Corinthians 14 - 15

Focus Word: Enthusiasm

Your mind is amazing. I have been told we only use about 10% of our mental capacity.

Notice here how our mind also needs to translate our valuable thoughts in well spoken ways. We have to know our audience and tune in to them in such a way that our message is clear and understood. There is little use in great ideas if we can't communicate them effectively!

Let's answer the questions our culture is asking today. No sense congratulating ourselves in answering questions that no one is asking! Winsome words that show we love people will always be needed.

Also, take note of the crux of what we need to center our minds on: The resurrection of Jesus.

If this is not true we are all fools! Great passage in chapter 15.

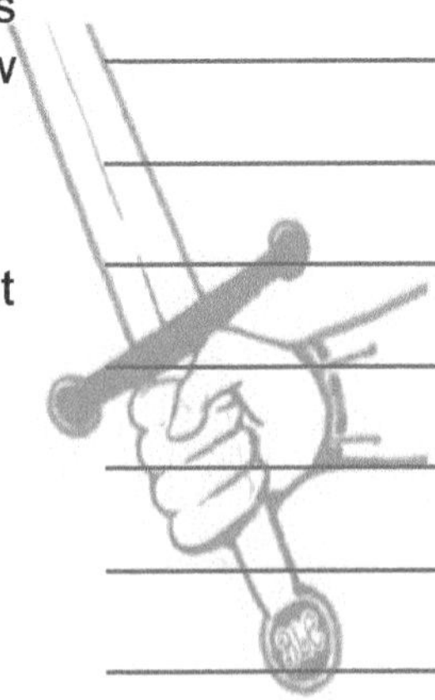

Authority Systems

People don't like to be told what to do. It is easy to become independent and self sufficient. When we feel independent and self-sufficient we begin to think we have all the answers!

A school needs teachers who deserve our support and parents who recognize the need for their children to learn to respect (teacher) authority.

God designed systems of authority because He is a God of order. We must continue to wrestle with the awareness of and willingness to submit to God-given authority and it's place in our lives, as well as in our children's lives.

The American dream is big on progress and success. People have been pretty driven over the years to make their own way and do their own thing. Although there are many benefits to such individuality paired with hard work, responsibility and morality, it can also lead to self-centeredness and vanity that sends many Americans into a tailspin.

Read the following passages:

Ephesians 5:22-6:9 I Peter 3:1-7 I Peter 2:21

Who has authority in your life? Who is teaching the next generation the value of authority and the need for strong family systems? Where is honor and respect taught and modeled in our culture today? Who has the right to speak into the life of children and guide and direct them towards truth?

Authority is created and given by God. Let's seek to "do authority" right whether we are a leader or a follower!

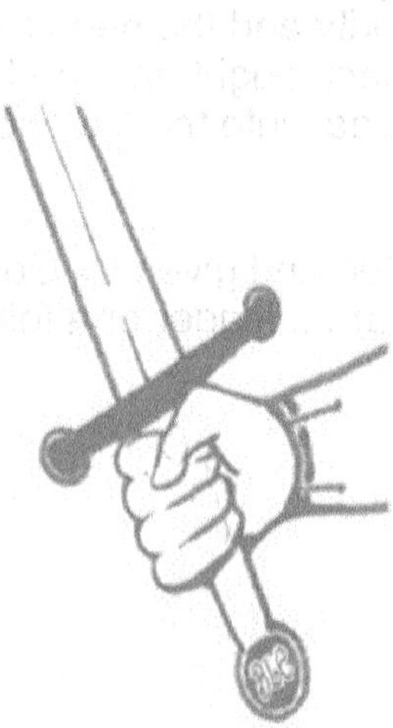

Week 37

Date: ________________

Good News

Bible Reading: Isaiah 46 - 52

Focus Word: Gentleness

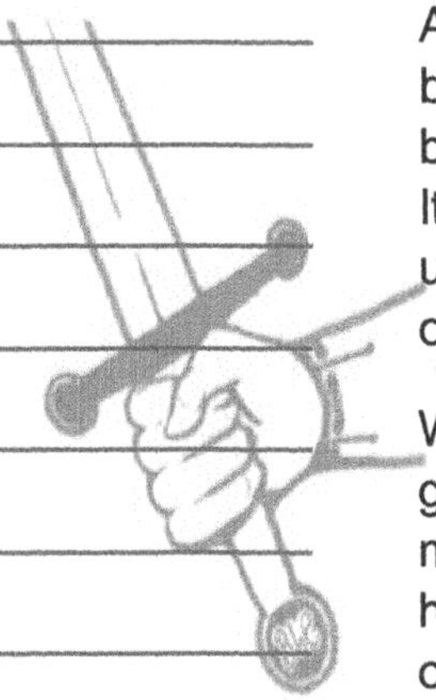

Everyone likes good news!

But good news has to be understood in context.

We cannot be happy about good news if it is a lie, or short lived, or based on totally wrong understandings of how the world works.

In fact, if the truth is bad news and it awakens us to the misconceptions we are living under, then that tough truth is actually good news. Because of that truth we can adjust and live with knowledge.

A majority vote may decide who becomes the mayor of your town but it doesn't decide what it true! It is silly to base our beliefs and understanding on some majority opinion.

We have to tie ourselves to a greater truth than just that which makes us happy or most free. We have to go beyond simple majority opinions. So what is your good news?

Date: ________________

Jesus Died for You

Bible Reading: Isaiah 53 - 60

Focus Word: Godliness

Isaiah basically tells us the story of the death of Jesus nearly 1000 years ahead of the event.

Call it crazy, unbelievable. Supernatural. The Bible is filled with this kind of amazing stuff.

So what is going on here? Why did God take such a difficult path? A supernatural God can and does that which He decides is best.

He had and has a plan. And yes, He loves you so much. Jump into the plan He has for you.

Come, all of you, come if you are thirsty and drink the kind of water that only Jesus can offer.

Get your mind around the idea that we will not always figure out God. Be encouraged again that God's Word "will not return empty. He will accomplish His purposes. (Isaiah 55:8,11)

Date: ________________

Ph.D in Wisdom

Bible Reading: Proverbs 16 –18

Focus Word: Resourceful

Proverbs is full of wise words.

So many themes here:

Teachers.

Parents.

Friendship.

Communication skills.

Marriage.

Consequences of foolishness.

Write out some of your favorites today and take some time to think about them.

Date: ________________

Effective Work

Bible Reading: I Corinthians 16 - II Corin.1

Focus Word: Responsible

I think about my work all the time. It is very important to me. I think we need to consider what we do and why we do it often.

We need to make a living, but are we seeing fruit in what we do? Does our work add to your life or the lives of those around you?

Is there something else I should be doing with my life? Is it possible my work is not about me at all, but how I can refresh others?

As you think about the places that training for your work and your actual work have in your life, remember I Corinthians 16:13-14. Be on your guard, stand firm, and to be courageous and strong! Do everything in love!

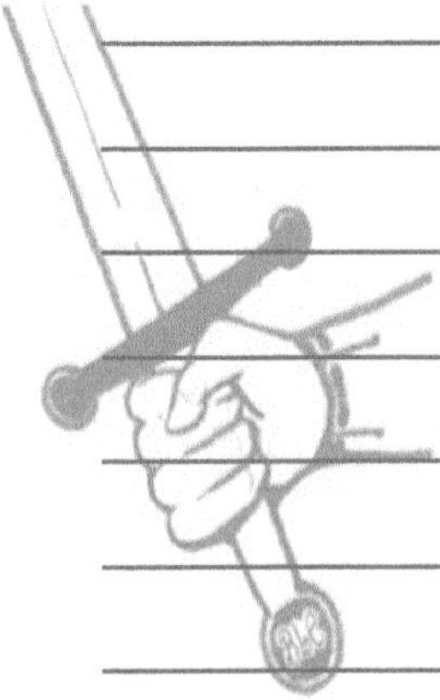

Date: ____________________

Switched Price Tags

Bible Reading: II Corinthians 2 - 4

Focus Word: Dependability

I heard a story of a couple of kids going into a hardware store at night and switching price tags (this was before barcode technology) as a prank. They thought they were so funny. Things like candy cost 100's of dollars and expensive tools were less than a dollar.

Is that not what has happened in our world today!?

The culture has made it so we do not see clearly and our minds are so messed up we do not even realize the negative course we are taking. The gospel doesn't look like good news and the life Christ has for us doesn't look attractive.

We value things not worth much and we overlook people around us who are priceless!

I want to build my life on a dependable system of His Truth!

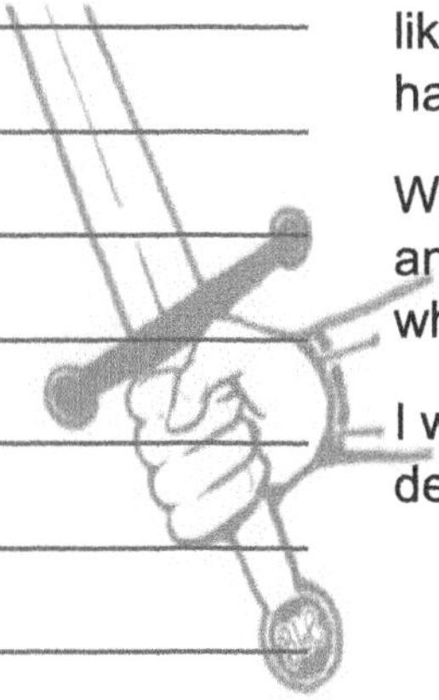

Week 38

Date: ________________

Jesus Proclaims Who He is

Bible Reading: Isaiah 61 - 66

Focus Word: Acceptance

The book of Isaiah gives countless examples of prophecy that has been fulfilled. Again and again Jesus told those who were listening that the prophecies were being made complete through Him! In one instance Jesus quotes the verses in chapter 61 during a trip to the temple in Jerusalem.

Look at what His purpose is and what He brings to you and me! It really is good news!

Yes, I have faith! But, I want to increase my faith!

Give people some grace, some space, because this concept is not so easy to understand and accept.

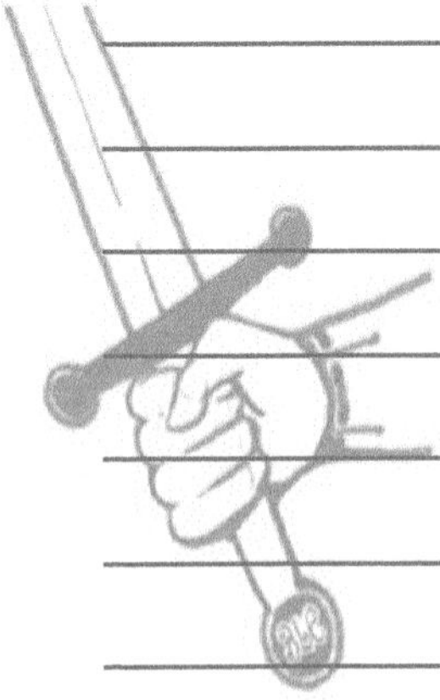

Date: ________________

Known Before Birth

Bible Reading: Jeremiah 1 - 5

Focus Word: Mindful

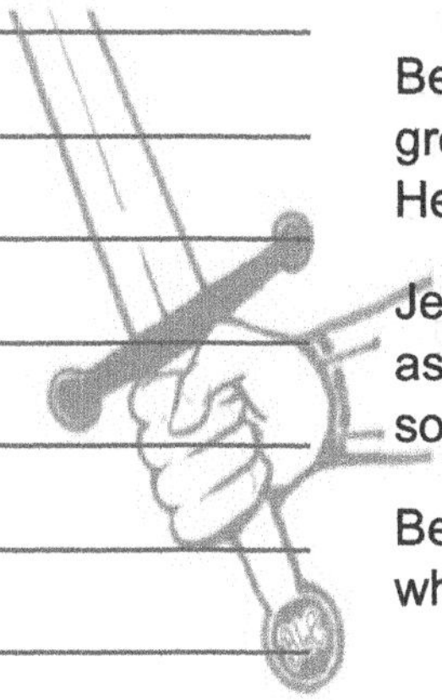

Jeremiah is proclaimed as a person God had in mind way before he was born.

When I read verses like that I have a tough time "being okay" with abortion.

But it does make sense that a sovereign God would have great care and knowledge about His people. You get a sense that when God calls you to do something, He prepares and equips you to do it! It was part of His plan so of course He designed your journey to prepare you for what He has for you!

Be ready, be willing, God has great things in mind for you, and He will use you!

Jeremiah had some very tough assignments. You and I will get some tough ones as well.

Believe that you can accomplish what God lays before you!

Date: ________________

Lists and Rules

Bible Reading: Proverbs 19 - 20

Focus Word: Courageous

How do you deal with legalism?

The problem behind legalism is that rules and "thou shalt nots" crowd our understanding of what Christianity is. It often looks more negative than positive. Often there is little space left for grace or forgiveness. But not all rules are bad!

You read Proverbs and you will come out with lists of what to do and even more lists of what not to do.

Rather than see rules as bad, consider them as boundaries to help you steer through life. Allow the rules to guide you in a way that gives you freedom, freedom to be successful and freedom to practice best behaviors under the blessing of God's plan. It is your spirit and your motivation that is the key.

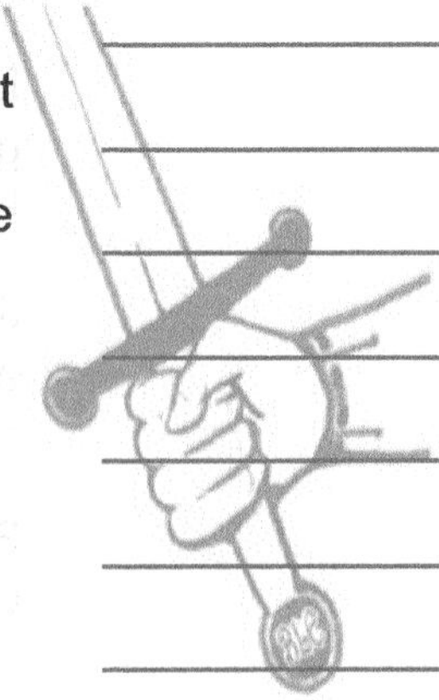

Date: ________________

Bouncing Back

Bible Reading: II Corinthians 5 - 7

Focus Word: Perseverance

We have discussed the idea of resilience before. Whatever tough times you come upon and whatever circumstances and problems present themselves as life goes along remember the apostle Paul says do not lose heart!

There were times in Paul's life where nothing seemed right. Everyone appeared to be against him, but he held strong to his convictions.

Life can be tough. As bad as you and I may think we have it, usually someone somewhere has it far worse! In the end we might feel the groans of discouragement and find ourselves wasting away, but the truth is we can overcome and be renewed through the Holy Spirit.

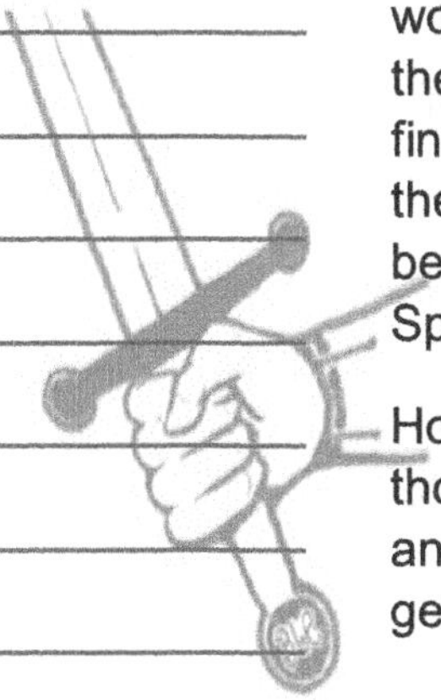

How might I be a part of equipping those around me with resilience and be able to bounce back when I get discouraged?

Date: ____________________

Excel

Bible Reading: II Corinthians 8 - 10

Focus Word: Discerning

Doing your best is a godly, impressive thing to do!

But its not just about worldly success, do well in the spiritual stuff too:

Faith

Speech

Knowledge

Passion

Love

Giving

No matter what you do people will notice your competence and excellence when you get this stuff right!

One piece of advice from II Corinthians 10 when looking to take the next step on this list:

Take captive every thought! Try to be like Jesus by meditating on Scripture and thinking like Jesus!

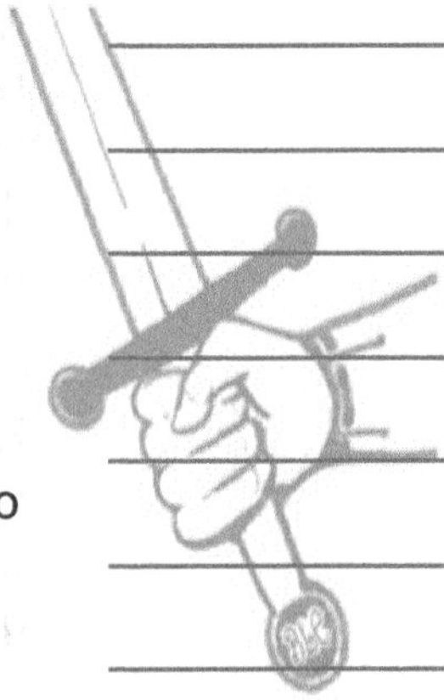

Time Flies When You Are Having Fun!

It seems like just yesterday my boys were little babies. I have loved watching them grow up, but wow, has it gone fast! I used to think I was one of the young guys, now I find myself the oldest person in most of my meetings!

Read the following passages:
Acts 13:36 Esther 4:14 Psalms 103:15-16

Are you purposeful about the way you use your time? Do you ever get in a funk and think that you can take care of it later? There will always be another day.

How long can we look the other way and assume someone else will solve the problem? Sometimes we agree there is a problem, but it doesn't effect me, so I am not going to worry about it.

Does the Body of Christ need to take more responsibility for the culture we live in? Has our silence and our inactivity allowed for the negative, anti-Christian culture to take over? Can we stop the loss of Biblical principles in our schools and our government? What is the place of the church in the midst of racial divisions and suffering?

Maybe we cannot do everything, but we can do some things. Maybe Mordecai speaks to us? For such a time as this…

Throughout history in the more difficult times the greatest leaders have stepped up. The conditions we have before us today may actually create the "perfect storm" for some really great things to be achieved!

What are you waiting for? Time is passing by!

Week 39

Date: ________________

Cultural Temperature

Bible Reading: Jeremiah 6 - 11

Focus Word: Faithful

Times are changing.

People are not what they used to be. The culture has taken some huge turns for the worst. It can be hard to sort out the truth from the lies.

The environment is changing and as discouraging as that can be, we need to be courageous to stand strong in such times. Israel certainly had days were the culture took a turn for the worst. It took men like Jeremiah to be courageous and speak the truth.

Walk in the ways of the Lord and He will direct and guide you.

Consider the seriousness of a wayward culture and what we must do.

Know that He is faithful!

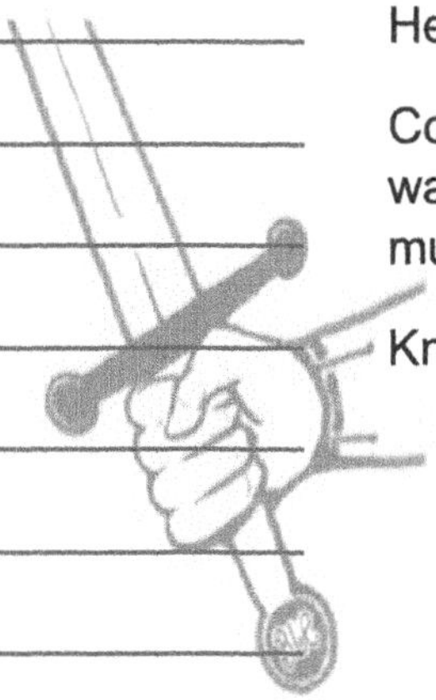

Date: ____________________

Humanism

Bible Reading: Jeremiah 12 - 18

Focus Word: Friendship

I am amazed at what mankind can do. Genesis speaks to capabilities of image bearers of God.

But we often become trapped into believing we are at the center of our world and nothing can stop us our advance. The problem is that this kind of thinking often leaves God out of the picture!

Watch out! These humanist beliefs are all too present in our culture and you can find yourself slipping into them without even thinking about it!

It is so important that we guard our hearts and minds.

Jeremiah 17 is a great chapter to think and ponder.

I pray that this journal and the reading of God's Word keeps you steadfast and focused on the right priorities.

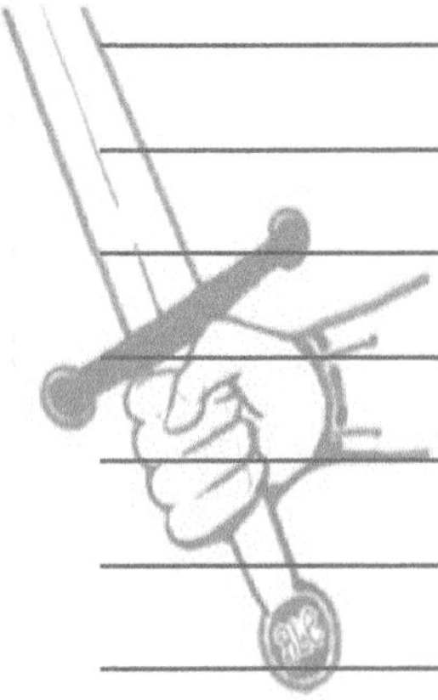

Date: ________________

Train a Child...

Bible Reading: Proverbs 21 - 23

Focus Word: Generous

Proverbs 22:6 tells us that if we train a child in the ways of the Lord, and when he or she is older they will do the right things.

I hear that "promise" evaluated all the time. People like to argue that its really the child's choice in the end. Maybe instead of being skeptical of this promise we need to examine the idea of training.

What kind of training?

What is involved in this training?

Have we really done all that is necessary to train out kids correctly?

No need for guilt trips, but let's purpose to do this job of raising the next generation well. Let's train our children up in the way of God and then trust that they will make the right decisions later.

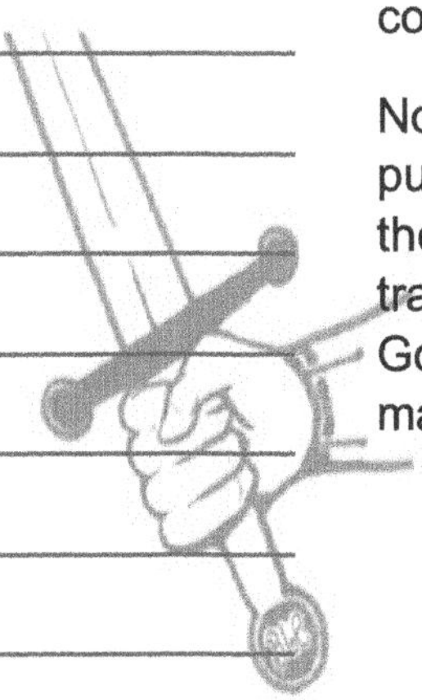

Date: ________________

Tricked

Bible Reading: II Corinthians 11 -13

Focus Word: Helpful

As I go through God's Word I notice several issues seem to come up a lot. And things often repeated are supposed to be important, right?

You will see this idea of deception dealt with a lot in the Bible.

It is so easy to think that others might be deceived or tricked, but not me! But look out! Satan is one tricky being!

On another note, I wonder what Paul's thorn was? Remember this phrase—"when I am weak, He is strong!"

Self-examination is good. Examine where you may be being deceived. Examine your weaknesses and seek help and guidance to overcome them.

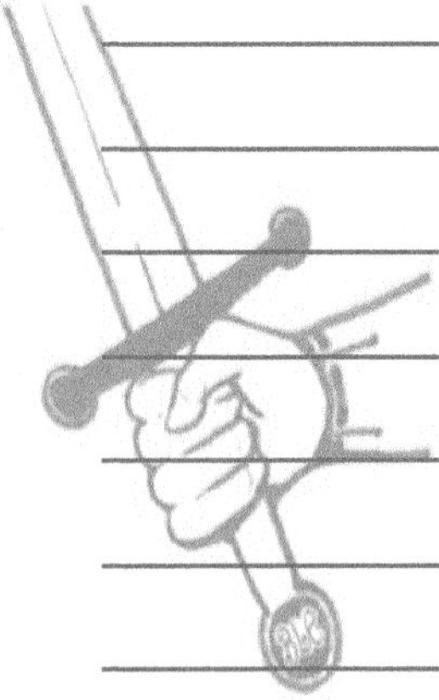

Date: ________________

Paul's Journey

Bible Reading: Galatians 1 - 2

Focus Word: Obedient

Track this guy named Paul.

He grew up to be a religious Pharisee that was probably very intelligent and then has a huge conversion story that completely turns his life around.

Then he was mentored by Barnabas. He became passionate about the gospel and teaching right doctrine. He was even willing to confront Peter on a matter.

He concludes that he is dead, and that any life worth living is Christ in him, the hope, and the glory.

Not saying this approach is the perfect way for all of us, but Paul is definitely an "in your face" kind of guy! He gave up everything for the Gospel!

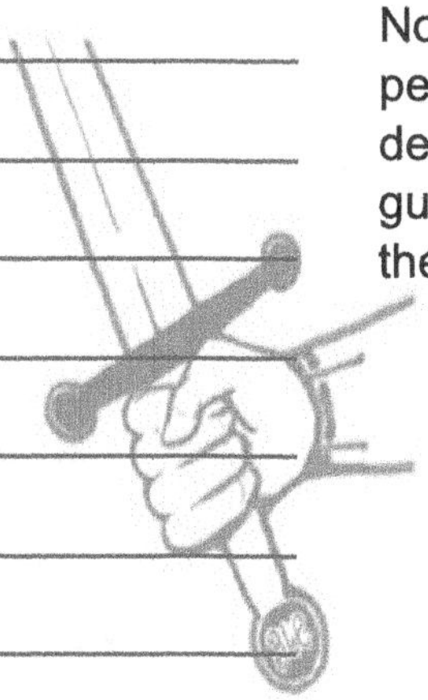

Week 40

Date: ________________

Dig In

Bible Reading: Jeremiah 19 - 26

Focus Word: Respectful

It has been quite difficult for Christians to realize that we are not the cool thing in this culture any more.

What should we do? We see the culture changing and we begin to consider ...

Accommodation. Escape. Or even fighting back in some angry ways.

But we are now more and more in the position that many Christians have been in throughout most of history…

Strangers. Cultural outsiders.

We have to figure out how to flourish and be a blessing despite our situation.

Bring beauty, display creativity, meet needs, and show mercy!

Dig down, dig in, dig deep!

Date: ________________

Prosperity

Bible Reading: Jeremiah 27 - 33

Focus Word: Self-control

Many people will quote Jeremiah 29:11 as their favorite verse. How amazing to think that the Lord has plans for you in which He sees you prospering! God has a hope and a future for you!

Don't miss this!

You matter!

Your circumstances matter!

Don't get all self-indulged in this fact, but apply this now to the bigger picture and the issues that God is working in and around you.

Not that it is easy, in fact it often times is just as hard, but we need to get on the same page as God.

He will prosper you!

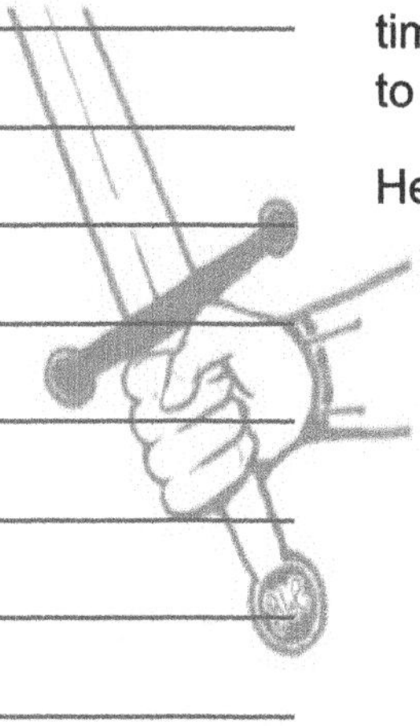

Date: ________________

Building Material

Bible Reading: Proverbs 24 - 25

Focus Word: Virtuous

The wise man builds his house upon the rock!

I have had opportunity to build and remodel several houses. It is a fun process, but every time I have needed a lot of help. I could not have done it without my father-in-law Wendell. Wendell was the best! Not only did we get a lot of work done, he taught me so much! And in the end we always had fun doing it.

Proverbs 24 tells a metaphor of life by building a house.

Check out the building material:

Wisdom

Understanding

Knowledge

These are powerful tools!

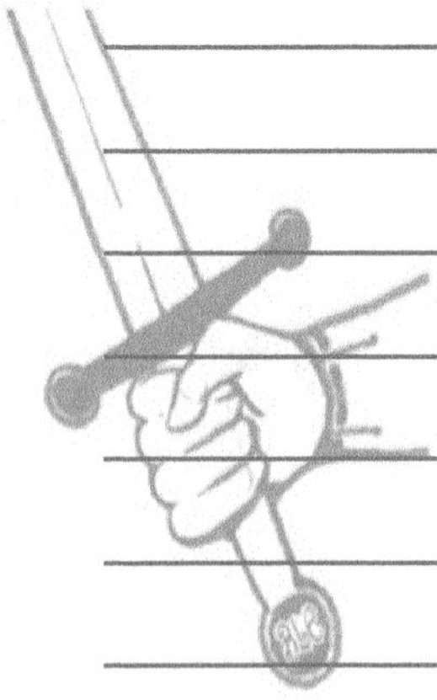

Date: ________________

Developing into What?

Bible Reading: Galatians 3 - 5

Focus Word: Sanctification

This journal is an exercise in reflective thinking. How do I get better? What does better even mean? Who decides? What is the metric?

Christ-like character is described throughout the Bible, but it is very pointed in Galatians 5! There are fruits of the Spirit that help us to be virtuous.

How are you doing on the virtue scale?

Just as a carpenter, or any other skilled workman needs to practice their skills to perfect their trade, we need to practice virtues so we are becoming more and more like our heavenly Father.

Make this journal a part of your spiritual discipline practice plan. Unite with God and His Word to build your moral character!

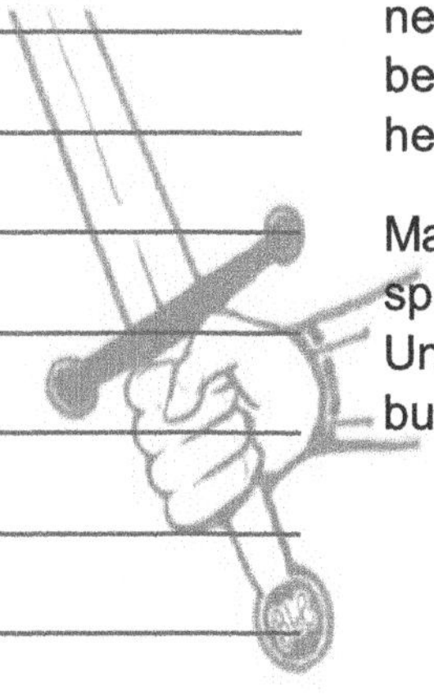

Date: ________________

Doing Good

Bible Reading: Galatians 6 - Ephesians 1

Focus Word: Wisdom

I love the frozen lemonade from Chick-fil-A! But I have a problem with this icy treat: brain freeze! Too much of a good thing all at once!

You may have brain freeze with this section. So full! So beautiful! So awesome! See if any of these topics can stick with you through the day.

Quick Hits from today's reading:

- Restore a fallen one with gentleness

- Judge yourself before you make big claims to others

- Reaping and sowing

- Chosen

- Enlightened heart

- Jesus and authority

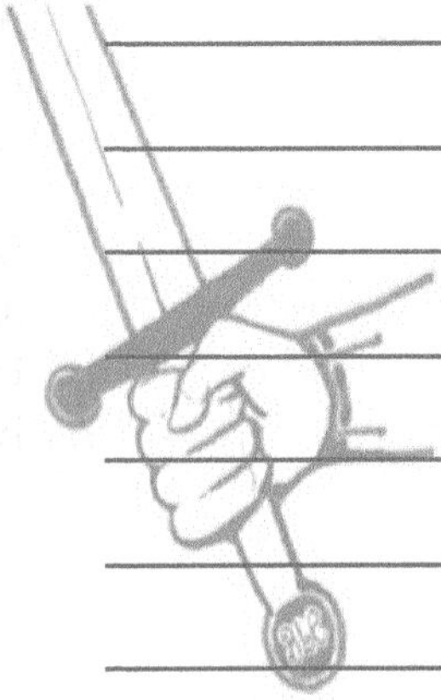

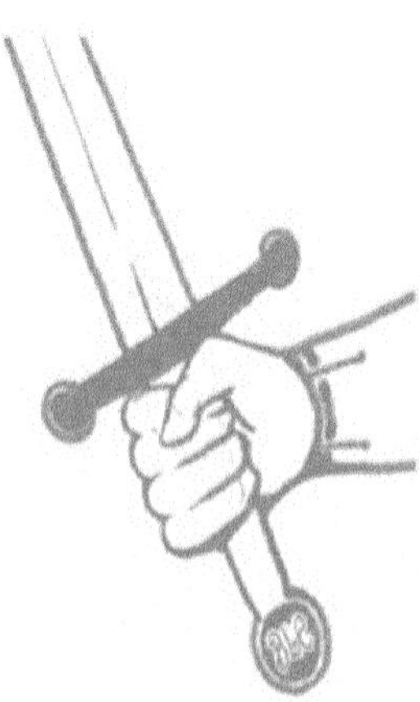

Week 41

Date: ________________

Gloom and Doom

Bible Reading: Jeremiah 34 - 43

Focus Word: Careful

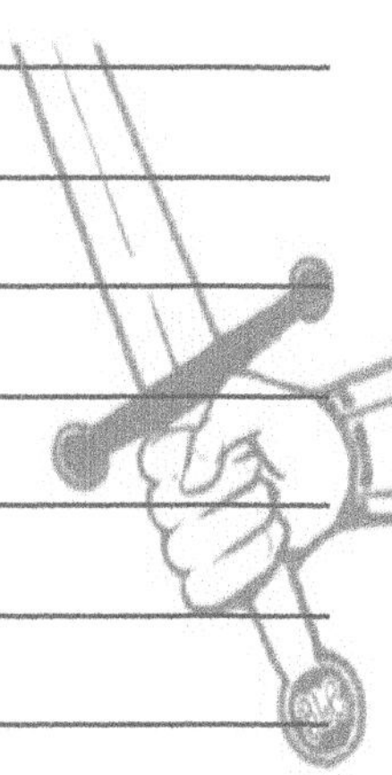

There is a lot of negativity out there. Just look at the problems going on during Jeremiah's life and ministry!

At the beginning of chapter 37 you will find that the King, his attendants, and most of the people paid no attention to the words of the Lord as spoken by Jeremiah.

I hate to keep beating that drum, but it does look very similar to what we are up against today!

Later we find Jeremiah in a cistern—a nasty prison just for him.

I believe there is a lot of hope and room for your growth and maybe even prosperity. But we better be prepared for a time when things do not go our way and the fact that we follow Jesus is a negative to those around us.

Stay close to Jesus!

Date: ________________

Prayer

Bible Reading: Jeremiah 44 - 49

Focus Word: Alert

I am excited about the trip my wife and I took to Israel! WOW!

Seeing the land of the Bible was another reminder that there is so much to learn concerning our faith, the Bible, and Jesus Christ our Savior, as we dig into the Old Testament (and New Testament).

The Bible certainly makes for challenging reading. Sometimes the truth is painful and hard to grasp. But as you understand more, you will see how all this comes together for a perfect picture of the Jesus who loves you so much!

Let's review the "ACTS" prayer system that has been so helpful to me over the years:

A-adoration

C-confession

T-thanksgiving

S-supplication/requests

Try it out!

Date: ________________

Friendship

Bible Reading: Proverbs 26 - 28

Focus Word: Prepared

Keep walking through these life giving verses, words of affirmation, and tidbits of wisdom and knowledge.

Proverbs 27:17 is a classic!

Just like rubbing iron against iron can make it sharper, friends can make each other better.

I have a friend, Brent, who is just amazing. We shared some deep things early in our careers when we were both just young married guys. That vulnerability and a love for Jesus, His Word, and other similarities has made us life long friends (30 plus years).

I have had a lot of good people to be around, great family, but an iron sharpens iron "lifer" is hard to find.

I cherish my friend Brent.

Seek and pray for such a friend! Be that kind of friend to others!

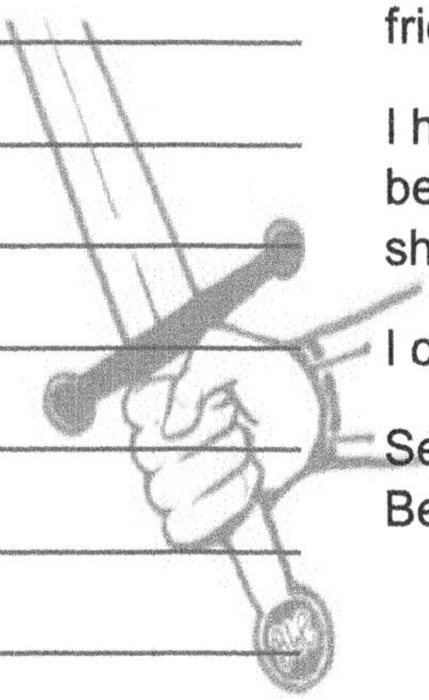

Date: ________________

Power Chapters I

Bible Reading: Ephesians 2 - 4

Focus Word: Loving

Take in Ephesians, you are going to love it!

Consider that it was God who created you. It was God who put you in the circumstances you are dealing with now. God did it exactly how He wanted it!

You are His workmanship created for the purpose of doing good works.

Life may be tough, but remember you are God's "plan A" and you are capable to get it done!

Remember, your salvation is based on grace. Its not all up to you to make everything right. You get to be a part of God's work and the jobs He has planned and laid out for you.

Paul's prayer in Ephesians 3:14-21 is for us! Wow! Amen!

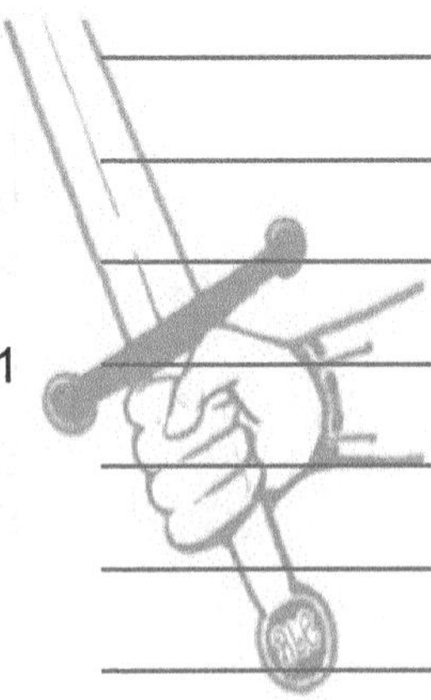

Date: ______________

Power Chapters II

Bible Reading: Ephesians 5 - 6

Focus Word: Integrated

Okay, husbands and wives, pay attention to this!

Love, submit, respect!!!

At my school our mascot is the knights. I am so glad we get to be knights because we talk about Ephesians 6:10-20 all the time.

I love to think through with the kids the metaphor of the armor and how each piece (including prayer) is integral to our success in this life.

You get a sense that this is a serious battle and only those who are ready and prepared will do well! I want to be ready and I want to do well! We need the full armor of God!

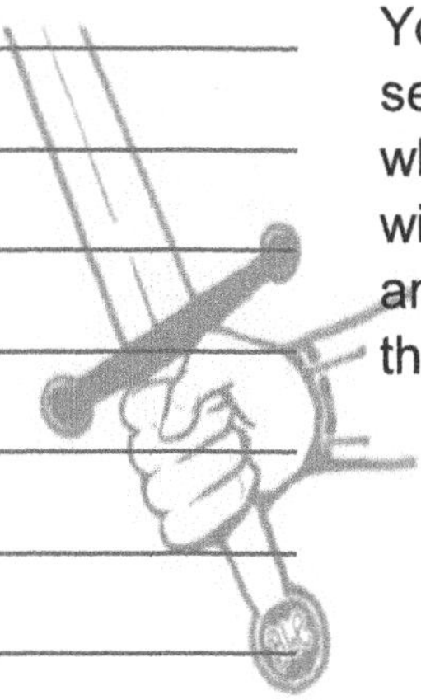

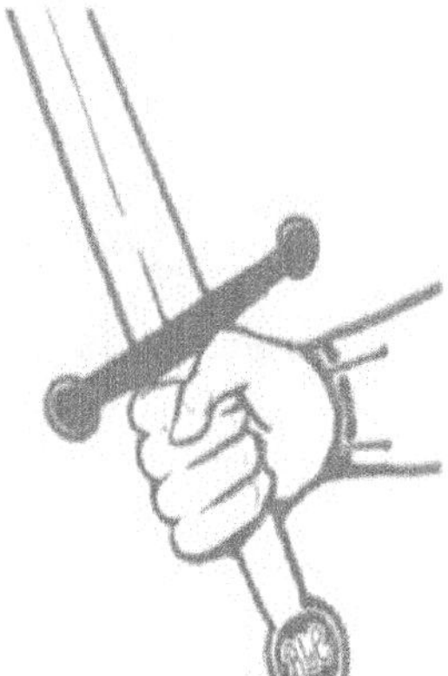

Week 42

Date: ________________

Prosperity Doctrine

Bible Reading: Jeremiah 50 - 52

Focus Word: Optimism

"If you do the right stuff, if you live in the spirit, if you pray right and have enough faith, then all good things will come your way."

That is the idea behind the health and wealth prosperity doctrine. The prosperity gospel has certainly been twisted over the years, but God does offer us abundant life in Him if we live like He commands us to!

Life will not magically become easy, but we have got to make an effort to do what we can.

Eat right and exercise. Look your best. Work on your mind and become wiser. Treat people honestly and have good friends. Invest in, and enjoy your family. Be a good worker and a leader. Grow in the Lord. Serve others.

The abundant life is good!

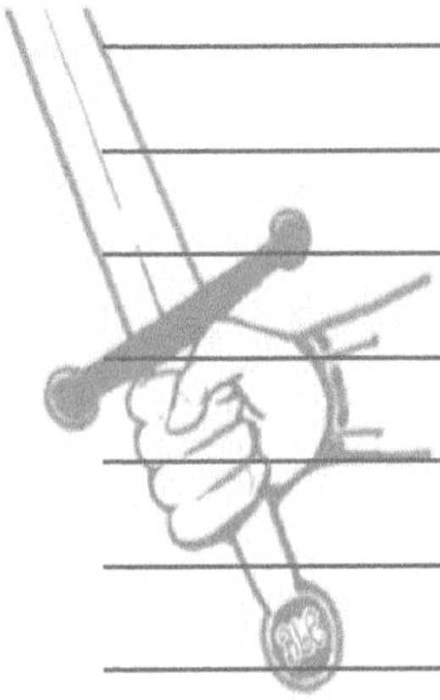

Date: ________________

Great is Thy Faithfulness

Bible Reading: Lamentations 1 - 5

Focus Word: Separated

Jeremiah was the weeping prophet.

Do you hurt when God's ways are ignored?

Do you hurt when you see sin getting the best of people?

Do you hurt when bad stuff happens to others?

Do you hurt when people you know reject Jesus?

There definitely is a place for weeping.

This empathy can give you power and strength to jump up and declare you will do something about it.

"Great is Thy Faithfulness," a great hymn of the faith written by Thomas Chisholm, comes from Lamentations 3:22-23.

Date: ________________

The Power of Vision

Bible Reading: Proverbs 29 - 30

Focus Word: Rich

Do you have vision?

Are there things that you see that are just not right and need to be fixed? Are you able to dream and consider a better way, a bigger plan, a solution that really helps others?

By the way, I think it's even okay if you have a big vision for making money! Just use it right! I am praying for purposeful entrepreneurs who use their wealth for the kingdom of God!!

My Dad is a great example of this to me. He is diligent to succeed so that he can be generous in his giving. Think about it, if you have the gift to give, you better have the gift to make.

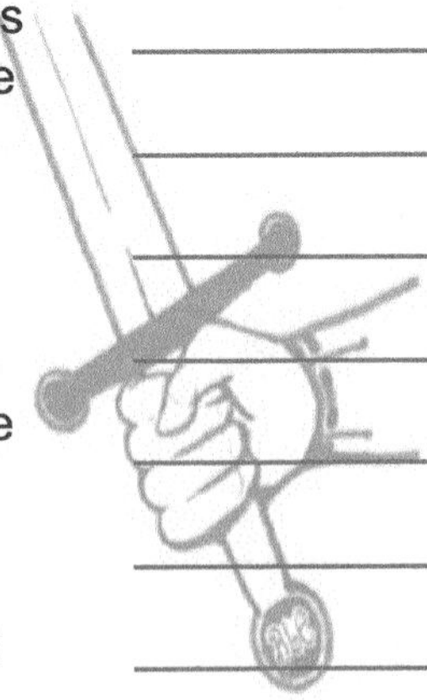

I want the people in the body of Christ to be loaded with talent, good ideas, resources, and have a knack for making big things happen!

Walk with God closely, don't get sidetracked, but shoot for the moon!

Date: ______________

Ten Thousand Hours

Bible Reading: Philippians 1 - 2

Focus Word: Perseverance

What does it mean to workout?

The runner is always thinking about more miles and the weight lifter wants to spend more time in the gym. Working out isn't just for your muscles. What about studying and memorizing for that test, that proposal, or the business plan you hope the bank accepts?

So what is expected when you workout your salvation?

Psychologist Anders Ericsson did a study that Malcom Gladwell talks about in his book *Outliers: The Story of Success*, where he "proves" the best of the best musicians spend 10,000 hours to perfect their skill! No one bumps ahead with less time and everyone who puts in the time in-fact succeeds! Even the talented need hard work and dedication!

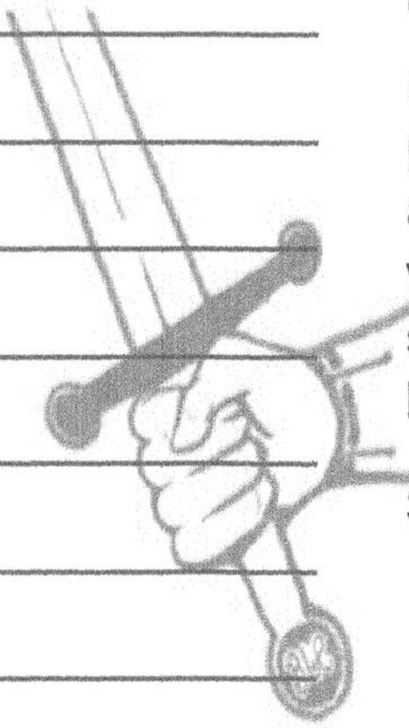

So are you giving "it" your best?

Date: ________________

Press On!

Bible Reading: Philippians 3 - 4

Focus Word: Blessed

Memorize the "press on" verses in Philippians 3:12-14!

Forget the stuff you need to forget (while remembering the right stuff), and move forward, make progress on purpose, to the righteous goals you have, and do something you can be proud of!

If you live like that, you will have a lot to rejoice about!

And while you are pushing, shoving, making things happen, find contentment along the way.

Our God, your heavenly Father, will meet all of our needs as you go! All of them! Every last one!

Let's press on toward the goal to win the prize for which God has called us heavenward!

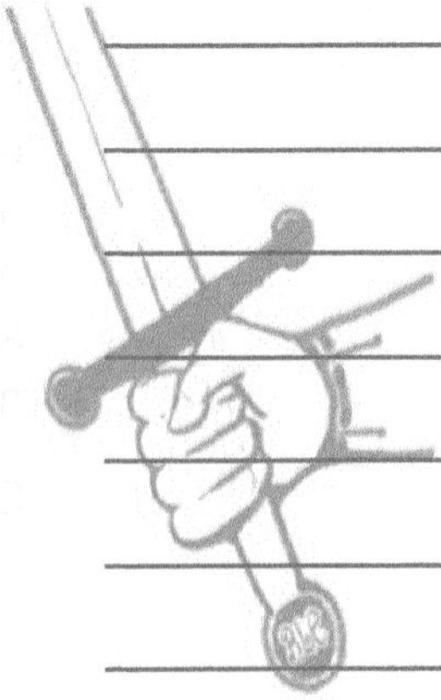

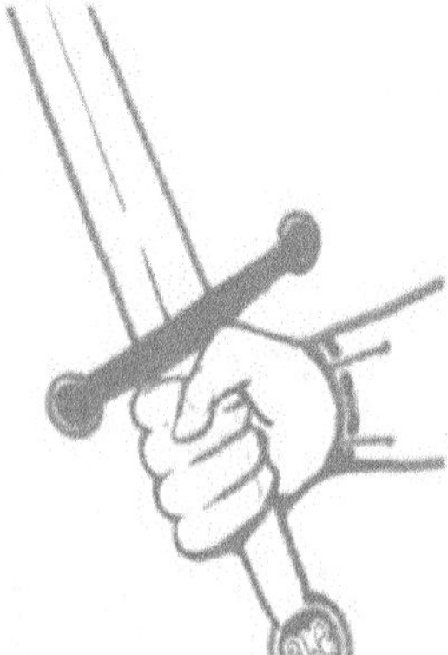

Week 43

Date: ________________

Calling

Bible Reading: Ezekiel 1 - 13

Focus Word: Self-starter

Ezekiel is major prophet #3.

1. Isaiah
2. Jeremiah
3. Ezekiel
4. Daniel

Have you been "called?"

It is a weird question. Often times you will hear when someone decided to be a minister or a missionary that they were "called" to such special occupations.

I know I have felt that "calling" for my work as a Christian school leader. I will also tell you there were days I was pretty sure the whole thing was crazy and I must have misheard!

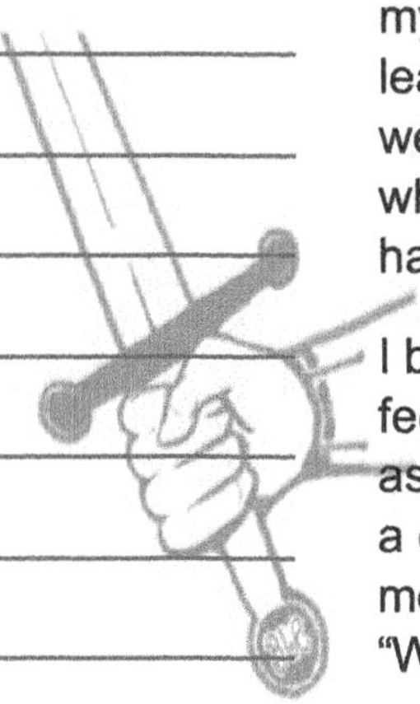

I believe it is possible that you can feel a call to a number of work assignments. You may also have a different calling for different moments in your life. Ask God often, "What do you have for me?"

Date: ____________

Calling #2

Bible Reading: Ezekiel 14 - 20

Focus Word: Focused

I believe that God speaks to His people in different ways.

It might be more typical to have a sense, something deep in your spirit, that points you to a certain decision.

This "move of the spirit" may be dramatic or it may be subtle. It may be about work or ministry. It could be about a short term mission trip, or being a part of a particular church or Bible study.

Be open to what God is saying to you.

I believe as you read through His Word and understand it more intimately He will nudge you in areas based on your reading.

Let me also say if you feel that God is saying something to you counter to His Word and its principles, then I would write that off. Our mind can play tricks on us! The Bible is a great guide!

Date: ________________

Annette

Bible Reading: Proverbs 31

Focus Word: Beautiful

Yes, that is my wife!

Yes, she is beautiful!

Yes, she is amazing and is the epitome of the Proverbs 31 woman!

Yes, I am the luckiest, most blessed guy I know.

And don't just take my word for it, her four boys know it too!

Proverbs 31 is powerful. Let us all look for these attributes. Let us all be about learning and growing these qualities in ourselves.

Let's also realize the value and the wonder of the two distinct sexes and how God ordered that part of our family for our good! The amazing creativity and perspectives that comes from the differences between men and women is something to rejoice in, not some shackle to be dismissed as sexist.

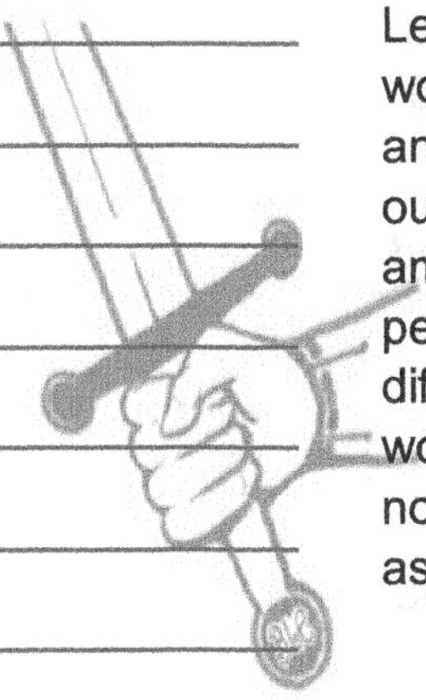

Date: ______________

Science

Bible Reading: Colossians 1 - 2

Focus Word: Personable

I love the scientific method. I think it helps provide answers for many things and we ought to follow it. But when you get to the supernatural, the scientific method does not always hold up.

There is so much that science cannot explain. Consider Colossians 1:15-17: "...He is before all things, and in Him all things hold together." (NIV)

Even down to molecules and atoms—God holds them all together!

One more thing. I cannot leave this section without telling you that Colossians 1:28-29 is my personal mission verse.

Proclaim! Admonish! Teach! And do it strenuously with Christ!

I love to be part of teaching, admonishing, growing, and discipling others. It is a work, a calling, that I am very proud of and I believe it is an honorable and valuable way to spend a life!

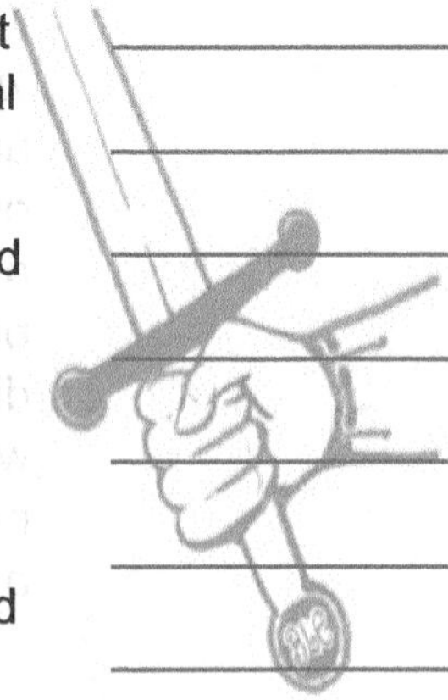

Date: ______________

Rules

Bible Reading: Colossians 3 - 4

Focus Word: Smart

There are smart things that you can do and there are really stupid things you can do.

There are good choices and there are bad choices.

There are wise decisions and there are foolish ones.

There are ways to make progress and there are other ways to send you in the wrong direction.

Paul is loading you up with helpful ways to navigate life.

These words are inspired by a Holy God. These words are better, stronger, much more helpful than just good advice!

Work on this list. Write them down, put a system in place to grow and attain the various admonitions.

Be watchful and thankful!!

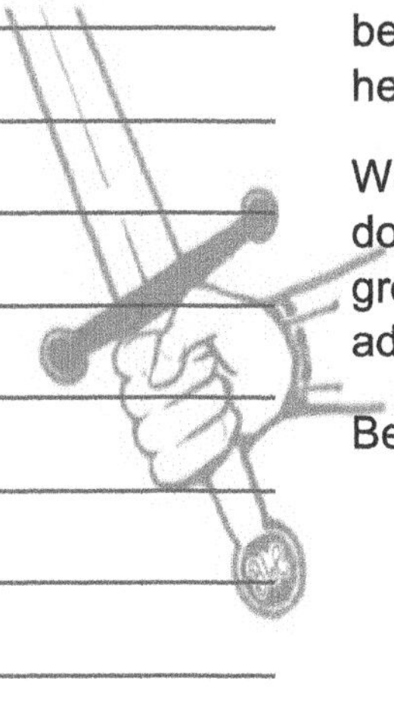

Treasure

"For where your treasure is, there your heart will be also."

Matthew 6:21 (NIV)

I used to think that was just a slick way for preachers to guilt me into giving. Now I realize that I give to the things I love, appreciate, honor, and respect. The things I value are worth my time, talents and treasure.

So what do you treasure?

What are you investing in?

Ever thought about investing into people?

How about investing in teaching and growing the next generation?

Week 44

Date: ________________

Standing in the Gap

Bible Reading: Ezekiel 21 - 28

Focus Word: Future

There are a lot of gaps in this world and God is looking for people like you and me to fill that gap.

Okay, you have heard it 100 times, go fill the gap, do the hard thing, jump out there and be amazing.

I remember the day my son Isaiah saw people jumping out of airplanes in Colorado Springs (we were there to visit Focus on the Family) and he said, "what do you have to do, to get to do that?"

Four years later he was at the Air Force Academy as an MVP runner on the Division 1 Track and Cross Country team and today he is currently a First Lieutenant.

It takes training, discipline, and preparation to be amazing.

Redundancy alert: You will never become what you are not now becoming.

Dream big and then work out the plan! Be a gap filler! You are needed!

Date: ________________

Watchman

Bible Reading: Ezekiel 29 - 34

Focus Word: Present

What you do right now matters.

The present matters. We educators are so tuned into a future that looks better (brought on by better understanding and technology), but the current process is also very important.

The watchman on the wall has to do his job or the whole castle, even the whole city, could be destroyed.

If people don't respond, we cannot help that, but let's not turn silent. Let's proclaim the truth of God and hope for our country and our culture.

Ezekiel does a great job explaining our role in the book that bears his name.

Help the lost sheep!

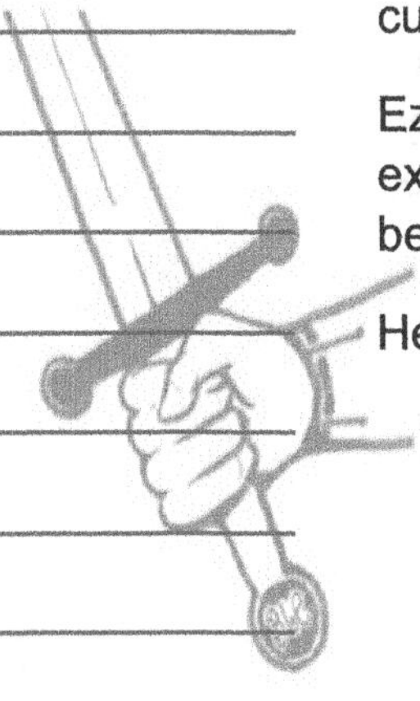

Date: ________________

Meaninglessness

Bible Reading: Ecclesiastes 1 - 3

Focus Word: Past

Researchers say this passage is Solomon talking about trying so many things, so many paths and finding them all empty.

It is a poetic, thoughtful way to address the issues that grab our attention. We all have weaknesses and areas that we are more susceptible to than maybe others are.

Be alert and aware!

Do not let the things of this world take you away form the more meaningful issues of life and your walk with God.

One more thought: I love the idea of time. Yes, time is clicking away. Use your time well. Time is a rare, unrenewable resource.

Tick, tick, tick...

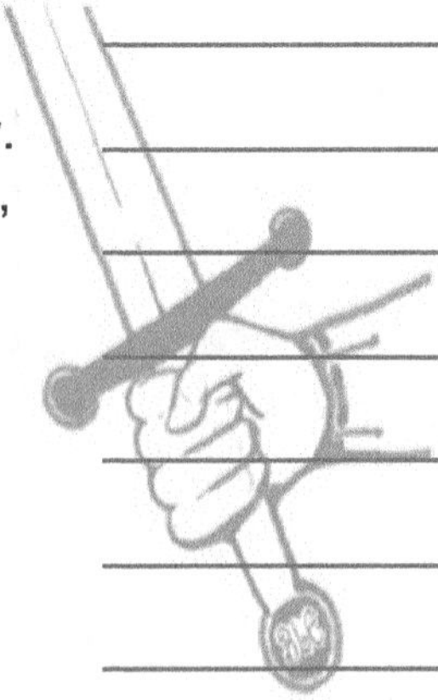

Date: ______________

Pleasing God

Bible Reading: I Thessalonians 1 - 3

Focus Word : Convincing

This idea presented in I Thessalonians, to please God and not man, is very similar to our study yesterday in Ecclesiastes. Focus on the right stuff: God and His kingdom!

It is so easy to get bogged down in the world of pleasing others. There are certainly times where you need to consider how you are being perceived by others, but be sure not to let your focus slip from Jesus!

We are so quick to become obsessed with pleasing our boss, our friends, or that new relationship we want to cultivate. But we are here to please God, not man!

Working for the glory of God leads to many people well served. Even if this leads to praise from others, we must keep our eyes on Him so we do not veer towards the praises of men.

Date: ________________

Make it Work!

Bible Reading: I Thessalonians 4 - 5

Focus Word: Well done!

God's Word is here for our good!

Martin Luther fought for our chance to read the Bible in our own language. That means we needed the Bible translated and then reproduced, so that normal people like you or me could have it! What a blessing.

The "priesthood of believers" means we can read God's Word and personally experience teaching from the Spirit through the message. You can follow God's plan, gain wisdom and insight, and grow. More than likely, this process will continue till the end of time.

So good job!

May you use this year's learning and grow so as to jump into a productive and effective future!

Nurture a habit of learning and growing. Commit to a life of learning and discovery as you walk God's path for you!

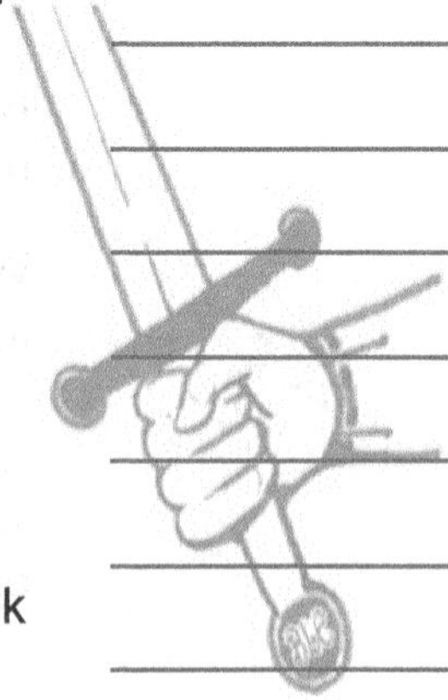

Week 45

Date: ______________

Save Me From Myself

Bible Reading: Ezekiel 35 - 43

Focus Word: Testimony

I have been told that trying to save a drowning man is one of the hardest things to do.

I am not a lifeguard but I understand that when someone is drowning they go crazy trying to figure out how to survive and will flap about and beat against the one who is trying to save them.

Like that drowning person we can be our own worst enemy!

Check out Ezekiel 36:24 and see how the Lord desires to pull us out, to save us, and to give us a new heart! He wants to free us from ourselves!

Check out the Valley of Dry Bones passage in Ezekiel 37. Only God can put life into dry bones. Only God can bring breath to our lips or lead us in the way we should go. He does miracles even when there seems to be no hope, even when we are nothing but dry bones!

You and I need Him so much!

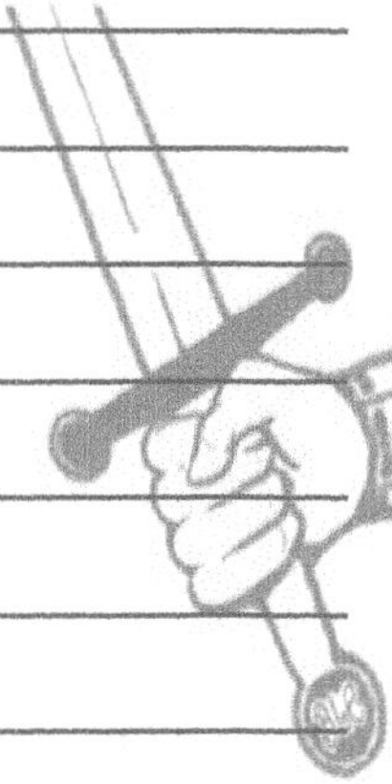

Date: ________________

Gratitude

Bible Reading: Ezekiel 44 - 48

Focus Word: Persistence

I recently read an article about the Ohio State wrestling team. It appears they are going to have a great year with a potential National Championship in their sights. They have an amazing wrestler who has a shot at being a four time national champion. If he is successful, he will join an elite group of four previous such champions. The interviewer asked, what would possibly hold him back?

The coach said the thing that holds all great men back, the always lurking attitude of arrogance, complacency, worry, fear, and lack of discipline. Then he said his wrestler did not display any of those issues because he was appreciative of his opportunities and displays a grateful attitude.

Is that not awesome? The cure to horrible, self-defeating traits is an attitude of gratitude!

Are you thankful?!

Date: ________________

Small Groups

Bible Reading: Ecclesiastes 4 - 6

Focus Word: Deep Thinker

How are we to make the Church an authentic, helpful organization?

Do you get excited about going, participating, and giving your time and money to your church?

You may have heard Ecclesiastes 4:14 during a wedding ceremony. "Though, one may be overpowered, two can defend themselves. A cord of three strands is not quickly broken." (NIV)

Consider today how important people are to you. Or at least consider how important they could be to you! Get to know others and be willing to be vulnerable and to be known. Keep each other accountable and work towards godliness.

Contentment is only possible as you invest in God and others.

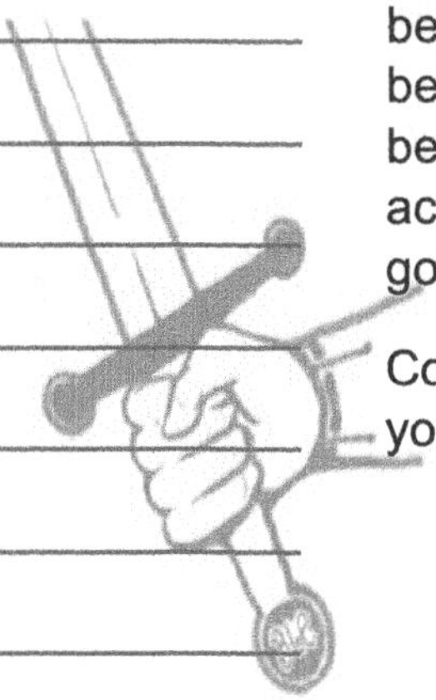

Date: ________________

Purpose Driven

Bible Reading: II Thessalonians 1 - 3

Focus Word: Fruitful labor

Paul starts off this letter with a prayer.

Paul in a sense prayed for us 2000 years ago that we would fulfill our purpose, the desires of our heart, that we would accomplish great things for the Lord and be a blessing to others!

I love the idea that no matter where you are, right now, no matter how smart, or spiritually motivated..

YOU CAN GROW!

Stand firm and hold on to the teachings you are receiving. Once again, these teachings will come by your reading of God's Word, by your associations with other believers, and with your church!

Never tire of doing good!

Date: ________________

Mentoring

Bible Reading: I Timothy 1 - 3

Focus Word: "Greater Things"

Paul was a mentor to Timothy. He had great expectations for Timothy.

Paul wanted to teach and prepare Timothy to lead and be helpful and valuable as a next generation church leader.

Here in Paul's letter we get the inside scoop through a lot of great instruction. Paul leaves Timothy lists, rules, and good ideas to make a church strong.

Excellence in behavior, in your academics, work life, family, becomes part of the attraction people will have for the life you live and the God you serve!

Invest in others while you yourself are being mentored. You can do even greater things as you plug into the good life Jesus prescribes for you.

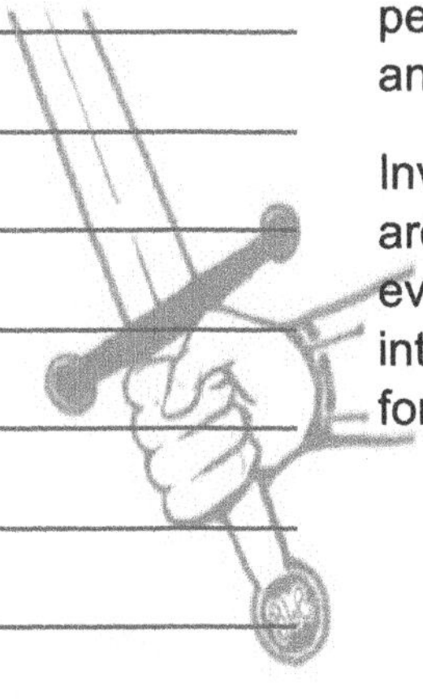

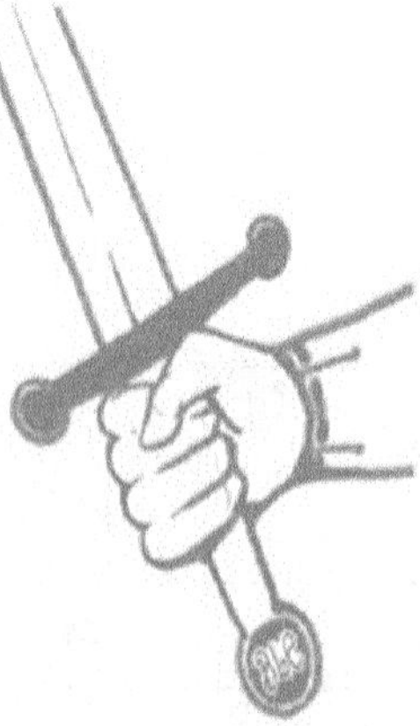

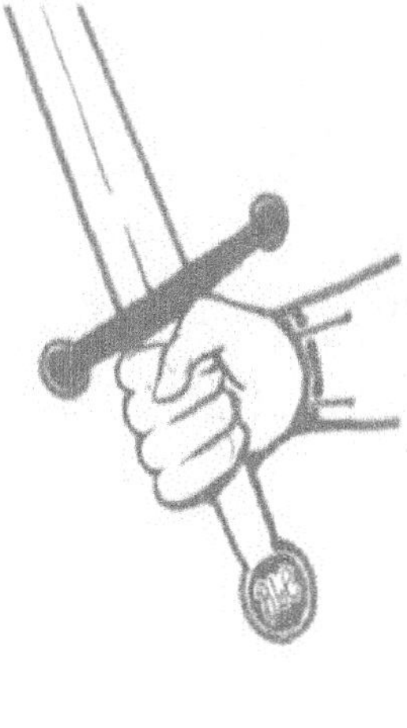

Week 46

Date: ________________

None Better!

Bible Reading: Daniel 1 - 4

Focus Word: Leadership

The challenge before Daniel was immense. If he received a pep talk before getting carted off to Babylon it might have gone like this:

"We need you to lead. We need you to be a person of integrity! We need you to develop yourself and become a mover and a shaker in difficult situations. We need you to be an agent of change.

You need to be personable and winsome. You need to be influential. You will not be able to pull this off with out big, tough, consistent, decisions that you purpose in your heart to follow through on!"

After what was surely a difficult path, the king told Daniel he was 10 X better than any others he had worked with in that particular role.

Are you willing to do what it takes to be the best?

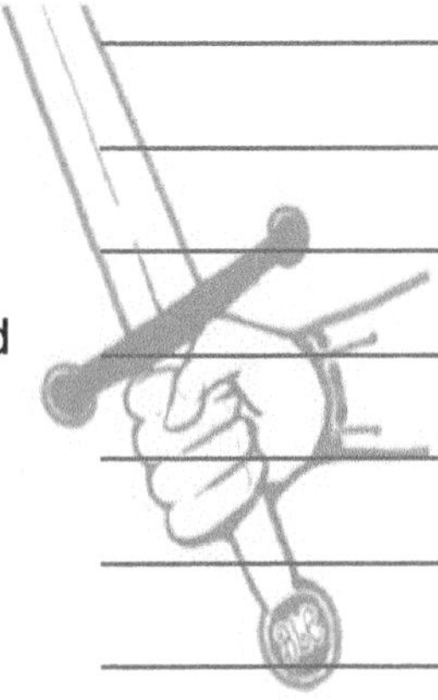

Date: ________________

Keen Mind

Bible Reading: Daniel 5 - 8

Focus Word: Dominion

I love the prophet Daniel.

I think why I like him so much is because we are introduced to him when he was just a boy!

He was not always a "face the lions" stalwart, godly man. Rather he took the talents God had given him, stayed faithful, and became the man of God we remember him as.

God gifted him with a keen mind, much knowledge and understanding. He was smart, but I would imagine he worked hard. I like to think he was always learning.

In Daniel 5:12 we see that he could solve difficult problems.

I believe with God's help we too can solve difficult problems.

Be a problem solver rather than a problem maker! Choose wisdom!

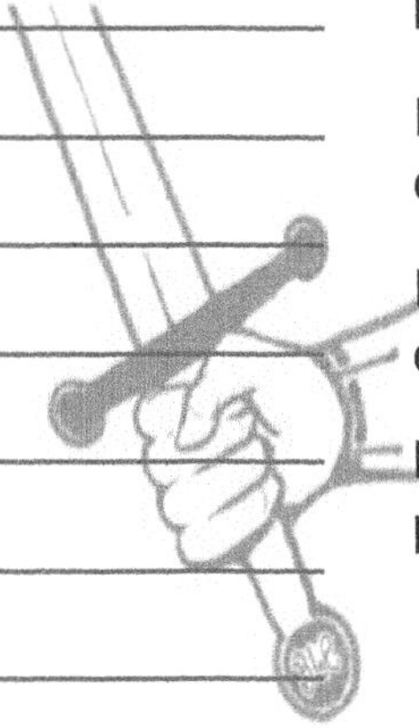

Date: ________________

Midlife Crisis

Bible Reading: Ecclesiastes 7 - 10

Focus Word: Grace

This guy in Ecclesiastes is questioning everything!

I think the idea behind a midlife crisis is that people will build a life on all the wrong things and find a lot of success, or some forms of success that the world has told them would be great. And then things start falling apart...

The character and values underneath the "success" were not nearly what they should have been.

Priorities get all mixed up.

One moment it all makes sense, then stuffs collapses and it's "What am I doing?!"

So if you are the old guy—finally, let's focus on the right stuff! And for the young person—avoid this goofiness!

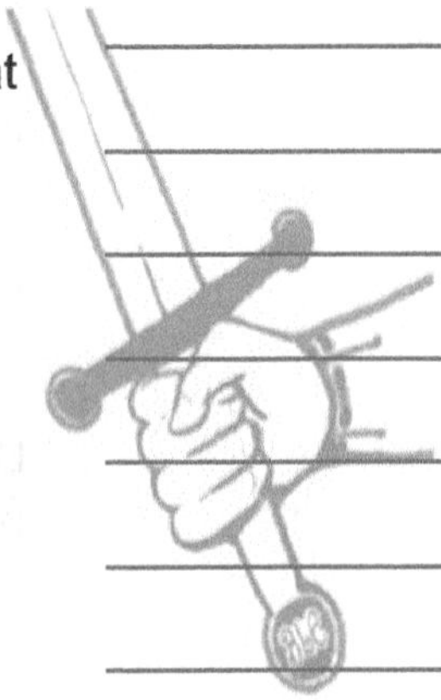

Date: ________________

Fight

Bible Reading: I Timothy 4 - 6

Focus Word: Good works

Press on.

Run the race.

Put on the armor.

Train yourself to be godly.

Fight.

I see a lot of aggressive, forward thinking, movement, in the words of Paul.

I see a huge value in learning, staying sharp so as not to be deceived, and hard work.

I read the book of Timothy and I want to sign up for the greater cause!! Bring it on!!

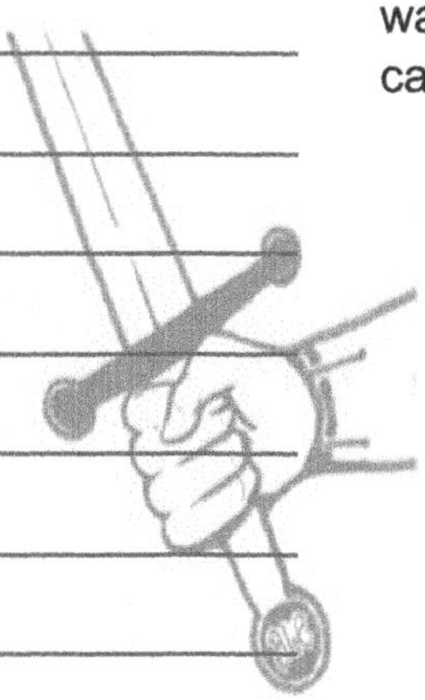

Date: ________________

Thoroughly Equipped

Bible Reading: II Timothy 1 - 4

Focus Word: Called

Another power packed passage! I love the stuff about a workman approved.

My son Josiah graduated from law school this year. Just took his bar exam. He is getting ready to serve in the Air Force as a JAG officer.

He is an amazing, diligent kid (young man). I am so proud of him. He has been in school for 20 years! That is a huge investment of time and resources! But he is ready. It is time to go to work. Prepared and ready.

The whole desire and purpose for this journal is right here in II Timothy 3:16 —

"All scripture is God-breathed and is useful for teaching, rebuking, correcting and training in righteousness, so that the servant of God may be thoroughly equipped for every good work." (NIV)

Strive to be thoroughly equipped for every good work!

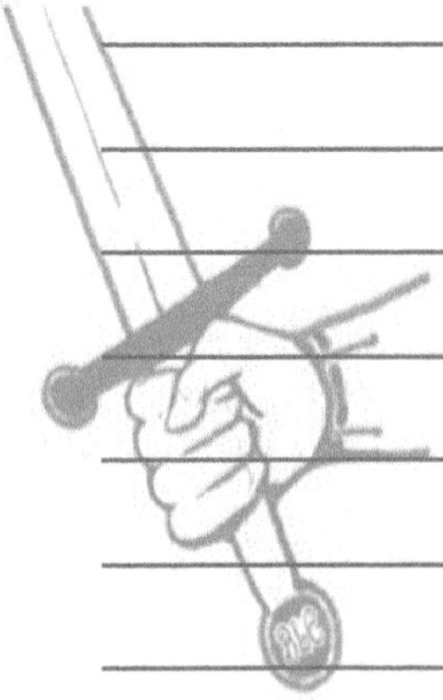

Week 47

Date: ________________

End Times

Bible Reading: Daniel 9 - 12

Focus Word: Reaping and Sowing

At some point this world started. It has not always been like it is now. Does it surprise you that a day is coming that it will be over?

There is a lot of speculation concerning the end times. We will jump into that when we read Revelations.

Look at Daniel 10:12 and think about how Daniel responded when he was a young boy in the first part of the book.

God reminded him of his attitude and his purposeful mindset that he had possessed since he was a kid. God had been using him ever since.

That is right, God used Daniel for a life time. He used him in various secular situations. Daniel was called to stand firm for God in countless challenging situations through the years.

Daniel figured out how to glorify God every time!

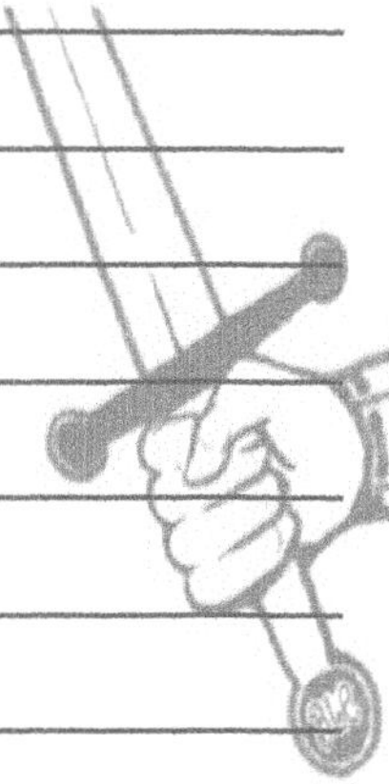

Date: ______________

Minor Prophets

Bible Reading: Hosea 1 - 10

Focus Word: Apologetics

You will now start reading through the 12 "minor" prophets.

They still have a lot to say, but the books are short. Let's start with Hosea.

One crazy story to highlight here is when Hosea was asked to marry a prostitute to help him understand God's love for His people. Hosea's wife was an example of how God loves His people even when He is treated so disrespectfully.

Love is powerful. God loves us even though we deserve nothing.

Hosea sure had it rough. Sometimes the smart guy is considered a fool and the inspired man looks like a maniac. It is an upside down world.

Search for truth and know the scriptures! God's love and understanding far exceed man's abilities.

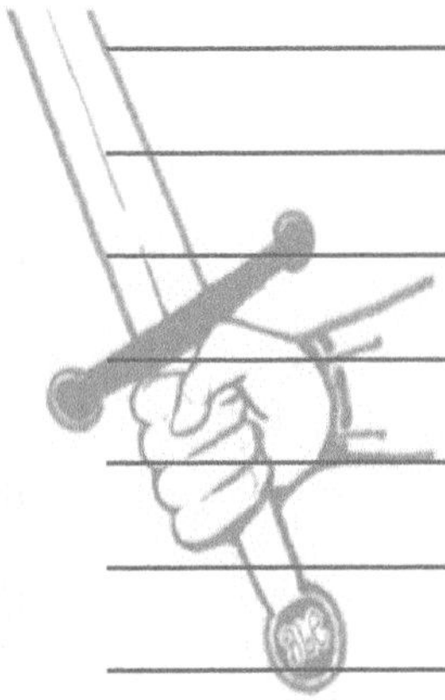

Date: ______________

Summary Statement

Bible Reading: Ecclesiastes 11 - 12

Focus Word: Skilled

Solomon goes from one issue to another and finds no solutions and a lot of loose ends.

He concludes there is a lot of meaninglessness going on with so many of our pursuits.

These thought processes, and his experiences help him to make a simple summary of how to make life work!

For some reason we often want to double check and try everything else before we get to the humility that God wants for us. We finally realize, "Okay, I do not know, I am not God, what do I need to do!?"

Life can be pretty complicated, so it is nice to make it real simple and just follow God. Just keep His commandments!

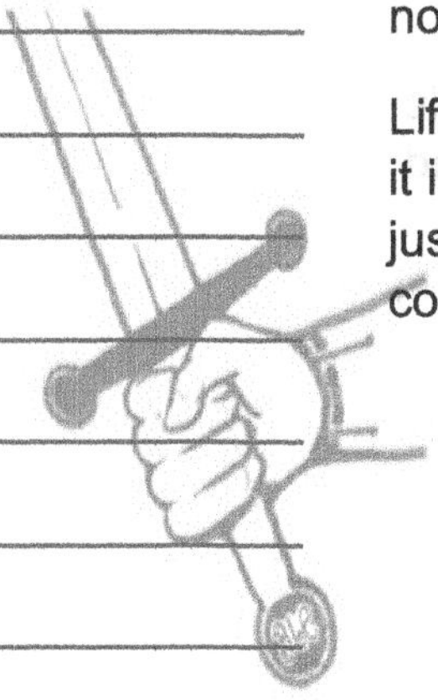

Date: ________________

Titus

Bible Reading: Titus 1 - 3

Focus Word: Trained

Paul is sharing several great tips to his friend Titus.

We can again see lessons on good conduct and expectations for leadership.

No doubt there is a need for leadership. The harvest is great but the workers are few.

I like the Titus 1:6 designation of how a good family looks.

Our Christian faith played out in the close nit, real world, authentic confines of the family is a pretty good indicator of spiritual maturity and sincerity.

We all need grace, so stay humble as you pursue positive sowing and reaping. Be mindful of sound doctrine and mentoring while being mentored.

So what does a productive life look like?

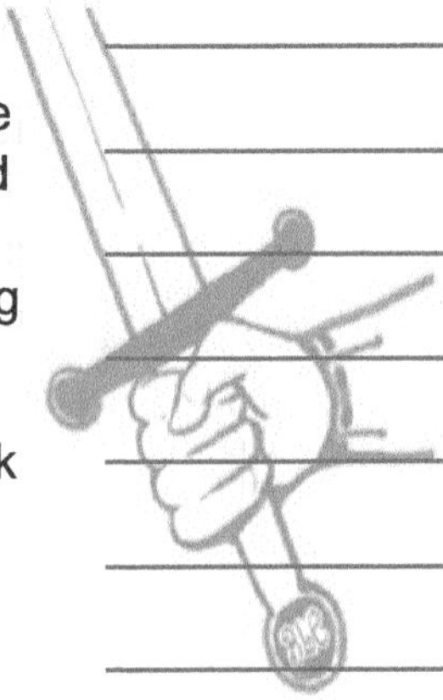

Date: ________________

Put Your Faith Out There

Bible Reading: Philemon 1 to Hebrews 2

Focus Word: Appreciation

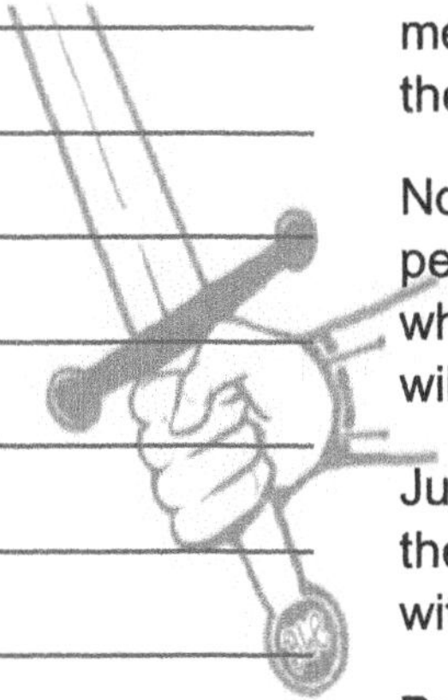

As you engage the world and come into contact with real people you will grow in the effectiveness of your delivery of the gospel and the reasons you believe what you do.

All those failures and successes you will have as you go will keep you learning and growing. If at first you don't succeed, try, try again.

My third son Noah is a computer programmer. I cannot believe the focused attention he gives to a project no matter how many hours it takes. In his mind failure just means you are one step closer to the solution.

No matter what your job or personality is like, be someone who refreshes others. And yes, it will require some people skills!

Jump into Hebrews and see how the author honors you as a human with gifts and abilities.

Praise the Lord with excellence today!

Week 48

Date: ________________

Wisdom

Bible Reading: Hosea 11 - 14

Focus Word: Teamwork

I believe as you work to know God and His Word you will grow in wisdom.

It may feel like two steps forward and one back, but never give up. Keep growing!

Part of wisdom is getting your focus off yourself and serving others. It is a great joy to make a contribution to those around you. Life is so much more meaningful and fun when you can give value to others whether it is a neighbor, boss, family member or friend.

With the wisdom and practical insights that God gives you, bless others!

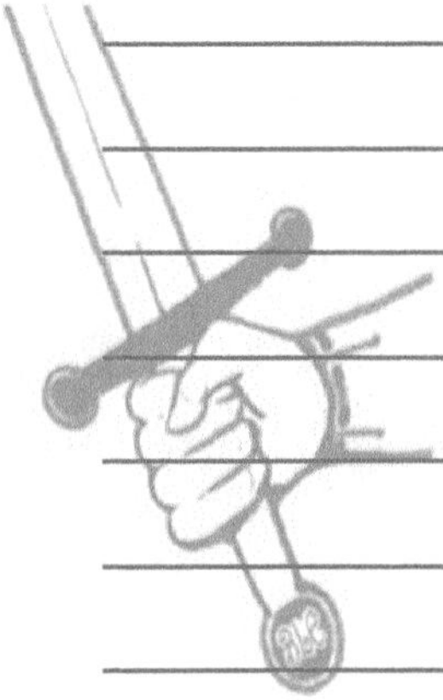

Date: ____________

Crazy Events

Bible Reading: Joel 1 - Amos 3

Focus Word: Work-ethic

So a flood sounds fantastical! Parting the Red Sea is unbelievable!

Sorting through the number of supernatural things in the Bible is a big task. Some of it is hard to understand. It takes faith!

Here in the book of Joel we find a crazy plague of locust that is destroying the land.

I have not experienced a plague of epic proportions but I have seen tornados that tear down everything in their path. And I have heard about tsunamis and volcanoes wreaking havoc.

Who can know what is next?

Don't let it paralyze you but be aware: We live in a fallen world.

Trust in God and His goodness.

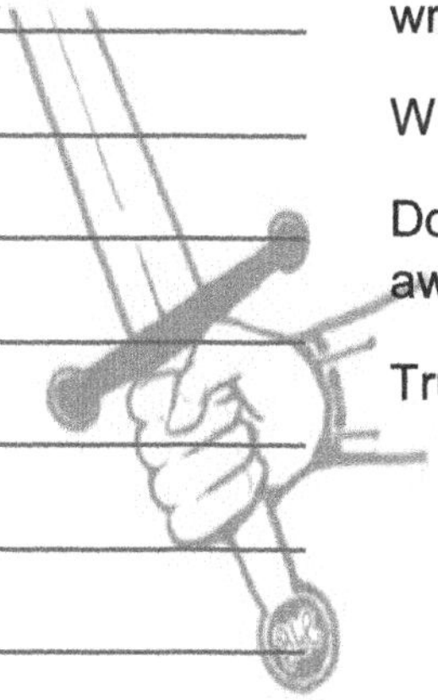

Date: ______________

Blessed Person

Bible Reading: Psalms 1

Focus Word: Forceful

I came back to Psalms 1 because it does such a great job of summarizing the good life!

We all want the good life, but are we willing to do the day by day stuff that gets us to it?

I see this problem in high school students. At a time in life when individuals can be so emotional or unwilling to consider long term effects, high school students make decisions that totally change their future.

Consider long term issues! The good life requires making the right choices, possibly even as a kid in school.

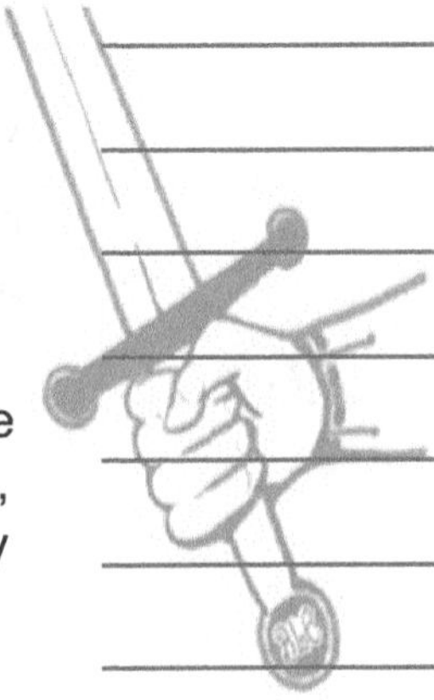

Think your next big decision through completely and carefully, then choose wisely!

It is a funny thing that when we are young our parents seem so stupid, but the older I got the smarter they became!

Date: ______________

Rest

Bible Reading: Hebrews 3 - 6

Focus Word: Competitive

I am always in a hurry.

My problem, a real weakness, is that I speed too much. I have had a few speeding tickets (more than a few). When I see a police car my foot automatically goes to the break!

God gives us rest when we do things right, when we follow His way. For example, when I am going the speed limit, I can pass by my police friends and smile and wave. I can relax! I am doing the right thing. Nothing to be worried about!

Hebrews chapter 4 will give you a nice perspective on Sabbath rest. And don't miss the value of God's Word in Hebrews 4:12-13.

Powerful!

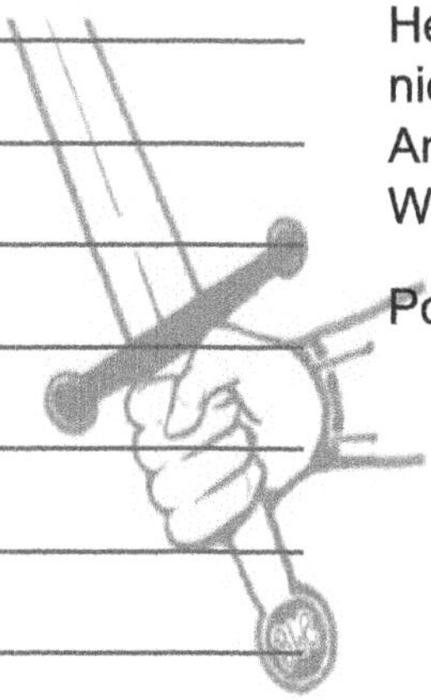

Date: ________________

Spur On One Another

Bible Reading: Hebrews 7 - 10

Focus Word: Heart for God

Hebrews is a deep tough book to take in.

Please consider writing out questions you have as you go through your Bible reading and then later ask your pastor or someone you trust and respect.

I get excited by chapter 10 where we are called to persevere. You can hear the call to action and the excitement of meeting needs.

If a spur is designed to get a horse to moving faster, then a spur to a friend is to encourage them to live out their faith with joy and focus.

We have the power to help our friends and family move in the direction of an abundant life.

Meet together and spur each other on...often!

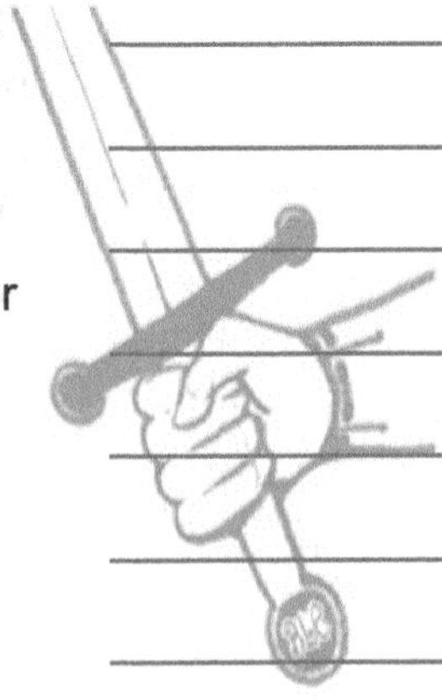

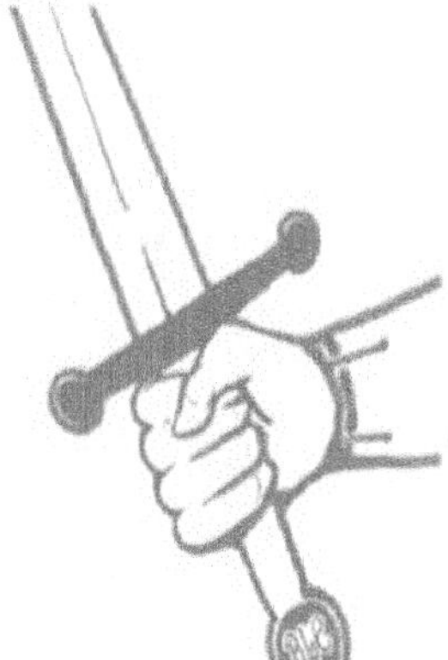

Week 49

Date: ________________

The Problem Is Us

Bible Reading: Amos 4 - 9

Focus Word: Growing

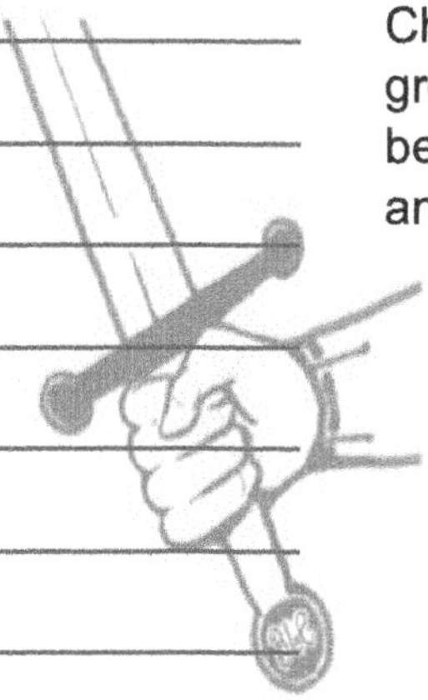

The little guy in Lord of the Flies realizes that the evil that his buddies are worried about is not some danger out there, but it is in themselves! They are the problem!

Amos gives us the feeling that if the believers, the God followers, would do what they are supposed to do we would be much better off.

The problem is not the pagans, the bad guys, the enemy….but rather the people who should know better!

How do we build up the body of Christ! How do we make our group attractive and strong? Let's be great ambassadors for Christ and His Word!

Date: ______________

Whiny Jonah

Bible Reading: Obadiah 1 - Jonah 4

Focus Word: Loving

Most people know the story of Jonah and the whale, at least the little kid story version.

Dig a bit deeper and you see Jonah was fighting against God's plan for his own life and a whole group of people whom Jonah happened to not like.

In the end, Jonah did not think the Ninevites deserved to be saved. Even after Jonah was given grace and a second chance, he did not think it should be available to this other group of "bad" people. God had to set him straight!

Where does discrimination creep in and make us judgmental? Have you ever thought you had good reason to hope the worst for someone or some group of people?

What does it mean to love the least of these?

Date: ________________

Faith Chapter

Bible Reading: Hebrews 11 - 13

Focus Word: Honorable

Faith is being sure of a hope we have that is not seen. Faith is how you receive Jesus Christ into your heart.

Salvation—the belief that Jesus died for us and loves us, and has a plan for us, just like He said over and over, and in so many ways.

Pick out a couple of your favorite heroes of the Christian faith.

Notice that some of those listed as heroes, in many ways were not very impressive. God can do some amazing things through weak people!

Next, do not grow weary, and do not lose heart. Here is the kicker; God disciplines those He loves.

OUCH!

Been disciplined lately?

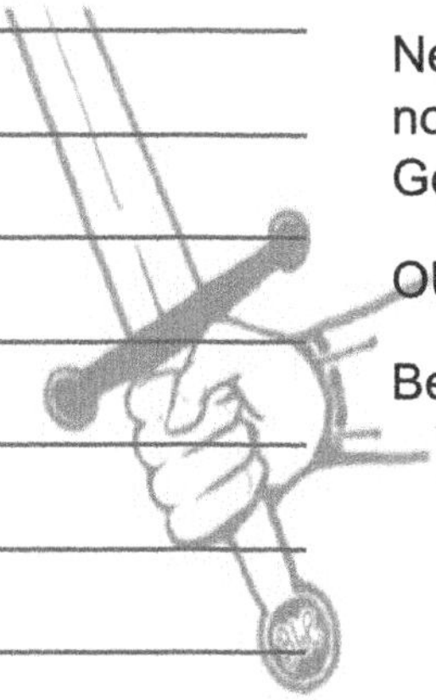

Date: ____________

Trials

Bible Reading: James 1 - 3

Focus Word: Generous

I hope there is no real-life pattern to this one, two shot!

Yesterday it was discipline and today its trials!

Trials are difficult circumstances made to test and challenge you. Trials might be something you instigate or it may be circumstances you had nothing to do with at all And unfortunately, it is a matter of "when" not "if" you will face trials!

You have to be tough. You have to persevere. You have to have an eternal perspective.

You might not be able to change the issues that brought you here, but you can decide how you will react from now on!

Pay attention and listen!

Date: ________________

Plan Away

Bible Reading: James 4 - 5

Focus Word: Reliable

Plan. Plan hard. Really think it through. Count the cost. Get organized. Budget.

Education is a long term planning process.

This whole journal is about planning and taking the proper steps for growth and living out God's best.

One little problem....

You have no idea what is going to happen tomorrow! There is a lot we cannot control.

Because we have so little control over our lives, there may be a temptation to throw up your hands and not plan anything. Some may argue it is sinful to attempt to control every detail of your life. But in my experience, the greater sin in this balance is not planning and executing well the plans we make. Do your best and trust God!

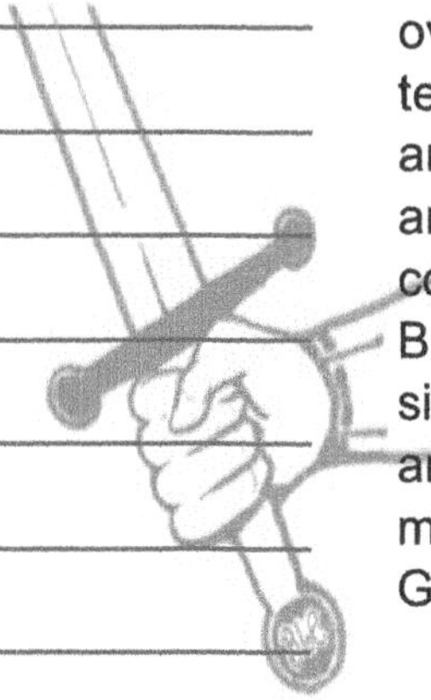

Week 50

Date: ________________

Micah

Bible Reading: Micah 1 - 7

Focus Word: Consistent

Micah is my youngest son.

He is such a blessing! We named him Micah because of Micah 6:8. What does God require? Act justly, love mercy and walk humbly with Him! What a quality way to describe a God follower!

My son can do so many things. He can write. He loves philosophy and theology, and he loves God's Word. He has a gift with people and knows how to make people feel comfortable while also getting them to think deeply. He is also a great runner! He is on his way to being fully equipped for God's service!

Not always sure what to do? Follow Micah 6:8 and clarity will come!

We need to internalize this verse and make it part of our everyday life. Someone who knows what is good and acts in justice with love and mercy while still remaining humble is certain to be a powerful tool for God to use!

Date: ________________

Bullies Get Their Due

Bible Reading: Nahum 1—Habakkuk 3

Focus Word: Cheerful

I hate it when the bad guys win!

But the truth is they rarely win. Stuff catches up with the bully.

Eventually.

Don't get sucked into their bad thinking or their wrong behaviors. That can be really tough when life is rough and the bad guys seem to be enjoying the spoils of their ill gotten gain! The injustice just seems to be too much!

Cry out to the Lord. Tell him what you think and what you believe should happen.

Then listen. Let the Holy Spirit direct your path, maybe even change your attitude or perspective. Maybe you don't know everything about the situation. Have patience and humility!

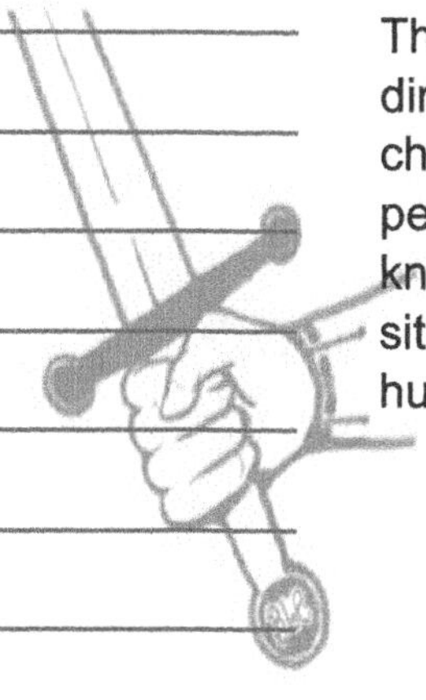

Date: ________________

Love and Marriage

Bible Reading: Song of Solomon 1 - 2

Focus Word: Good friend

Solomon wrote Song of Solomon. But when did he write it? Before all the wives and concubines?

It does give us an understanding of love and physical expression. You get a real sense of the beauty of the physical body! But let's be clear: This book is rated R!

Sex is an important issue and I hope you can do the sex thing right! God is clear that sexual immorality should have no place in the life of the Christian.

And if you are waiting, let me just join Solomon in telling you that once you are married, it is the best! Studies are so clear and consistent that married people have the best sex!

Commit to doing sex God's way!

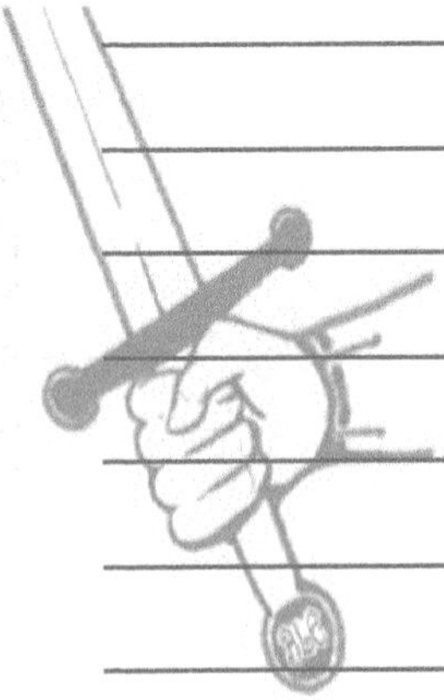

Date: ________________

Prepare the Mind for Action

Bible Reading: I Peter 1 - 5

Focus Word: Encouraging

The educator gets to shout here in I Peter! This is what we do! We want to prepare minds for activity.

Use your brain (your heart, soul, and spirit all have a part too), and learn! Prepare yourself for service to God, prepare yourself for a life well-lived.

Children don't just start out life as geniuses. We all begin uneducated and ignorant. Guess what? That is okay! It is normal.

But parents and teachers must come around the obedient, humble child, and help them to grow!

I love I Peter 2:12—where Peter calls us to live such a good life that pagans will be unable to accuse you of anything. No one will believe them because of our reputation for righteousness!

Unfortunately, I often fall short of this mark, but it is a great goal to strive for!

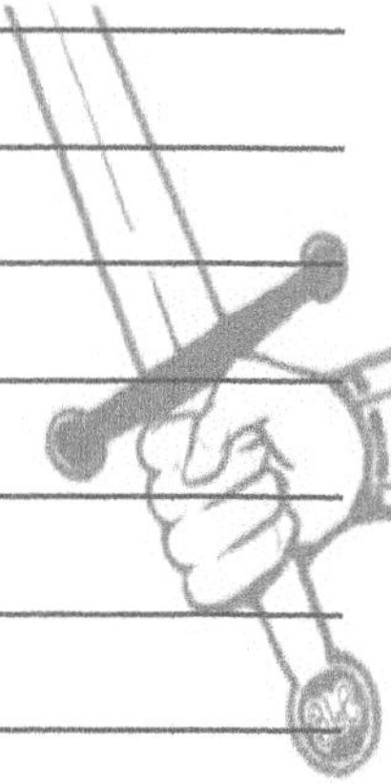

Date: ____________________

Principles of Education

Bible Reading: II Peter 1 - 3

Focus Word: Truth Seeker

Peter sure gives us a great list of Christ-like characteristics to aim for! These should be end result of a great Biblical education!

- Faith
- Goodness
- Knowledge
- Self-control
- Perseverance
- Godliness
- Brotherly kindness
- Love

Wow! This is great stuff! Effective! Productive! Becoming a person who can be used by Christ in a mighty way! This is how to be smart, wise, and educated.

This is it!

How is your list shaping up?

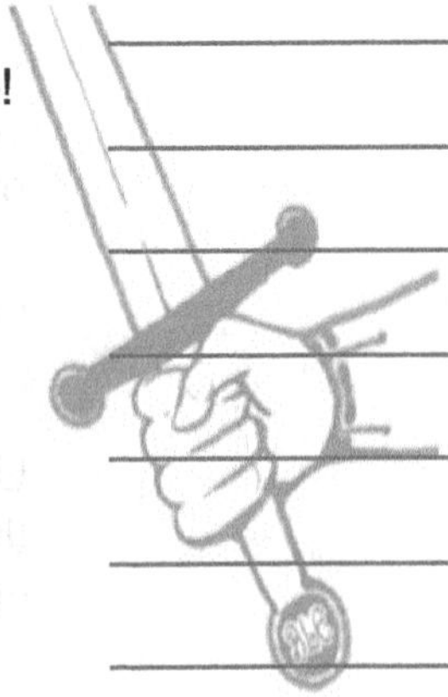

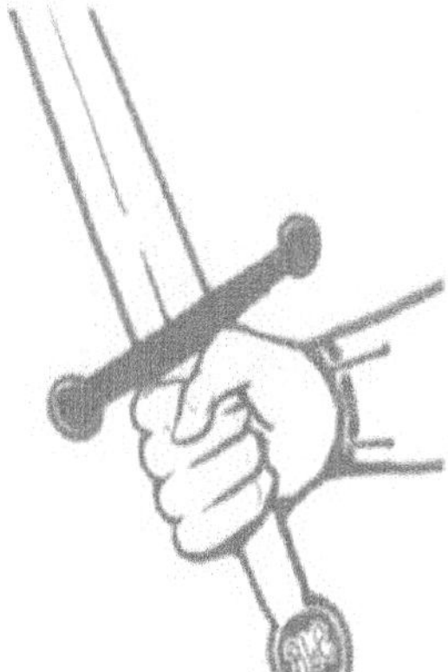

Week 51

Date: ________________

Body Of Christ

Bible Reading: Zephaniah 1—Haggai 2

Focus Word: Fighter

I think the possibilities, the strength and power, that is at our disposal in the Body of Christ is amazing! The potential to do good is enormous!

Can we actually get our act together and see it come to pass? Unfortunately we often struggle to cooperate. I know we have not done a very good job in the political arena.

It is so tough to be unified.

Zephaniah 3:9 gives me encouragement! Once we have purified lips and a desire to call on the name of the Lord, we can serve shoulder to shoulder!

What great imagery to hope for and work towards. Unity.

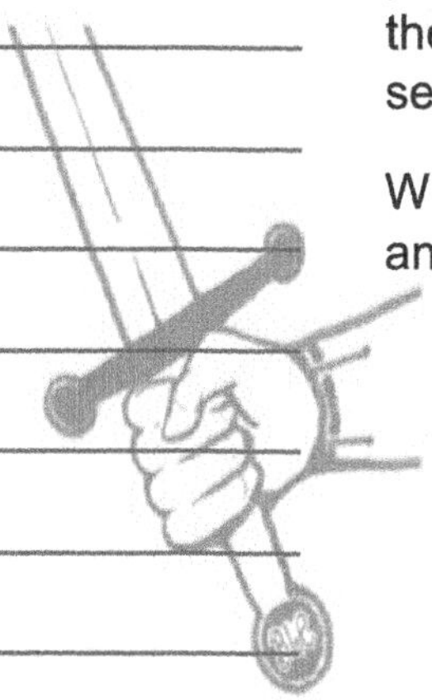

Date: ________________

Serving Others

Bible Reading: Zechariah 1-14

Focus Word: Willing

The focus of a journal is **YOU**!!

That really is the idea, to invest in yourself, to follow God's path for you, and to make adjustments and be all that you can be!

But lets not forget others! A component of this growth process is that we are serving others.

Serving others means to be concerned with the disadvantaged, the oppressed, and the poor.

How much time do you give to others? How much money do you give to those in need? How are we supporting ministries that help and heal?

Am I compassionate or have I become calloused?

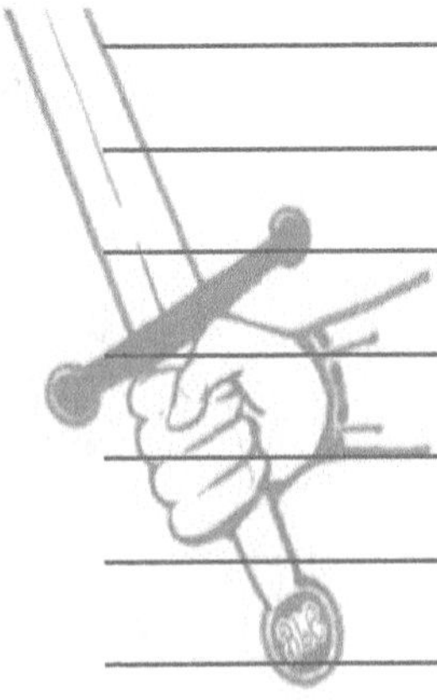

Date: ________________

Singleness

Bible Reading: Song of Solomon 3 - 5

Focus Word: Fruits of the Spirit

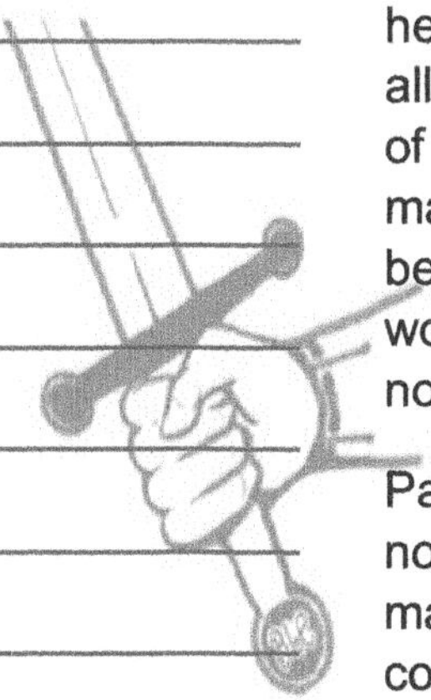

The statistics suggest the state of singleness, as opposed to marriage, is on the rise.

Some just have not found the right person. Others feel called to singleness. But a big reason for the rise in singleness is that there is a greater willingness to live together unmarried which in the past hardly existed in this country. Divorce is still rampant as well.

I just want to take a moment to shout it out that the family is valuable! The family is awesome!

There is room for single people to help and protect families. Let us all participate in the strengthening of the family, parenting, and marriage. Let us all commit to being good uncles and aunts and work to see our Christian families nourished.

Paul sees singleness as a gift, but not the norm. No matter our marital circumstances let us each commit to strengthening the family.

Date: ________________

Walking with Jesus

Bible Reading: I John 1 - 5

Focus Word: Steward

Walking with Jesus is about obeying His commands.

The key to obedience is LOVE.

When we start with the Father's love to us we can't help but want to love Him back. We can't help but follow the path He lays out to love others as well.

A few other pieces of advice for walking with Jesus:

- Fight against worldliness.

- Be careful that you are not led astray.

- Ask for big things and see what God does!

What are you praying for today?

Who are you praying for today?

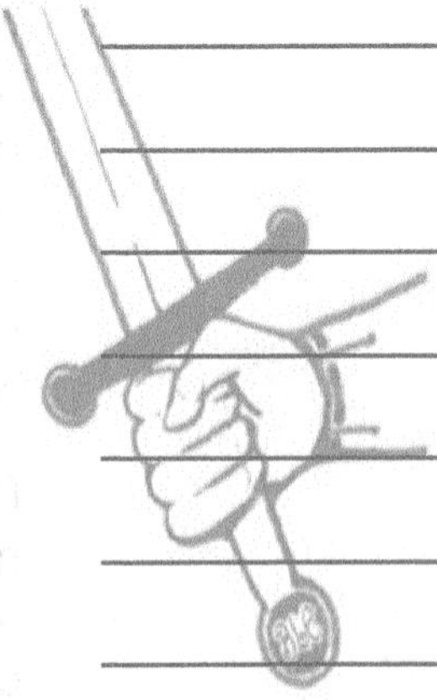

Date: ________________

No Greater Joy

Bible Reading: II John, III John, Jude 1

Focus Word: Legacy

Parents know this, there is no greater joy than to see our children walking with God.

I love to see my boys and their wives flourishing! The abundant life is a beautiful thing to behold!

I love to see my students walking with the Lord! I love to see my church family serving the Lord faithfully and living the good life.

Are we willing to teach and mentor godly principles that encourage children to make proper choices? Are we willing to encourage our fellow Christians to make hard but godly decisions.

It is tough and sometimes we cannot even agree with each other on what those principles are!

Are we willing to have difficult, deep conversations which sometimes produce conflicts to get to a better conclusion?

Build the legacy; it is worth it!

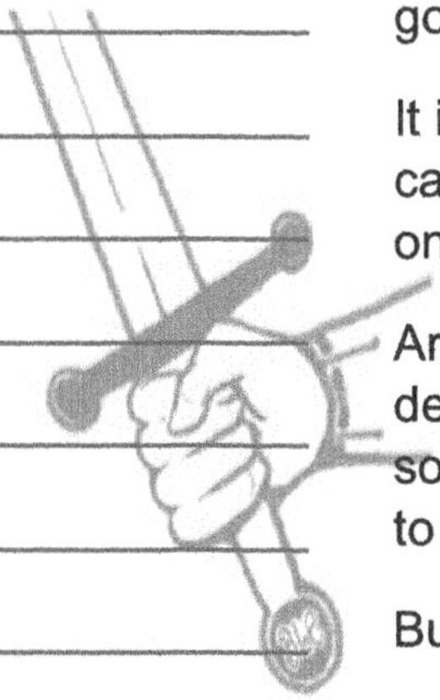

Week 52

Date: ________________

The Silent 400 Years

Bible Reading: Malachi 1 - 4

Focus Word: Biblical

Malachi is the last book of the Old Testament.

After this it will be more than 400 years before John the Baptist is on the scene and we move into the New Testament era with Jesus here on earth.

You have no doubt noticed me making a big deal out of family over the year. Notice what is says here in Malachi 2:13 and following. A faithful marriage is key to creating godly offspring!

The silent period is very interesting as during this time the Pharisees, Sadducees, Essences, and the Maccabees all exercise power and change the shape of the country and government before Jesus comes on the scene.

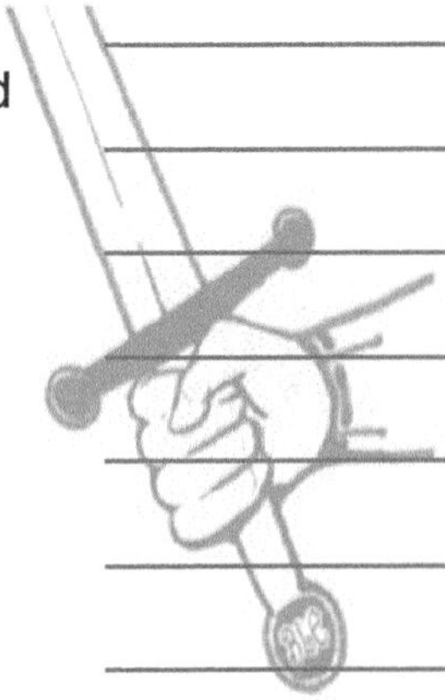

Date: _______________

Let There be Light

Bible Reading: Genesis 1 - 3

Focus Word: Commissioned

The Old Testament reading is done. Good job!

To go back to the beginning is to remember, in the beginning it was GOD!

God the Creator— He designed the whole thing, me, you, the system, and the way it works.

We are like little ants in comparison to His unending power and glory! How can a little ant running around as one among billions on an ant hill say, "No God, I will handle it all on my own terms." Talk about arrogance!!

The other thing that blows me away is His plan to use us, to allow us to be in dominion, to be creative.

Let us steward that responsibility well! Be a light in the darkness! Be the "City on the Hill!"

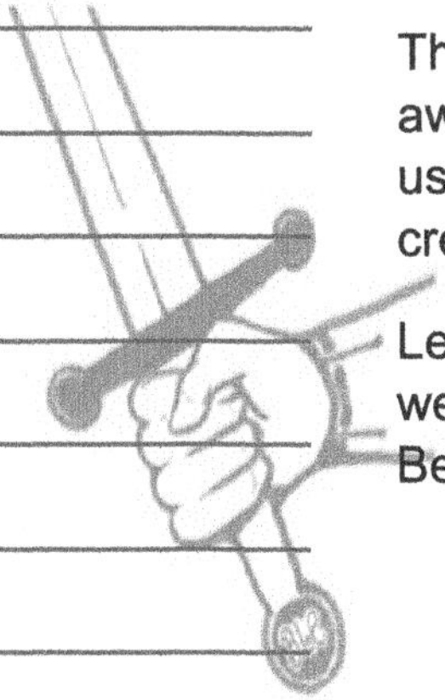

Date: ________________

Is That All You've Got?

Bible Reading: Song of Solomon 6 - 8

Focus Word: Partner

In the heat of competition people get cocky and tempers flame up. In the midst of rivalry sometimes the response is:

"Is that all you've got? Bring it on!"

I do not understand Solomon. I know he was wise and everything but all of his wives and concubines kind of blow it for me. Is that all you've got? How could you mess up like that, Solomon!

Hey, I am not an expert. And that is true over and over as I read God's Word. But keep reading! Keep asking questions. Do your research and homework.

In the end, we will learn so much but still not understand it all! We have to be willing to live with that tension.

Isaiah 55:8—His ways...

Date: ________________

Left Behind

Bible Reading: Rev. 1 - 11

Focus Word: Holy

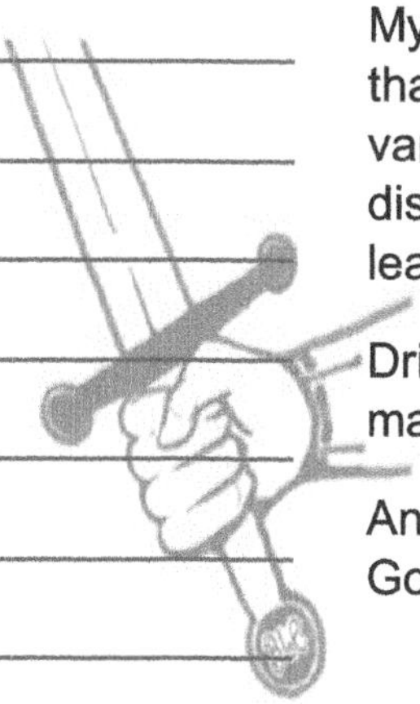

I had the privilege of meeting and talking with Tim LaHaye about three weeks before his death at 90 years of age.

He is famous for the Left Behind series, wrote over 90 books and sold more than 60 million copies.

He was a sharp, amazing servant. He was a leader and a family man. He also knew a lot about the book of Revelations.

He interpreted it through a dispensational, pre-tribulation point of view.

My point, much like yesterday, is that there are experts who have varying opinions and often end up in disagreement. Do what you can to learn from each point of view.

Drive carefully! But notice the majesty of God!

And know this: In the end, you and God win! Christ has prevailed!

Date: ________________

Praise and Worship Forever

Bible Reading: Rev. 12 - 22

Focus Word: Eternal

So if heaven is just me singing praise and worship songs forever, or even worse, hymns...Not a big appeal to me!

I believe there is more, and that most of the more is inexplicably wonderful! It is beyond our human thoughts!

A day is coming when we will experience what I call the joy of the teacher! You know, that hope every teacher has that her students will suddenly have a breakthrough moment and realize what they have been taught!

"Aha! Now I get it!"

I hope you like your book! But don't stop here! I believe that if you continue journaling and reading God's Word over and over, you will find new and meaningful nuggets to apply as life's circumstances continue to change causing your needs and insights to alter your focus.

Keep Growing!

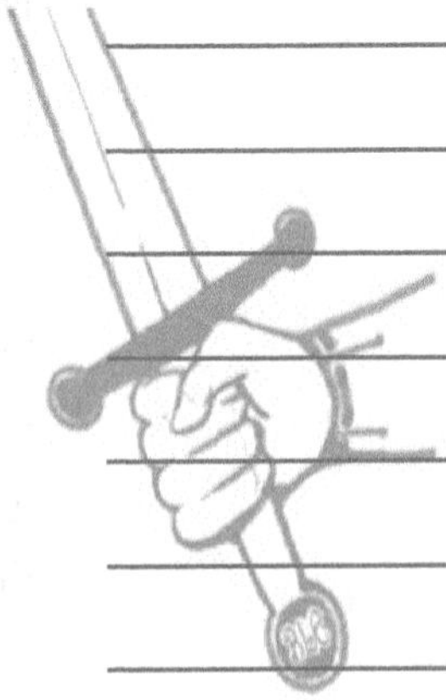

Indexing the key events/ideas

Index

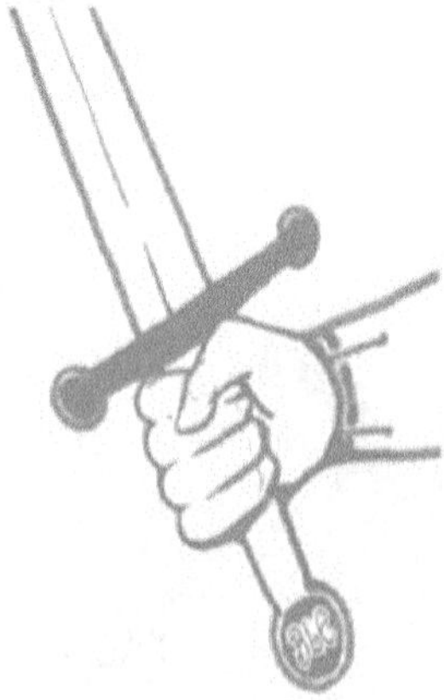

Index

Old Testament Readings:

1. Gen 1-8___
2. Gen 9-17___
3. Gen 18-24___
4. Gen 25-30___
5. Gen 31-37___
6. Gen 38-43___
7. Gen 44-50___
8. Ex 1-8___
9. Ex 9-15___
10. Ex 16-23___
11. Ex 24-31___
12. Ex 32-40___
13. Lev 1-9___
14. Lev 10-17___
15. Lev 18-25___
16. Lev 26-Num 4___
17. Num 5-10___
18. Num 11-18___
19. Num 19-24___
20. Num 25-32___
21. Num 33-Deut 2___
22. Deut 3-6___
23. Deut 7-11___
24. Deut 12-20___
25. Deut 21-28___
26. Deut 29-34___
27. Josh 1-8___
28. Josh 9-15___
29. Josh 16-23___
30. Josh 24___
31. Judges 1-5___
32. Judges 6-9___
33. Judges 10-16___
34. Judges 17-21___
35. Ruth 1-4___
36. I Sam 1-8___
37. I Sam 9-15___
38. I Sam 16-22___
39. I Sam 23-31___
40. II Sam 1-8___
41. II Sam 9-16___
42. II Sam 17-22___
43. II Sam 23—24___
44. I Kings 1-9___

45 II Kings 10-15___

46. I Kings 16-22___
47. II Kings 1-7___
48. II Kings 8-15___
49. II Kings 16-22___
50. II Kings 23-I Chron 2___
51. I Chron 3-7___
52. I Chron 8-15

OT Readings continued:

53. I Chron 16-23___

54. I Chron 24-29___

55. II Chron 1-10___

56. II Chron 11-18___

57. II Chron 19-27___

58. II Chron 28-34___

59. II Chron 35-Ezra 5___

60. Ezra 6-10___

61. Neh 1-8___

62. Neh 9-13___

63. Esther 1-10___

64. Job 1-12___

65. Job 13-21___

66. Job 22-31___

67. Job 32-42___

68. Is 1-8___

69. Is 9-24___

70. Is 25-31___

71. Is 32-39___

72. Is 40-45___

73. Is 46-52___

74. Is 53-60___

75. Is 61-66___

76. Jer 1-5___

77. Jer 6-11___

78. Jer 12-18___

79. Jer 19-26___

80. Jer 27-33___

81. Jer 34-43___

82. Jer 44-49___

83. Jer 50-52___

84. Lam 1-5___

85. Ez 1-13___

86. Ez 14-20___

87. Ez 21-28___

88. Ez 29-34___

89. Ez 35-43___

90. Ez 44-48___

91. Dan 1-4___

92. Dan 5-8___

93. Dan 9-12___

94. Hosea 1-10___

95. Hosea 11-14___

96. Joel 1-Amos 3___

97. Amos 4-9___

98. Obad 1-Jonah 4___

99. Micah –1-7___

100. Nahum 1-Hab 3___

101. Zep 1-Hag 2___

102. Zech 1-14___

103. Malachi 1-4___

104. Gen 1-3___

New Testament Readings:

1. Matt 1-3___
2. Matt 4-5___
3. Matt 6-8___
4. Matt 9-10___
5. Matt 11-12___
6. Matt 13-14___
7. Matt 15-17___
8. Matt 18-20___
9. Matt 21-22___
10. Matt 23-24___
11. Matt 25-26___
12. Matt 27-28___
13. Mark 1-2___
14. Mark 3-5___
15. Mark 6-7___
16. Mark 8-9___
17. Mark 10-11___
18. Mark 12-13___
19. Mark 14___
20. Mark 15-16___
21. Luke 1___
22. Luke 2-3___
23. Luke 4-5___
24. Luke 6-7___
25. Luke 8-9___
26. Luke 10-11___
27. Luke 12-13___
28. Luke 14-15___
29. Luke 16-17___
30. Luke 18-19___
31. Luke 20___
32. Luke 21-22___
33. Luke 23-24___
34. John 1___
35. John 2-3___
36. John 4___
37. John 5-6___
38. John 7___
39. John 8___
40. John 9-10___
41. John 11-12___
42. John 13-14___
43. John 15-16___
44. John 17-18___
45. John 19-20___
46. John 21___
47. Acts 1-2___
48. Acts 3-5___
49. Acts 6-7___
50. Acts 8-9___
51. Acts 10-11___
52. Acts 12-13___

NT Readings continued:

53. Acts 14-16___
54. Acts 17-19___
55. Acts 20-21___
56. Acts 22-23___
57. Acts 24-26___
58. Acts 27-28___(29)
59. Rom 1-2___
60. Rom 3-4___
61. Rom 5-6___
62. Rom 7-8___
63. Rom 9-10___
64. Rom 11-12___
65. Rom 13-14___
66. Rom 15-16___
67. I Cor 1-3___
68. I Cor 4-6___
69. I Cor 7-9___
70. I Cor 10-11___
71. I Cor 12-13___
72. I Cor 14-15___
73. I Cor 16-II Cor 1___
74. II Cor 2-4___
75. II Cor 5-7___
76. II Cor 8-10___
77. II Cor 11-13___
78. Gal 1-2___
79. Gal 3-5___
80. Gal 6-Eph 1___
81. Eph 2—4___
82. Eph 5-6___
83. Phil 1-2___
84. Phil 3-4___
85. Col 1-2___
86. Col 3-4___
87. I Thes 1-3___
88. I Thes 4-5___
89. II Thes 1-3___
90. I Tim 1-3___
91. I Tim 4-6___
92. II Tim 1-4___
93. Titus 1-3___
94. Philemon 1-Heb 2___
95. Heb 3-6___
96. Heb 7-10___
97. Heb 11-13___
98. James 1-3___
99. James 4-5___
100. I Peter 1-5___
101. II Peter 1-3___
102. I John 1-5___
103. II John, III John, Jude 1___
104. Rev 1-11___
105. Rev 12-22___

Poetry and Wisdom Readings:

1. Ps 1-7___
2. Ps 8-14___
3. Ps 15-18___
4. Ps 19-23___
5. Ps 24-29___
6. Ps 30-33___
7. Ps 34-37___
8. Ps 38-41___
9. Ps 42-45___
10. Ps 46-50___
11. Ps 51-55___
12. Ps 56-60___
13. Ps 61-66___
14. Ps 67-70___
15. Ps 71-73___
16. Ps 74-78___
17. Ps 79-82___
18. Ps 83-88___
19. Ps 89-91___
20. Ps 92-97___
21. Ps 98-102___
22. Ps 103-105___
23. Ps 106-108___
24. Ps 109-115___
25. Ps 116-119:40___
26. Ps 119:41-119:176___
27. Ps 120-129___
28. Ps 130-136___
29. Ps 137-142___
30. Ps 143-147___
31. Ps 148-150___
32. Prov 1-3___
33. Prov 4-6___
34. Prov 7-9___
35. Prov 10-12___
36. Prov 13—15___
37. Prov 16-18___
38. Prov 19-20___
39. Prov 21-23___
40. Prov 24-25___
41. Prov 26-28___
42. Prov 29-30___
43. Prov 31___
44. Ecc 1-3___
45. Ecc 4-6___
46. Ecc 7-10___
47. Ecc 11-12___
48. Ps 1___
49. Song of 1-2___
50. Song of 3-5___
51. Song of 6-8___

Index, summarize, categorize, and track.

Index

Index

About the Author

Dan Bragg grew up a farm boy in Ohio where he was blessed with a wonderful family that valued God, each other, and working hard.

During his college years at Taylor University he grew as a Christian, fell in love with learning, and found his true love Annette!

Dan and Annette have been Christian school educators for 32 years and love the ministry that God has given them. Dan is thankful to have earned a Doctorate of Education in Educational Leadership at Liberty University. He also holds degrees from Wright State University and Grace Theological Seminary.

Dan and Annette are proud of their children. Together they have raised four boys who are doing wonderful and amazing things. This idea of passing faith and values to the next generation is the real deal in the Bragg home. They are also very excited about the amazing girls (finally girls!) that are coming their way through marriage.

Dan is currently school superintendent at Legacy Christian Academy in southwest Ohio and loves to play a part in the lives of the students and families that God sends his way.

In his free time Dan enjoys reading, watching movies, and running. He has especially enjoyed chasing after his boys while they ran track and cross country races from the time they were young through their college years and beyond. Dan is passionate about learning, leading, and inspiring others in their walk with the Lord.

Please contact him at **www.bleabundantlife.com**, on Facebook or email at danbragg85@gmail.com. if you are interested in more information about Biblical Leadership Enterprise (BLE) or having Dr. Bragg speak to your church, school, or organization. Dr. Bragg loves to talk about education, board development, Biblical integration, marriage, parenting, personal development and growth.

Journals can be purchased at selected bookstores or online.

LCA